AF905055

Corporations and Partnerships in Italy

Corporations and Partnerships in Italy

Third Edition

Federico Pernazza

This book was originally published as a monograph in the International Encyclopaedia of Laws/Corporations and Partnerships.

Founding Editor: Roger Blanpain
General Editor: Frank Hendrickx
Volume Editor: Koen Geens

Wolters Kluwer

Published by:
Kluwer Law International B.V.
PO Box 316
2400 AH Alphen aan den Rijn
The Netherlands
Website: lrus.wolterskluwer.com

Sold and distributed in North, Central and South America by:
Wolters Kluwer Legal & Regulatory U.S.
7201 McKinney Circle
Frederick, MD 21704
United States of America
Email: customer.service@wolterskluwer.com

Sold and distributed in all other countries by:
Air Business Subscriptions
Rockwood House
Haywards Heath
West Sussex
RH16 3DH
United Kingdom
Email: international-customerservice@wolterskluwer.com

DISCLAIMER: The material in this volume is in the nature of general comment only. It is not offered as advice on any particular matter and should not be taken as such. The editor and the contributing authors expressly disclaim all liability to any person with regard to anything done or omitted to be done, and with respect to the consequences of anything done or omitted to be done wholly or partly in reliance upon the whole or any part of the contents of this volume. No reader should act or refrain from acting on the basis of any matter contained in this volume without first obtaining professional advice regarding the particular facts and circumstances at issue. Any and all opinions expressed herein are those of the particular author and are not necessarily those of the editor or publisher of this volume.

Printed on acid-free paper

ISBN 978-90-411-9468-8

e-Book: ISBN 978-90-411-9489-3
web-PDF: ISBN 978-90-411-9510-4

© 2017, Kluwer Law International BV, The Netherlands

All rights reserved. No part of this publication may be reproduced, stored in a retrieval system, or transmitted in any form or by any means, electronic, mechanical, photocopying, recording, or otherwise, without the prior written permission of the publisher.

Permission to use this content must be obtained from the copyright owner. More information can be found at: lrus.wolterskluwer.com/policies/permissions-reprints-and-licensing

Printed in the United Kingdom.

for my father's freedom of thought and for my mother's courage

The Author

Professor Dr Federico Pernazza (born on 20 June 1966) studied law at the *Università di Roma La Sapienza* (1985–1990). In 1996, he obtained his PhD in Comparative and European Private Law with a comparative study of the corporation law of France and Italy. Subsequently, he has conducted post-doctoral researches in Germany, France and United States.

Since 1998, Dr Pernazza has taught International Commercial Law, Private Law of the European Community, Comparative Private Law, Comparative Private Law of the Economy in various Italian Universities, such as Università di Roma La Sapienza, LUISS Guido Carli in Rome, Università di Genova, and Università di Cassino. In 2005, he was appointed Associate Professor of Comparative Private Law at the Università del Molise, where he currently teaches both Comparative Private Law and International Trade Law. In addition, he was visiting professor at the Université de Franche-Compté (France) in the years 2007–2011, at the Julius-Maximilians-Universität Würzburg (2014 and 2015), and at the Universidad de Granada (2016).

Professor Pernazza has been a member of the Rome Bar since 1993 and is a member of the Commission for International relationships of the Consiglio Nazionale Forense and a consultant for the Chamber of Commerce and Industry of Paris. He has published more than one hundred articles in Italian, English, and French on Comparative Private Law, European and European Member States' company law, commercial contracts, directors' liability, financial markets, bankruptcy, and fair trade.

He is the author and editor of several volumes on the same subjects and has participated as a speaker before numerous national and international congresses in Italy, England, France, Germany, Denmark, and Brazil.

The Assistant Authors

Antonello Ciervo (born on 2 September 1981) studied Law (2000–2005) at *Luiss Guido Carli* in Rome. He obtained his PhD in Public Law at *Università di Perugia* in

The Author

2009 and has been a member of the Rome Bar since 2009. He obtained National scientific qualification as associate in the sector 12/C1, *Constitutional Law* (2013). Livia Ventura (born on 9 April 1984) studied Law (2003–2008) at Luiss Guido Carli in Rome. She obtained her PhD in Comparative and Uniform Busines Law at 'Sapienza' Università di Roma in 2013 and has been a member of the Rome Bar since 2013. She is an S.J.D. Candidate at Temple University Beasley School of Law in Philadelphia. The author acknowledges Avv. Emanuele Faraci and Pier Paolo Picarelli LL.M. for their precious contributions.

Table of Contents

Table of Contents

List of Abbreviations (Italian and English)

AGCM	*Autorità Garante della Concorrenza e del Mercato*
CC	*Codice Civile* ('Civil Code')
CIPE	*Comitato Interministeriale per la Programmazione Economica* ('Inter-ministerial Committee for Economic Planning')
CNEL	*Consiglio Nazionale dell'Economia e del Lavoro* ('National Council for Economy and Labour')
CONSOB	*Commissione Nazionale per le Società e la Borsa* ('National Commission for Companies and Stock Exchange')
CPC	*Codice di Procedura Civile* ('Code of Civile Procedure')
CSM	*Consiglio Superiore della Magistratura* ('Superior Council of Judges')
EC	European Community
EEC	European Economic Community
EEIG	European Economic Interest Group
EU	European Union
EFIM	*Ente Partecipazioni e Finanziamento Industrie Manifatturiere* ('Industry Holding and Financing Company')
ENEL	*Ente Nazionale per l'Energia Elettrica* ('National Electricity Company')
ENI	*Ente Nazionale Idrocarburi* ('National Hydrocarbons Company')
INA	*Istituto Nazionale Assicurazioni* ('National Institute for Insurance')
IRI	*Istituto per la Ricostruzione* ('National Institute for Industrial Reconstruction')
ISTAT	*Istituto Nazionale di Statistica* ('National Statistics Institute')
IVASS	*Istituto per la Vigilanza sulle Assicurazioni* ('Institute for Surveillance over Insurances')
MEF	*Ministero dell'Economia e delle Finanze*
NATO	North Atlantic Treaty Organization
OPA	*Offerta Pubblica di Acquisto* ('Public Offer of Acquisition')
OPS	*Offerta Pubblica di Scambio* ('Public Offer of Exchange')
S.A.p.A.	*Società in accomandita per azioni*

S.a.s.	*Società in accomandita semplice*
SBD	Special Bargaining Delegations
SE	Società Europea ('Societas Europaea' or 'European Company')
SIM	*Società Intermediazione Mobiliare* ('Companies of Authorized Security Dealers')
SME	Small and Medium-sized Enterprises
S.n.c.	*Società in nome collettivo*
S.p.A.	*Società per azioni*
S.r.l.	*Società a responsabilità limitata*
S.r.l.s.	*Società a responsabilità limitata semplificata*
S.B.	*Società benefit*
S.t.a.	*Società tra avvocati*
S.t.p.	*Società tra professionisti*
TAR	*Tribunale Amministrativo Regionale* ('Administrative Regional Court')
TUB	*Testo Unico Bancario* ('Banking Sector Consolidation Act')
TUF	*Testo Unico delle disposizioni in materia di intermediazione finanziaria* ('Finance Sector Consolidation Act')

General Introduction

§1. General Background of the Country

I. Geography

1. The Republic of Italy is a southern European State with a geographical extension of 301,338 square kilometers, a population of 60,599,936 inhabitants, and a demographic density of 201.1 inhabitants per square kilometer (figures updated as of 30 November 2016).

Italy borders France to the west, Switzerland and Austria to the north, and Slovenia to the east. There are two micro-States located within the territory of Italy, San Marino and the Vatican City. The Municipality of *Campione d'Italia*, an enclave located in Italian-speaking Switzerland, is also a part of the Republic. The capital city is Rome, and the official language is Italian.

2. Italy is a founding member of the European Union (EU), The North Atlantic Treaty Organization, the Council of Europe, and the Western EU. It is a member of the United Nations (for the 2017–2018 biennium, it is also a non-permanent member of the United Nations Security Council) and belongs to the Group of Eight (G8).

II. Social and Cultural Characteristics

3. Although Italy is to a great extent homogeneous from a linguistic and religious perspective, the country has a variety of cultural, economic, and political differences. The population of Italy is mainly concentrated in coastal and low-lying areas of the peninsula, where the most heavily populated cities are located. The numbers of immigrants and foreign residents in Italy have increased substantially (especially in recent years). According to Italian National Statistics Institute (ISTAT) figures, on 1 January 2016, they reached a total of 5,026,153 (not counting naturalized persons with dual nationality), which is 8.3% of the total resident population.

4. The birthrate in Italy (ISTAT figures) was 9.2 per thousand in 2014. At the regional level, the highest rate is found in Trentino Alto Adige (10.2 per thousand), followed closely by Lazio (9.6). In third place are three regions: Campania (9.5 per thousand). The lowest rates are in Liguria, Molise (7.4 per thousand), and Sardinia (7.6 per thousand).

5. The average number of children per woman, 1.39 in 2014, makes Italy one of the countries with the lowest fertility rate in the world.

6. As far as the language is concerned, Italian belongs to the group of eastern Romansh languages of the Indo-European family. There are many different dialects in Italy, some of which are, from a historical perspective, Romansh languages in their own right, as they are autonomous evolutions of the variety of Latin spoken in various regions.

7. Like all national languages, modern Italian is a dialect that has managed to establish itself as the official language in a much bigger area than its region of origin. In this case, it was the Florentine dialect spoken in Florence that prevailed, not so much for political reasons as for the cultural prestige it had acquired. Indeed, Tuscan – or, to be more specific – distinguished Florentine (with enhancements borrowed from Sicilian, French, and Latin), was the language of three of Italy's most important authors of the 13th century: Dante Alighieri, Francesco Petrarca, and Giovanni Boccaccio. It was, of course, also the 'cultured' language of the City of Florence, so admired for its centuries-long cultural prosperity and its splendid architecture.

8. In the autonomous Province of Bolzano, German and Ladino have equal status with Italian, the official language of the State. The same applies to French in the Valle d'Aosta, where French is commonly spoken. Furthermore, a number of historic linguistic minorities are recognized and protected by both the State and the regions concerned, such as Sardinian, Friulian, Tyrolese, and Occitan.

III. The Political and Constitutional System

A. *The Constitution*

9. Italy is a 'democratic Republic founded on labour. These words appear in Article 1 of the Constitution, which went into force on 1 January 1948.

In the wake of the Second World War, the form of the State was chosen in an institutional referendum held on 2 June 1946 at the same time as the members of the Constituent Assembly were elected. Eighty-nine per cent of those entitled to vote took part in this referendum, including women who exercised their right to vote for the first time. Fifty-four per cent of the votes cast were in favour of the Republic (approximately 12 million), exceeding the votes cast in favour of the monarchy by over 2 million.

10. The Italian Constitution is a written, rigorous, and lengthy constitution.

11. The Constitution is contained in a written legislative text, as is usually the case in the legal experiences of both civil law and common law countries (apart from the United Kingdom).

12. The Italian Constitution is defined as 'rigorous' insofar as a special parliamentary procedure has to be followed to reform its contents (the normal standard majority is not sufficient), and any provisions with legal effect that are in conflict with the Constitution must be eliminated by a special jurisdictional proceeding at the

Constitutional Court. The constitutional reform proceeding envisaged in Article 138 of the Constitution is particularly complex.[1]

13. Article 139, however, provides that the republican form of State is not open to constitutional revision.

14. Finally, the Italian Constitution is lengthy in that it contains provisions encompassing many areas of civil life and goes further than simply indicating legislation on the sources of law. It in fact opens with twelve articles dedicated to fundamental principles and then consists of two parts dedicated respectively to the rights and duties of citizens and to the legal system of the Republic. Altogether, the Constitution consists of 139 articles.

It should, however, be stressed that the provisions of the Constitution are partly programmatic in nature, and as such acquire relevance purely in terms of guiding the legislature or providing an assessment of the legitimacy of acts of law. The process of consolidation of the principles indicated in the Constitution by embodying them in ordinary law is known as implementation of the Constitution. This process cannot yet be considered as having been concluded. Furthermore, the constitutional legislature decided to go back in Republican history in certain matters to extend and supplement these principles by adopting constitutional provisions (supplements to the Constitution approved in the same way as the constitutional revision proceeding). Examples of these two types of intervention, that is, implementing and supplementing constitutional norms, are, for instance, the facts that the Constitutional Court was set up only in 1955, the Superior Council of Judges (CSM) was activated in 1958, and the ordinary regions were set up in 1970 (although four special regions were set up in 1948 and the Friuli-Venezia Giulia region was set up in 1963). Finally, the abrogative referendum was set up under a law passed on 15 May 1970.

B. The Executive Power

15. The organ that represents executive power is the government of the Republic, which is formed by the President of the Council and by the ministers, who, before assuming their duties, are sworn in by the President of the Republic. The government has to win the confidence of the two Houses (the Chamber of Deputies and the Senate), which may either confirm it or revoke it in the form of an appropriately justified motion passed by roll call.

---

1. Article 138 of the Italian Constitution states that:

Laws amending the Constitution and other constitutional laws shall be adopted by each House following two successive debates held at intervals of not less than three months, and shall be approved on an absolute majority of the members of each House of Parliament on the second vote.

The said laws have to be submitted to a popular referendum within three months of their publication, whenever so requested by one-fifth of the members of one of the Houses or five hundred thousand electors or five Regional Councils. The law submitted to referendum shall not be promulgated unless it is approved on a majority of valid votes.

No referendum shall be held if the law has been approved on the second vote by each house of Parliament on a two-thirds majority of members.

16. The President of the Council of Ministers directs, and is in charge of, general government policy. The ministers are collectively responsible for the choices of the executive but are individually responsible as far as the acts of their ministries are concerned.

17. The history of Republican Italy has been characterized by a great number of governments (fifty-six in fifty-eight years, starting with the first Constitutional Legislature, which began on 23 May 1948). After the electoral reform in favour of a majority voting system (in which, however, 25% of seats in the two Houses are still awarded proportionally) in 1994, there have been significantly fewer governments, and they have lasted much longer.

18. The auxiliary organs of the government are the National Council for Economy and Labour (CNEL), the *Consiglio di Stato* (Council of State), and the *Corte dei Conti* (National Audit Office). CNEL is formed by experts and representatives from the various categories of production. It provides advice on the matters, and in accordance with the duties, assigned to it by law. It is vested with legislative initiative and can thus contribute towards economic and social legislation by presenting parliamentary bills.

19. The *Consiglio di Stato* is a judiciary and administrative advisory body responsible for ensuring justice in the administration. It is formed by seven divisions: the first, second, third, and seventh divisions play a consultative role vis-à-vis the executive, whereas the fourth, fifth, and sixth divisions play a second-level jurisdictional administrative role (the first level of administrative jurisdiction is represented by the Administrative Regional Courts, the so-called TAR).

20. Finally, there is the *Corte dei Conti*, which preventively monitors the legitimacy of acts of the government, as well as later verifying national budget management and the financial management of other public and semi-public agencies.

C. *The Legislative Power*

21. The organ representing legislative power is the Parliament, which is formed by the Chamber of Deputies and the Senate of the Republic.

22. The Chamber of Deputies consists of 630 members, who are elected by universal and direct suffrage. Any electors who, on election day, have reached the age of 25 may be elected as deputies. The Senate of the Republic, which is elected on a regional basis, is formed by 315 members. Any electors who have reached the age of 40 may be elected as senators.

23. The members of Parliament remain in office for five years. They represent the nation and exercise their functions on the basis of an unrestricted mandate.

24. Furthermore, the President of the Republic may appoint as senators for life (no more than five) any citizens who have honoured the country through special distinctions achieved in the social, scientific, artistic, and literary spheres. All former Presidents of the Republic are appointed senators for life by right.

25. With Costitutional Law n. 3/2001, the Italian Parliament approved an important change to Title V of Part II of the Constitution, regarding Italy's territorial organization. The law introducing the reform has reinforced the regionalist framework of the country, primarily by reversing the order of pre-eminence in the formation of laws established in Article 117 of the Constitution. Whereas prior to the reform, Article 117 in fact restricted itself to listing the matters in which the regions had the power to pass laws concurrently, leaving the State with jurisdiction to pass laws in all other matters, it now lists all matters that come within the exclusive jurisdiction of the State, together with certain matters that come under the concurrent jurisdiction of both the State and the regions, leaving the regions with general or residual jurisdiction over any matters that are not specifically listed.

26. In the text of the Constitution, the aforementioned reform also formally recognized the City of Rome as the official capital of the Republic. It gives the municipalities pre-eminence in administrative matters and introduces principles based on vertical subsidiarity between the various levels of government of the Republic and on horizontal subsidiarity between local authorities and citizens, while also adopting principles of fiscal federalism and providing for an equalization fund for the less-developed areas of the country.

D. The Judicial Power

27. Judicial power is exercised by ordinary judges who form an order that is autonomous and independent from all other State powers: the judiciary. The judges administer justice in the name of the people and are subject only to the law. Their representative self-governing body is the CSM, which is chaired by the President of the Republic. The first president and the general attorney of the *Corte di Cassazione* ('Supreme Court') are members by right of the CSM, while two-thirds of the other members are elected by all the ordinary magistrates and one-third by Parliament sitting in joint session. In its turn, the plenum of the CSM elects as vice-president one of the members appointed by Parliament.

28. The jurisdictional organs are organized in three levels: the Tribunal, the Court of Appeal, and the *Corte di Cassazione*. The power of the latter court is restricted to evaluating the legitimacy of impugned decisions. For minor issues, the *Giudici di Pace* (justices of the peace) have jurisdiction in place of the Tribunal.

29. As far as tax disputes are concerned, jurisdiction is vested in the Fiscal Provincial Commissions at the first level and the Fiscal Regional Commissions at the second level. The decision of the Regional Commissions may be challenged before the *Corte di Cassazione* in case of breach of legal principles..

IV. The Economic System

30. Although the text of the Republican Constitution contains no programmatic declarations in the sphere of the economy, Italy's economic system is a capitalist system. In this system, until at least the late 1980s, an important role had been played by State-controlled policies designed to provide social safeguards for the weakest sectors of the population (the so-called welfare State).

Under Article 41 of the Constitution, private economic initiative is free, but it cannot be exercised in contrast with social utility or in such a way as to jeopardize human safety, freedom, and dignity. Furthermore, ownership may be either public or private. Private ownership is in its turn recognized and guaranteed by the law, which also provides that it must have a social function and that it should be accessible to everyone (Article 42 of the Constitution).

Finally, the Constitution also acknowledges the social function of cooperation for mutual benefit and non-speculative purposes (Article 45 of the Constitution). Furthermore, it encourages and protects all forms of saving, regulating, coordinating, and monitoring the provision of credit in the form of an ordinary law.

31. Since the early 1980s, a process re-adjusting the State's presence in the economy has come about in all capitalist countries. This includes Italy, where the choice of a mixed economy has traditionally played a more significant role. Alongside the traditional State enterprises (railways, monopolies, and post offices), in the first half of the twentieth century, a series of management agencies (IRI, EFIM, ENI, etc.) were set up, which in 1956 were brought under the combined control of the Ministry for State Holdings and the Ministry of Industry. Municipal and regional enterprises operating in the gas, electricity, and transport sectors were also set up.

The 1990s heralded a period of privatization. The aim of this was to reduce public indebtedness and streamline the State-controlled enterprises. Therefore, in 1990, laws were passed regulating the privatization of the State-owned banks (Law No. 218/1990 and Legislative Decree No. 356/1990). In 1991, the post office administrations were privatized. In 1992, the State enterprise for telephone services was privatized. In 1993, the State's non-economic agencies were privatized, in particular, the social security agencies (Law No. 357). Then, Law No. 474 of 1994 inaugurated the procedure for privatizing State-controlled companies.

At the same time, Law No. 359 of 1992 transformed the National Institute for Industrial Reconstruction (IRI), the National Institute for Insurances (INA), the National Hydrocarbons Company (ENI) and the National Electricity Company (ENEL) into joint-stock companies, while also providing that other public economic agencies could be transformed into private joint-stock companies under a resolution passed by the Inter-Ministerial Committee for Economic Planning (CIPE), which would produce the same effects as those of an ordinary law.

32. Since 2007, the economy of Southern Italy has decreased at a rate twice that of the North: between 2008 and 2013, it was reduced by 13% compared to 7%. Between 2007 and 2014, 70% of unemployed Italy was in the South. The level of employment in southern Italy is the lowest compared to any other EU country but Greece: 40%; North is at the level of 64%. A national women's employment is 50%, in the South is 33%. With regard to the unemployment rate, in 2014, was 21.7% in the South, while at the national level was 13.6%. Between 2001 and 2013, the economy of the North grew by 2%, while the South has contracted by 7%.

ISTAT estimates that between 2001 and 2013 more than 700,000 people have moved into the northern Italian regions: 70% were aged between 15 and 34 years, about a quarter had a degree. Finally, according to ISTAT in the next fifty years, the migration from the South to the North and abroad could affect around 4.2 million people.

33. As far as the system of production is concerned, Italy has a large number of small and medium-sized enterprises and a small number of employees (according to ISTAT figures, one worker in three in Italy is self-employed).

In relation to the five major EU countries (Italy, together with France, the United Kingdom, Germany, and Spain), which alone account for approximately three-quarters of EU added value and employ two-thirds of all workers, Italy has the largest percentage of enterprises, 32.1%, and the lowest percentage of employees, 18.2%. We find the opposite situation in the United Kingdom, with 14.6% of enterprises and 25.7% of employees.

34. The sectors that contribute most to the country's economy are the so-called Made in Italy products: in particular leather and footwear – this sector alone produces more than three times the quota of added value of the other countries – clothing, textiles, and the manufacturing of bicycles and motor-cycles, with each sector registering quotas two or three times bigger than those of Italy's main European partners.

The apparent productivity of labour in Italian enterprises measured in terms of added value per employee is, according to ISTAT, below both the EU average and that of the major economies. It outperforms Spanish enterprises (but only in the services sector).

The biggest differences compared to Germany and the United Kingdom are registered in other sectors and in industry, too. Italian enterprises actually benefit from a cost of labour per employee significantly lower than that of the major European economies, in all the sectors considered apart from commerce.

In the tertiary sector, Italy performs relatively better in sea and land transport, postal and telecommunications activities, and wholesale trade.

35. Over the last ten years, there has been a greater propensity to import, especially on the part of small enterprises, while at the same time, there has been a lower propensity to export, especially on the part of enterprises operating in traditional sectors. In spite of this, there has been a substantial increase in export flows, which – even if considered the net of exchange rate and inflation dynamics – points to an increase in the value and quality of the goods exported.

36. We would like to wind up this general introduction with a set of statistics that will play a very important role as we proceed with our analysis, that is, the number of companies in Italy (including both partnerships and joint-stock companies). When the company law reform came into force in January 2003 (Legislative Decree No. 5–6 of 17 January 2003 implementing Law No. 366 of 3 October 2001), there were 67,098 *società semplice*, 647,934 *Società in nome collettivo* (S.n.c.), and 491,150 *Società in accomandita semplice* (S.a.s.).

As far as joint-stock companies (*Società per azioni* (S.p.A.)) are concerned, there were 63,399 *Società in accomandita per azioni* (S.A.p.A.). There were only 204 limited partnerships with share capital *Società a responsabilità limitata* (S.r.l.) whereas there were as many as 981,000 limited liability companies (which, according to unofficial estimates, had risen to over one million in 2006, thanks to the legislative reform).

§2. THE ORIGINS AND EVOLUTION OF ITALIAN COMPANY LAW

I. The Origins

37. The Italian term "società" comes from the Latin word societas, a general term used to indicate a group of people. The concept of incorporation and the idea of the societas being a distinct entity were in fact unknown in Roman times, and the only rules regarding the societas were those regulating internal relations between the soci.

38. In the Middle Ages, as economic activities and trading developed, the need for some form of organization led to the creation of companies with different names in Italy's major cities, and, in particular, in cities where maritime trade flourished, such as Amalfi, Pisa, Genoa, and Venice. The companies were usually based on the principle of unlimited responsibility typical of partnerships, but the commenda was also a widespread phenomenon. This was the form of organization that gave birth to the modern società in accomandita semplice.[2] The typical feature of this type of organization was that its members were divided into two categories: members engaged fully in the business such as merchants, and others, usually nobles or landlords, who financed the business and shared in its profits without fully sharing the burden of risk.

39. During the seventeenth and eighteenth centuries, the growth of trade on an intercontinental scale and the colonial policies adopted by European countries made it necessary to set up business organizations that could collect substantial amounts of money. To finance such organizations, which had both economic and political aims, kingdoms such as Britain, France, Holland, and other countries gave them special sets of rules. More specifically, investors were encouraged to underwrite the capital by introducing the principle of limited liability for shareholders, and the subscribed capital was embodied in transferable documents representing shares.

40. For both political and economic reasons, the phenomenon of the modern corporation emerged in Italy some time later. Prior to the unification of Italy in 1860 (Rome was included in 1870), the various Italian states and governments played no part in colonial policy, and their economies were based on agriculture.

When the Italian Codice civile (Civil Code (CC)) and Codice di commercio (Code of Commerce) were established in 1865, the French distinction between civil and commercial companies was resumed. This distinction hinged on the form of organization and the purpose of the company. As far as commercial companies were concerned, the codes regulated partnerships with unlimited liability (the S.n.c. and the S.a.s.), as well as private and public corporations (the società anonima). The 1882 Code of Commerce (the so-called Mancini Code) was characterized by a more modern and structural set of rules. Political control over companies was abolished, new rules were introduced to safeguard shareholders and third parties (the twenty-nine articles in force in 1865 rose to seventy-nine in 1882), and stricter rules were enforced, which also provided for preventive control of the articles of association by the courts.

2. In Part II, Ch. 3.

II. The 1942 Civil Code

41. The Italian CC of 1942 merged the previous civil and commercial codes. As a result of this, the società civile disappeared and the different types of companies were reorganized into two groups: companies based on groups of associates (società di persone) and companies based on capital and capital ownership (società di capitali). The basic distinction between the two groups is that of the shareholders' liability, which is usually unlimited in the case of the società di persone and limited in the case of the società di capitali. The former group includes the *società semplice,* the S.n.c., and the S.a.s., whereas the latter group includes the S.r.l., the S.p.A., and the S.A.p.A..

42. An important innovation came about with the introduction of a new type of capital-based company, the S.r.l.. The S.r.l., which draws its inspiration from the German corporate designation GmbH, is based on the association of a small group of shareholders who run a business benefiting from limited liability without collecting resources on the financial markets. The structure of the S.r.l. was in fact modelled to a large extent on that of the S.p.A., but its memorandum of association had a more limited structure. The S.r.l. is, nevertheless, the most common type of company in Italy.

43. In the Italian CC, companies are designed to run a business. The only exception to this is the società semplice, which cannot be used for this purpose but follows the original model of the società civile. A further exception to the profit- making purpose of companies came about with the introduction of the società cooperativa, a type of company the purpose of which is to directly meet a specific need of its shareholders (work, services, property) and not to maximize profits or dividends.

III. The Influence of European Union Law

44. In the original perspective of the CC, a company was generally defined as a contract, which meant that at least two people were needed to set it up. This fundamental approach has undergone changes thanks to the influence of EU law. When the Twelfth Directive was applied to companies with a single member, in 1993 the Italian CC introduced a new definition of company. Under this new definition, a company was no longer just a contract but could be set up either by contract or by other means, such as a deed of foundation by an individual or an entity. The rules regulating companies thus acquired a new function that was based on how the business was organized, irrespective of the number and capacity of its members.

The changes introduced by the EU legislature in the codified rules on companies are not limited to the Twelfth Directive. EU directives and regulations, as well as the decisions of the European Court of Justice, have had profound effects in some of the main aspects of company law, such as setting up, capital, disclosures, safeguarding minorities, mergers/demergers, and freedom of establishment. This is not the time or place to provide a description of European sources, but specific analysis will be made, profile by profile, of how they have contributed to Italian company law.

IV. Financial Market Law

45. Another basic development following the codification can be seen in the growing influence on company law of the requirements of the financial market. Since 1974, the aforementioned types of companies have been subject to special rules designed to inform and safeguard investors, which are typical elements of the financial markets. Such requirements have become more and more frequent in company law. We refer in particular to rules regulating such matters as shareholders' meetings, transferring shares, shareholders' agreements, powers of minority shareholders, duties of management, and the corporate governance of listed companies. These requirements also indirectly affect the rules regulating unlisted S.p.A.s and S.r.l.s.

Following the privatization (and sometimes the floating and listing) of State-controlled companies, a tendency emerged in the 1990s for the differences between the rules regulating S.p.A.s and S.A.p.A.s (the two types of companies admitted to the financial markets) to increase. Subsequently, Legislative Decree No. 58 of 24 February 1998 introduced a wider-ranging reform of the corporate governance of listed companies, increasing the powers of minorities, reorganizing rules on takeover bids, and reinforcing the role of the National Commission for Companies and the Stock Exchange (CONSOB).

V. The 2003 Reform of Italian Company Law

46. Under the rules of the 1942 CC, capital-based companies were regulated by a rigid, mandatory framework. This was unsuitable for the S.r.l., the most widespread type of company preferred for small and medium-sized enterprises. More flexibility was, however, also needed for unlisted S.p.A.s, which were often owned either by members of the same family or by a very small number of shareholders (four on average). Meanwhile, it emerged that capital-based companies needed better organizational and fiscal rules, in such a way as to encourage the conversion of partnerships, spread the benefits of limited liability, and provide access to a broader variety of financing.

47. Legislative Decree No. 6 of 17 January 2003 thus introduced a comprehensive reform of the part of the CC dedicated to S.r.l.s, S.p.A.s, S.A.p.A.s and società cooperative. Legislative Decree No. 5 of 17 January 2003 introduced special proceedings for company law litigations (abolished in 2009), while Legislative Decree No. 61 of 11 April 2002 has radically reformed the concept of criminal offences in this field.

48. The reform has reduced the number of mandatory rules, especially as far as the S.r.l. is concerned, but to a certain extent, also S.p.A.s. What this means is that the articles of association of an S.r.l. may tailor the company to suit the specific purposes of the founders concerning the structure of the governing bodies, including the option for shareholders to directly exercise the power of management with all the consequences this entails in terms of obligations and liabilities. Furthermore, the option of fiscal transparency of an S.r.l. may combine the benefits of partnerships' typical taxation system with the benefits of limited liability.

As a result, the reform has increased the differences between an S.r.l. and an S.p.A., in view of the organic structure that has been maintained in S.p.A.s. However, the traditional structure of S.p.A.s appears to have undergone a complete transformation. Two new optional structures have been added to the traditional one-tier system, which hinges on entrusting executive power to a board of directors appointed by a shareholders' meeting and monitored by a supervisory body with limited responsibilities (the collegio sindacale). These are: (a) a pure one-tier system in which executive and monitoring functions are distributed within the board of directors; and (b) a two-tier system modelled on the German Aktiengesellschaft.

49. Differences also exist in the new rules on S.p.A.s between private and State-controlled companies. The latter companies maintain in part the special system of rules for listed companies previously introduced by Legislative Decree No. 58 of 1998. Finally, the autonomy of companies with a mutual benefit purpose (the società cooperativa) has been maintained, but their internal organization and their auditing and tax framework have undergone radical changes.

50. Since 2003 several provisions have been enacted in order to continue modernizing corporate law. We refer in particular to rules regulating the *società a responsabilità limitata semplificata* (S.r.l.s.), introduced by Legislative Decree No. 1 of 24 January 2012, the reduction of S.p.A.s' minimum capital from EUR 120,000 to EUR 50,000, enacted by Legislative Decree No. 91 of 24 June 2014, and the new model of *società benefit* (SB), introduced by Law No. 208 of 28 December 2015, Article 1, paragraphs 376–384.

51. Following the reforms, the modernization of Italian company law now guarantees coordination between the need for flexibility and safeguards for shareholders, especially as far as listed companies are concerned. The increased freedom of shareholders has, however, made it necessary to regulate a variety of management systems and introduce a number of mandatory rules when companies issue financial instruments. The result of all this has been a general increase in the number of legislative provisions. Most of these rules are contained in Book Five of the CC, but there are also special laws that apply to listed companies and to companies engaged in particular types of business. If we are to have a complete picture of the subject, we shall need to coordinate Italian legislative provisions with both EU rules and the rules of a number of national authorities (Ministry of Justice, Bank of Italy, and CONSOB). The most important provisions will be mentioned in the relevant paragraphs.

§3. Definitions, the Notion of Company, Types of Corporations and Partnerships

I. Forms of Association

A. Association and Company

52. The company is a peculiar form of association: its main features are its business, which is to carry out an economic activity, and its purpose of profits sharing.

Article 11 and following articles of the CC contain general rules that apply to all forms of association in the absence of specific provisions. Companies, however, which are the most widespread form of such organizations, benefit from special provisions (Articles 2247–2548 CC). These provisions are supplemented wherever necessary by the subsidiary provisions generally applicable to associations.

In spite of this, the conducting of economic activities is not a privilege reserved for companies. Recent experience has shown that there are frequent instances of other types of organizations (not just associations) that run businesses or hold interests in economic activities. Associations are limited in that, because they are allowed neither to make profits nor to distribute them to the associates (the so-called profit-making purpose). If an association distributes dividends or in any other way pursues a profit-making purpose de facto, it will have to be classified as a company and in this case company law will apply.

B. Joint Ownership for Enjoyment and the Company

53. Joint ownership for enjoyment is also a different situation from that of a company. Article 2248 of the CC states that 'joint ownership established or maintained purely for the purpose of enjoying one or more properties is regulated by the provisions of Title VII of Book III'. The main feature of joint ownership for enjoyment is that the ultimate goal of the joint ownership is the enjoyment of the common asset. This is the only possibility provided to the joint owners, whereas in the case of companies, the purpose cannot consist only in enjoying the assets, which is simply a requisite for conducting the economic activity.

In the framework of the aforementioned distinction, it has been stressed that, whereas a company is normally a contract, with all that this implies in terms of the parties' obligations, joint ownership is simply a legal situation of common ownership. Other authors have maintained that, in the case of companies, the focus is on business, whereas in joint ownership, is on the assets.

C. Companies and the Joint Ownership of an Enterprise

54. A half-way situation between the aforementioned forms of association is that of the joint ownership of an enterprise, that is, the common ownership of a firm. The basic prerequisite to pure joint ownership is that the joint owners should not conduct the business (which is run by someone else or by only one of the joint owners). According to the prevailing doctrine and to recent decisions by the courts,[3] on the other hand, in cases in which the joint owners start to use the common assets to conduct a joint entrepreneurial activity, a company is established de facto.

II. Companies and Enterprises

55. Book Five of the Italian CC, which examines the general matter of lavoro (labour), regulates enterprises in Title Two (Articles 2082–2221). Title Five (Articles 2247–2510) and Title Six (Articles 2511–2548), on the other hand, focus on companies.

3. Corte di Cassazione, n. 3028 of 6 Feb. 2009 and Corte di Cassazione, no. 13291 of 27 Nov. 1999.

56. The CC does not provide a definition of enterprise but states that the entrepreneur is a person who 'professionally engages in an economic activity organized for the purpose of producing or exchanging goods or services' (Article 2082 CC). Enterprises may be carried out individually or jointly by two more persons. Under the contratto di società, pursuant to Article 2247 CC, 'two or more persons contribute assets or services in order to jointly conduct an economic activity and pursue the purpose of sharing the profits thus gained'.

57. It should be stressed, however, that not all contracts among entrepreneurs are qualified as companies (consortia, for instance, are not included) and that not all companies are necessarily enterprises, because the requisites of professionalism and organization, which are typical requisites of enterprises, are not fundamental in the case of companies. Enterprises cannot, for instance, be held to include so-called occasional companies, that is, companies formed to conduct an activity with a very short duration, which restricts their purpose to a pre-established series of acts, with no organization at all.

58. Another type of company that, in terms of its activity, cannot be classified as an enterprise is a company formed by professionals such as lawyers, public notaries, or medical practitioners. Even in cases in which such professionals are allowed to set up a company to conduct their activities, the legal nature of such activities cannot be compared with those of an enterprise, which means that their companies are not subject to the rules governing business enterprises.

III. The Partnership Agreement and the Single Member Company

59. The definition of contratto di società provided in Article 2247 no longer applies to each and every hypothesis. Under the original provisions of the CC, a company could in fact be formed only by contract, and it was classified as a contractual association. Today, following Legislative Decree No. 88/93 and the general reform in 2003, certain types of companies (S.r.l.s and S.p.A.s) may also be set up by unilateral deed, which means that the definition given in Article 2247 cannot always apply.

It has, however, been observed that, even in the case of a company set up by unilateral initiative, the principles of rules regulating contracts should be maintained and will apply if they are compatible. Indeed, under Article 1324 and unless otherwise provided, the provisions regulating contracts will be followed, if they are compatible, in unilateral deeds with an economic purpose between living persons. The special provisions covering single member companies will be investigated in the paragraphs dedicated to the different types of companies.

IV. The Contratto di Società and Its Elements

A. General Characteristics

60. Even after the introduction of single member companies, the contract continues to be the most frequent method of setting up companies.

The contratto di società can be defined as a contract among several parties who have a common purpose. Therefore, the articles provided by the CC for multilateral contracts apply, such as Articles 1420, 1446, 1459, and 1466. Under these articles, in cases of contracts with more than two parties in which the activity of each party seeks to achieve a common purpose, if one party's obligation is void, voidable, breached, or becomes impossible, the contract itself will not necessarily be void, voidable, breached, or impossible unless the participation of the party concerned is deemed essential.

On the contrary, some other rules of the general discipline of contracts do not apply to the contratto di società, such as those relating to the *inadimplenti non est adimplendum* exception and to termination resulting from breach of contract (replaced by those on exclusion) or hardship.[4]

As for it concerns the form, a partnership agreement is not a formal agreement as it can be finalized without signing any particular document, whereas special formalities have to be met in the case of capital-based types of companies.

There are usually three distinct characteristic elements in a contract:

(1) contributions;
(2) the joint exercising of an economic activity; and
(3) the purpose of sharing of profit between shareholders.

B. The Elements of the Contract: Contributions

1. Definition of Contribution

61. The term contribution refers to the associate's obligation to provide a direct contribution towards attaining the corporate purpose. Each associate must assume this obligation based on his or her participation in the company's activities.

Thanks to these contributions, the company is endowed with so-called risk capital and forms its initial assets. A minimum capital is required only in the case of capital-based companies.

2. The Object of the Contribution

62. The object of the contribution can be anything that has an economic value.

The associate may, therefore, contribute cash, goods (whether movable goods or real estate, tangible or intangible), or services (or even an undertaking to carry out a specific activity). The associate may also contribute a number of organized assets needed to carry out the business (i.e., a firm or a business unit) or a credit.

The contribution may not, however, come in the form of a negative undertaking, that is, an undertaking not to develop a competing business, as this can hardly be classified as an asset or a service.

---

4. Termination as a result of *eccessiva onerosità sopravvenuta* is unknown in the tradition of common law and can be equated with cases of termination for hardship or cases of frustration of contract.

There are special limitations applying to specific types of companies (S.p.A.s, S.A.p.A.s, and società cooperativa).

3. The Obligation to Contribute

63. The contribution does not necessarily have to consist of transferring the ownership of an asset. The use of the asset may also be transferred, giving the company the chance to earn the proceeds produced by the asset (e.g., the rent due on an estate).

Upon signing the contract the associates actually assume an undertaking with the newly born corporate entity to make their contributions, and it is then that the company becomes the associates' creditor.

4. Contribution, Patrimonio, and Capitale

64. Whereas the term patrimonio sociale (corporate assets) encompasses all of a company's legal relations, including receivables and payables, the term capitale sociale (company capital) represents the money value of the contributions.

Initially, the amount of the company capital and the amount of the corporate assets are obviously the same, because the company has no liabilities, and its only assets are the associates' contributions.

The assets may fluctuate immediately (to start with, because of expenses incurred in setting up the company and later as a result of the company's activities), but the capital will remain unaltered unless the associates decide to either increase it with new contributions or reduce it. In the case of capital-based companies, there may be rules providing for the capital to be reduced when the value of the assets falls below the value of the capital by a particular percentage.

65. The patrimonio (corporate assets), or to be more precise, its patrimonio netto (net worth of patrimonio, that is, the company's assets less its debts and liabilities), serves to guarantee the payment of the company's debts. The capital indicates the extent of the value which the partners have to maintain in the company and thus represents a portion of the patrimonio that cannot be distributed between or among them. This latter value may thus be considered by creditors as a minimum guarantee covering the company's debts.

66. The capital also serves a so-called organizational purpose. If no specific provisions apply, the associates' rights will be proportional to the amount of capital they have subscribed.

C. The Elements of the Contract: Jointly Conducting Economic Activity

67. The activity of a company may vary considerably. Its purpose must be to produce fresh wealth in terms of goods, services, or accrued value on existing goods, and it must comply with criteria based on profit or, more generally, on sound economic principles.

A typical feature of a company is that the economic activity must be conducted by jointly using common instruments to attain common targets. Whereas in unincorporated companies, management is personally guaranteed by the associates and the associates have the powers and duties of a manager, in incorporated companies, management powers are usually vested in a special body and kept separate from the responsibility of the associates.

D. The Elements of the Contract: The Purpose

1. The Objective Profit Purpose and the Subjective Profit Purpose

68. The purpose of a company is both to produce a profit (objective profit) and to distribute the ensuing earnings among the shareholders (subjective profit).

If the associates have made their contribution towards conducting an economic activity provided that any profits be reserved for charitable purposes, such an agreement cannot be classified as a contratto di società but will be treated as a different form of association.

69. In the case of a company, however, the profit does not necessarily have to be materially distributed among the shareholders, but it is essential that the associates gain an economic advantage in the form of a monetary increase, a reduction of expenses, or a higher remuneration. Companies that give their associates a direct mutual benefit without distributing dividends are classified as società cooperative (cooperatives), thereby distinguishing them from profit-making companies, in pursuance of the principle set out in Article 2247. The società cooperative are regulated by Article 2511 and the following articles of the CC.

70. Another example of companies not characterized by a profit-making purpose is provided by the so-called società consortili (consortia), the purpose of which is to benefit the entrepreneurial activities of their associates and improve their economic conditions as a result of either increasing earnings or reducing costs. The società consortili are regulated by Article 2615 and following articles of the CC.

71. Following the Law No. 208 of 28 December 2015 (Article 1, paragraphs 376/382) the Italian system accepted the possibility that all the types of companies described in the CC have a specific hybrid, or dual, purpose by obtaining the status of SBs. In fact, SBs in carrying out their economic activities shall pursue, in addition to the aim of producing and distributing profits, one or more aims of creating public benefit, by having a responsible, sustainable and transparent conduct vis-à-vis individuals, communities, territories and the environment, cultural and social heritage, entities and associations as well as other stakeholders.

72. Special rules apply to companies that are mainly owned by the State or by public entities or entities conducting activities of public interest and that have a profit-making structure (i.e., S.p.A.s) without having a profit-making purpose.

2. Prohibition of the Leonina Societas

73. An essential aspect of companies is sharing profits and losses, but the sharing does not necessarily have to be proportional to the contributions. However, any covenant whereby one or more shareholders are excluded from participating in profits or losses, the so-called leonina societas, is null and void (Article 2265).

74. Equally void are clauses that do not specifically exclude sharing profits and losses but that effectively prevent it, as, for instance, in cases in which an associate's entitlement to the profits is made subject to the achievement of a particular economic result that is in practice unattainable. In spite of this, clauses that establish priorities in repayment of capital upon the liquidation of assets are admitted.

V. Types of Corporations and Partnerships

A. The Principle of the Numerus Clausus

75. The Italian CC has significantly limited private autonomy as far as companies are concerned. Article 2249 in fact provides that companies conducting a commercial activity must follow the classification regulated in paragraph 3 and the following paragraphs of Chapter 5, that is, the category comprising the società di persone (*see* below), but not the società semplice, and all types of società di capitali (*see* below).

Consequently, the principle of the numerus clausus applies (i.e., the principle based on the restricted number of types of companies). Under this principle, a company that does not correspond to one of the types included in the list will not be admitted and the associates will not be permitted to 'customize' the rules of the type of company selected, by, for instance, combining them with the rules applying to a different type of company.

76. The 2003 reform has nevertheless drastically reduced the number of mandatory rules applying to the S.r.l. and, to some extent, to the S.p.A., thereby partly diminishing the importance of the numerus clausus principle.

B. The Choice of the Type of Company

77. There are no limits when it comes to choosing among the types of companies described in the Code, apart from the provisions of special laws and the ban on using the società semplice model (*see* below) to conduct a commercial activity.

Among the special laws that require a particular type of company to be adopted according to the type of activity, have to be mentioned those regulating some sectors such as banking, insurance, and other financial activities that must be carried out either by an S.p.A. or a società cooperativa.

C. Classification of Companies

1. Classification Criteria

78. There are three basic criteria on which the types of companies established under Italian law are based: the purpose, the nature of the activity, and the organizational structure.

As far as the purpose is concerned, there are: (a) profit-making companies, the aim of which are to produce a profit (so-called società lucrative); and (b) companies that pursue a mutual benefit for associates without having to distribute dividends (so-called società cooperative).

We also must distinguish the società semplice, a company that may conduct a non-commercial activity, such as the agricultural activity, from all the types of companies that can carry out commercial and non-commercial activities.[5]

As per the organisational structure the main distinction is between società di capitali and società di persone.

2. Società di Capitali and Società di Persone: The Corporation and the Distinction Between the Assets of the Company and the Assets of the Shareholders

79. In the category of società di capitali, there are the S.r.l., the S.p.A., the S.A.p.A., and the società cooperativa, whereas in the category of società di persone there are the società semplice, the S.n.c., and the S.a.s. .

80. The main difference between the società di capitali and the società di persone consists of the following elements: the importance of the capital and of the various forms of associates' organization forming a distinct legal entity (the so-called personalità giuridica) and the degree of legal separation between the company's and its associates' assets (autonomia patrimoniale). The former type of company in fact usually has a set of bodies with specific responsibilities, in which the rule of the majority applies and in which associates are vested with rights and limited liabilities in proportion to their share of the capital. In the latter type of company, on the other hand, the associates run the company personally as there is no rigid structure, any changes to the memorandum of association and to the partners must be agreed upon unanimously, and liability is unlimited regardless of the share associates own. Under the 2003 reform, the S.r.l. (*see* below) now occupies a hybrid position between the two categories, in that its shareholders may reduce the responsibilities of the governing bodies and directly exercise certain powers of management.

81. The distinction between companies with personalità giuridica and companies with no personalità giuridica, but with their own corporate assets, stems from the original approach followed by the CC that only certain companies can be considered to be autonomous legal entities, that is, entities with their own personalità giuridica.

82. This distinction is actually far less rigid because the società di persone, just like the società di capitali, have no limits in terms of exercising their legal activities (owning property, for instance, and access to courts). The distinction acquires importance from a practical perspective when it comes to the company's liabilities and the associates' debts. In companies with personalità giuridica, the obligations of the company and of the associates are separate, which means that the company's creditors cannot make

5. The distinction between commercial and non-commercial activities is based on Art. 2195, which makes registration at the compulsory for enterprises engaged in such sectors as industry, trade, transport, banking, insurance, and any auxiliary activities. The register is kept at the Chamber of Commerce, where the main details of business operations are registered. The registration has been extended to the *società semplice*, but the distinction is still relevant, because the purpose of the società semplice is limited to the non commercial activities such as listed in Article 2195 CC.

claims against the associates and that the associates' creditors cannot make claims against the company. In companies with no personalità giuridica, on the other hand, there is no clear separation between the obligations of the company and those of the associates. The associates usually have subsidiary obligations as far as the company's debts are concerned, and the associates' creditors can make claims only against dividends and only in exceptional cases obtain liquidation of the associates' stakes. These rules are not common to all società di persone. The autonomy of a company increases as it evolves from the società semplice towards the S.n.c. and thence to the S.a.s..

3. Società Benefit

83. SBs are the result of the legal transplant of benefit corporations from the United States to Italy. The first benefit corporations legislation was enacted in Maryland in 2010. Nowadays in U.S. 31 States and Washington, D.C. have passed legislation allowing for the creation of benefit corporations. Italy has been the first country in the world to introduce the new model of companies following the U.S. example by Law No. 208 of 28 December 2015, Article. 1, paragraphs 376–384. The S.B. model may be adopted by any of the types of companies provided by the CC (*società di persone*, *società di capitali* and *società cooperative*), in compliance with the relevant applicable provisions of each type. The unique features of SBs are: purpose, accountability of directors and transparency.

A SB must state its 'public benefit' purpose in the *contratto di società*. The 'public benefit' is described by law as the pursuit, while carrying out the companies' economic activities, of one or more positive effects, or the reduction of negative effects, for communities, territories and the environment, cultural and social heritage, entities and associations as well as other stakeholders, as individuals or groups of individuals directly or indirectly involved in the activities of the SB, being, *inter alios*: workers, clients, suppliers, lenders, creditors, public administration and civil society.

The public purposes shall be pursued through an administration finalised at balancing the interest of the associates or shareholders, the interest of those that may be impacted by the SB's business activity and the pursuit of the public benefit objectives. Directors of a SB have greater accountability because their duties are encompassed by a balancing test and they must act consistently with the public benefit purpose. The infringement of such obligations may be deemed as a breach of their fiduciary duties, consequently all the relevant provisions of the Italian CC and of the Italian laws regarding directors' liability and actions against directors shall apply.

Moreover, SB legislation ensures transparency through a mandatory annual reporting about the pursuing of public benefit, to be attached to the annual financial statements, and through the use of a third-party standard for the evaluation of the impact generated by the company's activity. The effective pursuing of the aims of public benefit is subject to the control of the *Autorità garante della Concorrenza e del Mercato* (AGCM) and in case of breach provisions of Legislative Decree No. 145 of 2 August 2007, regarding misleading advertising, and the provisions of the Legislative Decree, No. 206 of 6 September 2005 (the Italian Consumer Code) are applied.

VI. Partner Companies

84. The phenomenon of partner companies is globally widespread and Italy is not an exception. A partner company is generally admitted in law and confirmed by court rulings. An exception to the general principle of admissibility was represented by the ban opposed by the Corte di Cassazione (the Supreme Court in commercial lawsuits) to partnerships between società di capitali and società di persone. The Court held that those partnerships would in fact breach the rules on the members' liability. In the case held before the Supreme Court, the aim of the partner company was to combine the managing model of a partnership with the corporation's limited liability of members. More recently, the participation of a società di capitali in a società di persone has been explicitly admitted with the Company Law of 2003 (*see* new Article 2361, paragraph 2 CC).[6] According to the new discipline, the participation of a corporation (limited liability) in a partnership (unlimited liability) shall be approved by the general meeting and directors shall insert the information in the Supplementary Note attached to the balance sheet.

VII. Financial Companies and Holding Companies

85. The purpose of a financial company is to acquire shares from other companies and to hold, manage, negotiate, and distribute public or private securities. Holding companies (or companies leading a group) are to a certain extent different, as their purpose is to manage and coordinate the activities of subsidiaries and affiliates.

In its original wording, the CC only marginally regulated groups of companies. This deficiency has been remedied by the 2003 reform, which introduced specific rules regulating groups of companies and liabilities for holdings (*see* Part III, Chapter 1 on this subject).

VIII. Companies Formed by Professionals

A. The Issue of Compatibility

86. It is a much debated issue whether or not a company set up by professionals so as to jointly exercise their activity is admissible under Italian law. First of all, the problem has to do with the nature of the professional activity. The CC contains a number of provisions dedicated to the professioni intellettuali (intellectual professions), that is, professional activities requiring a high degree of knowledge and specific studies, the practice of which is regulated by law and requires an exam for admission to a professional roll. The CC does not qualify them as enterprises but imposes specific rules (bankruptcy measures, for instance, do not apply to professional activities).

87. Therefore, if we define a company as an association set up to jointly run an enterprise, professional activities cannot be included. But if we consider Article 2247,

6. The leading case is *Corte di Cassazione*, United Divisions, no. 5636 of 17 Oct. 1988. published in *Giur. Comm.* 1989, II, 5, in *Giust. Civ.* 1989, 1, 349 and in *Foro It.* 1989, I, c. 1285.

according to which the sole purpose of a company is to jointly conduct an economic activity, we can overcome the first obstacle.

The second problem that arises concerns the legal status of professional activities. Article 2232 requires that professionals exercise their activities personally, aided only by collaborators and assistants, as and when provided in the contract or by custom. Any such collaborators or assistants must in any case work under the guidance and responsibility of 'professionals'. The differences between this type of activity and the joint running of an enterprise typical of a company are, therefore, evident. In spite of this, economic development has led to more highly structured services in which individual capacities are not sufficient and new forms of cooperation are required.

88. Prevailing doctrine used to distinguish between protected professions (professions that can be practised only after admission to a professional roll (such as notaries, physicians, and lawyers)) and unprotected professions. The joint exercising of a professional activity by a company was only allowed in the case of unprotected professions. Recently, though, the legislation has started to extend the scope of companies to professional activities as well.

B. The Traditional Approach

89. An Italian Law of 1939[7] recommended that a group of activities practised by associated professionals should be referred to as studio (a term usually used to indicate the office of someone who practises an 'intellectual profession', in which the activity is described with such adjectives as 'technical, legal, commercial, accounting, administrative, and fiscal', followed by the names of all the associates). It banned professionals from setting up, operating, or running – in any shape or form – companies, institutions, offices, agencies, or other entities. On account of this ban, the courts agreed, almost unanimously, that companies formed by professionals were unlawful, regardless of their nature.

C. The 1997 Reform

90. In 1997, this ban was repealed, paving the way for companies to practise intellectual activities, even though then, as now, there were no specific provisions to this effect. Until such time as we have a general framework of rules, the debate as to whether companies of this kind can be formed will continue to be surrounded by controversy. A particular problem arises regarding the type of company concerned, which hinges on whether only the società di persone should be included or whether the capital-based model of a company may also be adopted.

The requirement for rules regulating specific activities has led to the introduction of special rules regulating companies practising professional activities, which are the first examples of a growing phenomenon.

7. Law No. 1315 of 23 Nov. 1939.

D. *Companies of Engineers, Auditors, and Lawyers*

91. The oldest example of associations of persons practising the so-called intellectual professions is that of companies of engineers (società di ingegneria). The activities of such companies go beyond the activities normally conducted by individual engineers as they also include preliminary studies, economic estimates, projects, and a series of activities inherent in constructing and selling buildings. The complexity and variety of such activities has persuaded the courts to equate them with an enterprise and allow the legal structure of a company to be adopted.[8] Consulting engineering companies were then regulated by the law on public procurement.[9]

92. A further example is provided by auditing companies. Under the 1974 reform of listed companies, compulsory auditing of companies was introduced. To this end, a register of companies was established (for companies set up as S.p.A.s), which operates under the control of the national authority for financial markets (CONSOB)).[10]

93. A highly significant and noteworthy innovation in this field has been Legislative Decree No. 96 of 2 February 2001, which, in accordance with EC Directive 98/5, has for the first time ever regulated companies formed by lawyers.

For such companies, a new type of association, the società tra avvocati (S.t.a.), was introduced that provides for specific rules of governance that must be supplemented, where necessary, by the rules regulating the S.n.c..

Most of the provisions on the s.t.a. follow the principles contained in s.n.c. rules. An exception is made with regard to the framework of invalidity which is based on principles typical of the società di capitali (*see* below) to protect clients and third parties.

94. In order to coordinate the principles of company law with the professional duties Law Decree 1/2012, converted by Law 27/2012, now permits lawyers (and other professionals with the same privilege) to keep secret information obtained within their activity in relationship with other professional members of the same company.

95. Unlike the associated firms of lawyers, which were regulated by the 1939 law, in which the associates were hired, the new companies formed by lawyers are directly liable for their professional activities. These activities can be exercised only by one or more associates endowed with the legal requisites, who are chosen by the client or else by the company. The associate or associates chosen will be personally and unlimitedly liable for the activities that they conduct, on a joint basis with the company, which will account for them through its assets. The other associates will not

8. The positive solution is confirmed in *Corte di Cassazione* ruling no. 5648 of 10 Sep. 1994, in *Riv. dir. Comm.*, 1995, II, 1.
9. Law No. 109 of 11 Feb. 1994, as amended in 1998 permitted the setting up of *società di persone, società cooperative* (only between associates admitted to professional rolls) and *società di capitali* (including non-professional associates, but laying down that activities typical of technical professions be exercised by professionals, who are personally liable).
10. Law No. 109 of 11 Feb. 1994, as amended in 1998 permitted the setting up of *società di persone, società cooperative* (only between associates admitted to professional rolls) and *società di capitali* (including non-professional associates, but laying down that activities typical of technical professions be exercised by professionals, who are personally liable).

be liable, except in cases in which the company fails to inform a client of the names of the designated associates.

The company will take its name from one or more associates with the additional words "e altri" (and others), if there are any others, and società tra professionisti (S.t.p.) (a company formed by professionals). The company will be registered in a special section of the companies register.

S.t.a.s, like S.t.p.s, are not subject to bankruptcy procedures.

96. Law Decree 223/2006, converted by Law 248/2006 has repealed law 1815/1939, and has permitted for partnership and society among professionals to offer interdisciplinary services. Moreover, Law 183/2011 has finally given further freedom to professionals who want to set up a company. They can now choose among all the types of corporations and partnerships, and cooperative too, provided by Italian law. Anyway there are some peculiar provisions:

- The aim of the company can only be the professional activity, carried out by professionals admitted to the respective roll (or, whether they are from another UE country, qualified according with their national law). Consequently the ban of a professional from his roll is a cause of exclusion from the company. Every professional can only be member of a single company at once.
- Non-professional members are admitted in case they are technicians that support professionals or investors, who contribute in the company share capital.
- Each professional performance shall be provided by a specific professional, and the customer shall have the opportunity to choose the one he prefers.
- The name of the company shall include the words 'società tra professionisti' (S.t.p.) (a company formed by professionals).

Amendments introduced by Law Decree 1/2012, converted by Law 27/2012, pointed out that, in presence of investors, professional members must at least hold a share capital corresponding to two third of the total votes. The breach of this provision is a cause of company dissolution. Furthermore, the memorandum of association shall include the company's commitment to subscribe a professional insurance policy. Lawyers are subject to the same provisions, set out by their professional law n. 247/2012.

97. A type of company commonly found in the framework of intellectual professions is the so-called società di mezzi. Such companies do not conduct activities typical of a protected profession but provide professionals with goods, instruments, and services. The società di mezzi carries out entrepreneurial activities and is subject to the ordinary rules regulating companies.

IX. The De Facto Company

98. The legal formalities that must be met in setting up a company will depend on the type of activities that are to be carried out. The società di capitali must be set up through a deed drawn up by a notary public. The società di persone is usually set up by a written agreement, frequently even by a deed drafted by a notary public, but the written form is not mandatoy, and the agreement may be formed also orally and proven by the conduct of the parties.

In the latter case, the company is defined as a società di fatto (de facto company), as its existence is based purely on the de facto conduct of the parties. In cases in which such a company is not commercial, it will be subject to file rules regulating the società semplice. A de facto company that conducts commercial activities will, on the other hand, be regulated as an irregular S.n.c. (i.e., the unregistered S.n.c.). In both cases, the associates will be jointly and unlimitedly liable.

Even though it has no legal status, the società di fatto has a number of rights and obligations, and it owns the assets formed by the goods contributed by the associates or produced by its activities.

If we are to ascertain whether or not a società di fatto exists, we will need to assess its activities and look for the elements typical of a company (contributions by associates, jointly conducting an economic activity, the affectio societatis, and agreements to distribute profits). Evidence of a partnership may also be found in funds used for a joint activity and in guarantees provided by the associates in respect to financing the activity. The fact that a firm is managed by a person other than the owner is not sufficient for a partnership to exist.

X. The Società Occulta ('Secret Partnership')

99. The fact that a corporate name is used in dealings with third parties is not an essential requisite for the existence of a company. In the same way, if partners carry out activities using the names of other people and the partners' names do not appear in dealings with others, this is not against the law.

A società occulta is held to exist in cases in which the associates of an unregistered entity agree to present their activities to third parties in the form of a one-person enterprise. In such cases, the activities are carried out on behalf of the partnership without using its name.[11] A secret partnership will exist as long as the clause imposing the secrecy of its existence is in force.

The secret partnership and the secret partners will be held accountable jointly with the partner appearing as the single entrepreneur for the obligations assumed by such entrepreneur, and the courts have unanimously held that the effects of bankruptcy must also extend to the secret partners.

The public advertising required in the framework of the existence of the società di capitali excludes the possibility of this kind of secret company being set up.

XI. The Società Apparente ('Dummy Partnership')

100. The società apparente is the exact opposite of the secret partnership. The società apparente indicates a situation in which two or more people pretend that they have set up a legal entity and jointly exercise an economic activity as partners, when in fact no such relationship exists between them.

11. Corte di Cassazione 12 Sept. 2016, ruling no. 17925.

In this case, to protect third parties, the courts consider that the partnership has actually been formed and in so doing establish a joint, unlimited liability on the part of the apparent partners. Furthermore, if the conditions arise, the partners are liable to personal bankruptcy.[12] Such a solution was thought to be excessive by part of the legal doctrine, because bankruptcy procedures apply to all creditors, including creditors who cannot rely on the existence of a company.

XII. The Società Occasionale ('Occasional Company')

101. Part of the legal doctrine is of the opinion that professionalism is not a requisite for a company. Consequently, the concept of a company might extend beyond that of a collective enterprise (*see* above) to include a company designed to perform just one economic operation; these kind of companies might not go bankrupt.

The concept of professionalism must not, however, be interpreted narrowly. Therefore, a company set up to perform a single economic operation cannot be held to be occasional, if the operation in question is complex and long-term. This means, for instance, that a company set up to build a block of flats and sell them cannot be a società occasionale.

Apart from the aforementioned example, the cases of companies that conduct organized economic activities restricted to single operations, as indicated in Article 2082, are quite rare.

XIII. The Company and the Associazione in Partecipazione

102. In accordance with Article 2549 of the CC, under the contract of an associazione in partecipazione, the associante gives the associato a share of the profits in its enterprise or in one or more businesses, receiving in exchange a specific contribution.

Unlike a company, in the associazione in partecipazione, the associato participates in the profits and losses produced by an enterprise, or by one or more firms, of another person, the associante, but has no other involvement in the business apart from the contribution.

The effects of the contract are restricted to the contracting parties, whereas relations with third parties are the exclusive domain of the associante, who is the only person to manage the enterprise.

103. We must distinguish the associazione in partecipazione from a company, especially a secret partnership, because in the latter case, there are corporate assets and the business is carried out jointly in accordance with the partners' deliberations; whereas in the former case, the partner is excluded from managing the enterprise or the single operation. As the associante is responsible for management (unless certain powers of management are delegated to the associato, who nevertheless exercises them in the name of the associante), the parties may establish the control that the

12. *Corte di Cassazione.* 13 Jun. 2016, ruling no. 12120, in *www.ilsocietario.it*; *Corte di Cassazione.* 22 Febr. 2008, ruling no. 4529, in *Guida al Diritto*, 2008, 19, 51.

associato can exercise over the enterprise or over the implementation of the business for which the association has been set up (Article 2552, paragraph II, CC). The associato is in any case entitled to receive a report on the business carried out or an annual report on operations, if the operations continue for more than one year (Article 2552, paragraph III, CC). The associato must act diligently and in good faith. He will share losses to the same extent to which he shares profits, but losses that he sustains cannot exceed the value of his contribution (Article 2553 CC). The parties may derogate from this provision, but a covenant based on the unlimited liability of the associato or on a pre-established limit on the loss in excess of the value of the contribution is held to be inadmissible. Excluding the associato from participating in losses is permitted, however.

§4. Sources and Hierarchy of the Law on Corporations and Partnerships

104. The system of sources of Italian company law does not differ from the general system of sources of private and commercial law, although certain sources play a greater role.

105. The Constitution makes no specific reference to company law, but company law guidelines can be found in the principles governing economic initiative, in the ownership of assets of economic importance, in services of pre-eminent general interest, and in rules on providing credit and on safeguarding/encouraging savings. The encouragement given to directly and indirectly investing savings in the share capital of the country's major production complexes (Article 47) is of particular significance, as it lays the foundation for legislation providing incentives and safeguards in this framework.

I. European Sources

106. EC law has played a decisive role in the last few decades. In this respect, EC regulations and, to an even greater extent, EC directives, have made a contribution, while more recently, the case law of the Court of Justice has had an important impact. In 1989,[13] Italy adopted an institutional mechanism designed to speed up the enactment and implementation of EC sources. Each year, Parliament approves a law (the EC law) containing measures that are required to adapt the Italian system of law to the EC system. The EC law may either directly implement the necessary rules or entrust this task to the Italian government, establishing the principles to which it must adhere. To this end, the Italian government may be authorized to issue a legislative decree or a regulation, which, however, thanks to the legislative mandate, also has the capacity to repeal laws based on legislative sources.

107. EC Law also affects Italian company law indirectly. The case law of the Court of Justice on the right for incorporated companies to be set up on a primary and secondary basis has made it possible to set up companies in one EC country for of

13. *Corte di Cassazione*. 13 Jun. 2016, ruling no. 12120, in *www.ilsocietario.it*; *Corte di Cassazione*. 22 Febr. 2008, ruling no. 4529, in *Guida al Diritto*, 2008, 19, 51.

exercise economic activities mainly or only in other EU countries.[14] This has given rise to a direct competition between national company law systems, which has persuaded the Italian Parliament (just as in other European countries) to carefully examine the Italian system to ensure that it does not create competitive disadvantages for the enterprises that are subject to it. Company law legislation over the last few years is thus heavily influenced not only by the policies that prevail within the EU, but also by those that prevail in the other national systems of EU countries.

II. National Sources

A. The Civil Code and Legislation on Company Law

108. In the framework of national legislation, the most important source continues to be the CC for company law. Titles 5 (Articles 2247–2510) and 6 (Articles 2511–2548) of the fifth book of the CC focus, respectively, on companies and on cooperatives/ mutual insurance companies. Title 11 contains a number of criminal provisions (Articles 2621–2641). The content of these provisions has, however, radically changed compared to the original text drafted in 1942, and numerous articles have been added by applying the technique of including articles with the same number but adding extra progressive Latin numbering (e.g., Article 2341bis, Article 2342*ter*, etc.).

109. From the 1970s onwards, special legislation has acquired an even more important role for company law as well, to the prejudice of the CC. In particular, the evolution of law on financial markets, banking law, and insurance law, which were only marginally regulated in the 1942 CC, has been made possible by special laws. As a result of the difficulty of using provisions stemming from a plethora of often uncoordinated sources, only later we find organic legislative texts covering entire sectors, known as 'Testo Unico' (consolidation act). As far as company law is concerned, the most important consolidation acts are those regulating: financial intermediation, the Finance Sector Consolidation Act (TUF), Legislative Decree No. 58 of 24 February 1998; banking sector, albeit to a lesser extent, the Banking Sector Consolidation Act (TUB), Legislative Decree No. 385 of 1 September 1993; and insurance, the Legislative Decree No. 209 of 7 September 2005. The TUF, in particular, contains a series of rules regulating the structure of governing bodies, the rights of shareholders, account audits, supervisory powers, and possible offences involving companies issuing securities listed on financial markets. These legislative provisions supplement, and sometimes derogate from, the provisions of the CC.

Legislative Decree No. 6 of 17 January 2003implemented an organic reform of the rules regulating joint-stock companies and cooperatives, which came into force in 2004. The new provisions have been included in the CC, either by replacing the previous provisions or by adding Latin numbering: e.g., after Article 2409, as many as nineteen new articles have been added, from 2409bis to 2409noviesdecies, regulating, inter alia, companies with one-tier and two-tier administration and auditing systems.

---

14. See, specifically, Court of Justice, 9 Sep. 1999. *Centros,* C-212/97; Court of Justice, 5 Nov. 2002, *Überseering BV, C.* 208/00; Court of Justice, 30 Sep. 2003, *Inspire Art,* C-167/01; Court of Justice, 13 Dec. 2005, *Sevic Systems AG,* C-411/03.

Thanks to this system, the number of articles of the CC unaffected by the reform could be left unchanged.

110. The criminal measures concerning commercial companies and cooperatives contained in the CC were also amended and supplemented during the same period (Legislative Decree No. 61 of 11 April 2002, which also implements Law No. 366 of 3 October 2001), while remaining in the CC.

111. Parallel to the company law reform, an important legislative intervention introduced a series of procedural rules designed to speed up litigation in this framework (Legislative Decree No. 5 of 17 January 2003, which also implemented Law No. 366 of 3 October 2001). In civil and commercial litigation, the Italian system has thus maintained the unity of jurisdiction reserved for the civil courts with the three levels of adjudication of the Ordinary Tribunal, the Court of Appeal, and the Corte di Cassazione, but it has also introduced special proceedings that were initially reserved for company law litigation but later extended to other areas of economic litigation. This has contributed to the creation of divisions and courts specialized in such litigation and judicial proceedings, which is still underway in Tribunals of larger dimensions and in the higher courts. Not having obtained its scopes, the special procedure for companies litigations has been abolished by the Law No. 69 of 18 June 2009.

B. Doctrine and Jurisprudence

112. Although company law is subject to increasingly detailed regulation, especially as far as listed S.p.A.s are concerned, case law, often guided by doctrine, has continued to play a very important role, especially in the years following the most important legislative reforms, such as those described above. In addition to the rulings of the Corte di Cassazione, the decisions passed by the Courts of Appeal and by the Tribunals of Milan and Rome often provide an important point of reference in the evolution of case law. The rulings can be easily accessed and are discussed in depth from a doctrinal perspective, in a number of specialized legal reviews (Rivista di Diritto Commerciale, Rivista delle Società, Giurisprudenza Commerciale, Le Società, Rivista di Diritto Societario).

C. Regulation of the Supervisory and Market Authorities

113. As far as listed companies and the financial instruments issued by them are concerned, an increasingly important role is being played by CONSOB and, to a lesser extent, by other authorities (Bank of Italy and Antitrust Authority). CONSOB, in fact, performs a supervisory function that consists of issuing regulations, providing an information service upon request, and organizing inspections and imposing sanctions. All such activities are legislatively regulated in the TUF. The law gives CONSOB a wide range of responsibilities designed to guarantee that operators, in particular, issuers, intermediaries, and auditors, behave in a transparent and correct manner. From a company law perspective, CONSOB's regulatory powers play a particularly important role in the framework of access to markets, takeover bids, accounts auditing, shareholders' meetings, and safeguards for minorities.

114. Finally, following the deregulation of financial markets, some of the rules concerning the admission of issuing companies and the trading of financial instruments are now covered by a set of rules adopted by financial markets management companies. Borsa Italiana S.p.a., the major management company, has also contributed to the elaboration of a Code of Self-Discipline on the corporate governance of listed companies.[15] Although the Code is not binding, it has created a significant impact on the conduct of issuing companies. Some of the provisions initially included in the Code of Self-Discipline have later been embodied in legislative provisions.

§5. International Private Law

115. Italian International Private Law is regulated by Law No. 218 of 31 May 1995. This law establishes the limits of Italian jurisdiction, the criteria by which Italian and foreign law are applied, and the validity of foreign rulings and deeds. There are no specific rules on jurisdiction for companies, but a special rule is dedicated to them as far as the applicable law is concerned (Article 25).

I. The Jurisdiction of the Italian Courts

116. Generally speaking, a dispute will come under Italian jurisdiction (Article 3 of Law No. 218/1995) in cases in which the defendant is domiciled or resident in Italy. In corporate matters, Italian jurisdiction will apply if the company has its registered office or a branch in Italy, or alternatively a representative authorized to appear in legal proceedings (Article 2204 CC). The Italian Court will also have jurisdiction in civil and commercial disputes according to the criteria established in the Brussels Convention of 27 September 1968, which was ratified by Italy under Law No. 804 of 21 June 1971 and in the European Regulation of the Council No. 44/2001 dated 22 December 2001. It should also be stressed that the Italian Courts have jurisdiction in actions for interim injunctions when the measure has to be enforced in Italy or the Italian Court has jurisdiction over the judgment on the merits. Moreover, the Italian Courts are competent according to different criteria in the framework of so-called voluntary jurisdiction if the case concerns an Italian citizen or dealings to which Italian law applies. The existence of the aforementioned criteria must be verified when the claim is filed, but the Italian Court will also have jurisdiction in deciding whether the required factual and legal prerequisites are satisfied at a later stage of the proceedings (Article 8 of Law No. 218/1995 and Article 5 of CPC .

117. Finally, the Italian jurisdiction will apply in cases in which the parties have so envisaged in a specific agreement, proven in writing, or in cases in which the defendant fails to raise the issue of a lack of jurisdiction in the first defence brief. Similarly, the parties may withdraw the dispute from the Italian Court, submitting it either to a foreign court or to arbitrators, provided that the agreement is proven in

15. The first Code of Self-Discipline (so-called Preda Code) came out in 1999 and was subsequently revised in 2002. A new Code of Self-Discipline was approved in 2006 and lastly amended in 2015. The documents can be read in <www.borsaitaliana.it>.

writing and the case concerns available rights (Article 4 of Law No. 218/1995 and Article 806 CPC).

118. Civil proceedings held in Italian Courts are governed by Italian law.

II. Applying the Foreign Law

119. In cases for which the Italian Court is obliged to apply a foreign law, the legal rules to be applied will have to be verified by the judge (Article 14 of Law No. 218/1995). The foreign law must be interpreted and applied according to its own criteria. Therefore, the judge can acquire information on the foreign law through the Ministry of Justice, benefiting from the instruments envisaged in international agreements, or through experts or specialized organizations. In case of extreme difficulty to find the rules he or she may apply another applicable national law according to different connecting factors or, if there is none, Italian law.

120. The foreign law should not be applied if it is contrary to Italian public order. Rules of public order are any rules that protect basic value and principles and are recognized and protected by the Italian legal system. In this event, either: (i) a different foreign law will be applied according to different connecting factors or, alternatively; (ii) an Italian law will be applied.

The Italian rule must be applied instead of the foreign rule identified according to the connecting factors, in cases in which the purpose and aim of Italian law so require (overriding mandatory rules; Article 17 of Law No. 218/1995).

III. The Law Applicable to Companies

121. Article 25 of Law No. 218/1995 establishes a common principle concerning the law applicable for 'companies, partnerships, foundations and any other public or private entity, even if not of an associative nature'. The principle thus applies, inter alia, to all types of companies, regardless of whether or not they have a legal status and regardless of whether or not they have been set up under an agreement or a unilateral deed.

Following the above-mentioned article the law applicable to companies is that of the State in the territory of which they were formally incorporated (the incorporation principle). Usually, this means that the Italian Court will apply rules of foreign law to disputes concerning companies set up abroad. In spite of this, Article 25 envisages that, irrespective of where they have been set up, Italian law will apply to companies that have their central administration or principal place of business in Italy. The central administration of a company is the place where decisions are usually made, even if it is not the same as the registered office indicated in the by-laws. The principal place of business refers to the prevalent activity of the organization, even if it is not the same as that specified in the by-laws.

According to the prevailing interpretation, the reference to the place of business principle does not mean that the foreign law established according to the incorporation principle will not be applicable, but that, if the aforementioned prerequisites arise,

Italian law will also apply. Italian law will, however, only be applicable as far as mandatory rules are concerned, in which case it will prevail over the foreign law. Apart from this provision, under the general principles, the foreign rule must not be applied if it is contrary to Italian public order or in cases in which the Italian rules apply insofar as they are 'overriding mandatory rules' (*see* above).

Furthermore, the rule specifies the sphere of application of the aforementioned principles. They will apply to such matters as: (i) the legal nature of the organization; (ii) the name of the company; (iii) the setting up, transformation, and extinction; (iv) the capacity, formation, powers, and operating procedures of the governing bodies; (v) representation; (vi) modalities of acquiring and losing the status of shareholders and the relevant rights and obligations; (vii) liability for the obligations of the company; and (viii) consequences arising from breaches of the law and of the by-law. The list of matters provided is, however, not considered to be comprehensive, and the sphere of application of the national law established according to the aforementioned criteria will also extend to other aspects inherent in those listed.

IV. The Application of Italian Law to Companies Set Up Abroad

122. Articles 2507 to 2510 of the CC establish a number of provisions concerning companies set up abroad, further integrating and highlighting the rules of private international law.

First of all, the obligations in respect to publicizing corporate deeds contemplated by Italian law will also apply to foreign companies that set up one or more branches in Italy. In this case, for each branch, the personal data and powers of the branch's representatives must be published at the Registro delle imprese. As far as third parties are concerned, the information published at the Registro delle imprese concerning the branch will apply, even if it conflicts with that published abroad. The registration office and number must be indicated in documents and mail, both for the registered office indicated in the by-laws and the branch. Joint-stock companies must also indicate the capital that has effectively been paid in and the capital appearing in the latest financial statements, as well as the other elements mentioned in Article 2250 of the CC. The relevant documents may be filed with the register in any official language of an EU Member State, together with their translations.

In the event of non-compliance with the aforementioned formalities, the persons who act on behalf of the company will account jointly and unlimitedly for the company's obligations.

123. Foreign companies are subject to the conditions and authorizations of Italian law only as far as the business carried out at the branch is concerned. Article 2510 CC nevertheless envisages that the general rules referred to above cannot prevent special laws from prohibiting, or submitting to special conditions, the performance of specific activities by companies in which foreign interests are represented.

Foreign companies that cannot be equated with any type of Italian company will be subject to the rules regulating joint-stock companies: (i) for the purposes of registering corporate deeds at the Registro delle imprese and (ii) as far as the liability of directors is concerned.

124. The application of Italian law, pursuant to Article 25, paragraph 2, of Law No. 218/1995 and Articles 2507/2510 CC, varies according to whether the companies concerned are set up inside an EU country or elsewhere. In the case of companies set up in countries not belonging to the EU, the aforementioned rules will not be subject to any limitation. The application of Italian law to companies set up in EU countries will, on the other hand, have to be assessed in light of the most recent case law of the Court of Justice.

From the Centros (C-212/97) case onwards, the Court of Justice has in fact adopted a rigorous approach when it comes to evaluating the national rules applicable to companies set up in another EU country to ensure that they do not give rise to an indirect restriction of the freedom of establishment. To avert any violation of the principle of freedom of establishment, the national rule must meet four conditions: (1) it must not be discriminatory; (2) it must be justified by imperative motives of public interest; (3) it must be such as to guarantee the achievement of the pursued purpose; and (4) it must not contain limitations over and beyond those that are necessary in respect to achieving the purpose. This approach has been further developed and detailed in various decisions, among which the Überseering (C-208/2000) and Inspire Art (C-167/2001) cases have contributed to specifying the residual frameworks in which the national rule of the host country can play a role.

For example, in view of Directive XI (Dir. 89/666/EEC of 21 December 1989), which provides for disclosure obligations on the branches of companies set up in an EU country, doubt now surrounds the legitimacy of Italian rules to the extent that they impose obligations over and beyond those envisaged in the directive. Today, the interpreter is now left with the task of identifying rules of Italian law that are susceptible to being applied to EU companies, within the limit that they may not lead to a restriction of the freedom of establishment. According to legal doctrine, the Italian provisions with the characteristics required by EC case law include the rules regulating groups (Article 2497 CC and following articles), the rules on shareholders' agreements (Articles 2341bis and 2341*ter*), and the rules regulating financial instruments (Article 2346 CC and following articles) and, more generally, the financial market.

V. Transferring the Head Office of an Italian Company Abroad

125. The final paragraph of Article 25 of Law 218/1995 looks into the different question of transferring abroad the statutory registered office of an Italian company and of merging an Italian company with an organization based abroad. In both cases, the prerequisite to finalizing such operations is that they should conform to the laws of the States concerned. The rule then goes on to stress that the operation must be valid and effective under any legal systems that are susceptible to application: this usually means the legal systems regulating the company in accordance with Article 25 and the legal system of the place where the registered office is to be transferred or where the organizations participating in the merger are based. The Italian Court require to evaluate the effectiveness of the operation and, therefore, to assess whether the legal systems involved permit such types of operations and whether they have been implemented in compliance with the prerequisites and procedures contemplated by the relevant systems. As far as the Italian legal system is concerned, transferring the registered office abroad is permitted and it is one of the hypotheses from which a dissenting shareholder is entitled to withdraw (Article 2437 CC for S.p.A.s and Article 2473 CC for S.r.l.s). International mergers are not specifically regulated by the CC, but in practice they come under the general rules envisaged for mergers.

Also, on the matter of mergers and demergers, a special set of rules applies to operations between companies of EU countries following Parliament and Council Directive No. 2005/56 of 26 October 2005 implemented in Italy by Legislative Decree No. 108 of 30 May 2008.

§6. Labour Law Implications

I. The Constitutional Principle

126. Although Article 46 of the Italian Constitution of 1948 acknowledges 'the right of employees to collaborate, according to the modalities and within the limits established in the by-laws, in managing companies', no provisions were introduced after the Second World War providing for compulsory forms of participation by employees or by their representatives in the governing or supervisory bodies of employer companies. Negotiations on the economic and regulatory aspects of labour contacts are, in fact, usually held on a sector-by-sector basis between the respective representative bodies of employees and employers. Consequently, the organization of commercial companies is not structured in such a way as to permit or contemplate the participation of the employees' representatives.

127. However, on the basis of the aforementioned constitutional requirement, the CC encourages employees to purchase shares in the company or in companies that control it or are controlled by it. To this end, Article 2441 CC envisages that under a resolution passed by the majority required for extraordinary meetings of shareholders, when new shares are issued, as many as one-quarter of them may be reserved for employees. To reserve a higher percentage, though, a resolution must be passed with the approval of at least half the share capital. In this hypothesis, and in other cases in which employees have access to ownership of the capital, they can benefit from the rights acknowledged to minority shareholders, especially in listed companies, which include designating some members of management and supervisory bodies (*see* Part I, Chapter 1, §6).

Apart from the hypotheses described above, the law does not give employees the right to appoint members of management or supervisory bodies or acknowledge them other forms of 'joint management' of the enterprise.

II. Information and Consultation Rights

128. Employees are, on the other hand, acknowledged to have information and consultation rights, which have gradually been adapted to EC sources in this matter.

Since the 1970s, the information and consultation of employees' representatives have been regulated in national industrial reconstruction and reorganization legislation. Under Law No. 223 of 23 July 1991, these forms of employees' involvement were envisaged in the special State dole and benefits procedures (file so-called Earnings Equalization Fund), to which enterprises employing more than fifteen employees can be admitted. Subsequently, under Legislative Decree No. 74 of 2 April 2002, the Italian legal system adapted to Directive 94/45/EC on the European company committee and on the information and consultation of employees in EC-level enterprises and groups.

129. Finally, Legislative Decree No. 25 of 6 February 2007 implemented Directive 2002/14/EC, which introduces a general framework for the information and consultation of employees. In Italy, information and consultation obligations apply, pursuant to the aforementioned legislative decree, to enterprises that employ more than fifty employees, but they must be specified in collective contracts in such a way as to harmonize the interests of the enterprise with those of employees. The information and consultation cover such matters as the economic progress and situation of the enterprise, employment within the enterprise, and, if there is a risk of job losses, the measures adopted to avert them and the decisions that might affect the organization of labour and labour contracts. The enterprise must provide the information sufficiently in advance to allow the employees' representatives to prepare opinions on the matters in respect to which the consultation is envisaged. The consultation must take place through the employees' representatives, at a company management and employees' representation level suitable for the question under review. The employees' representatives will express their opinion on the basis of the information received, and the enterprise will provide a reply with explanations. The purpose of the consultation is to reach and finalize an agreement on the enterprise's decisions. The employees' representatives are under an obligation to maintain the confidentiality of any information obtained during the course of information and consultation procedures. Violations of obligations on the part of the enterprise's senior managers and the employees' representatives will be punished in the form of pecuniary fines.

Part I. Corporations

Chapter 1. The Società per Azioni (S.p.A.) ('Public Company Limited by Shares')

§1. CHARACTERISTICS

I. Legal Status, Limited Liability, and Share Capital

130. The current wording of Article 2325 of the CC does not provide a definition of an S.p.A. but limits itself to asserting one of the fundamental characteristics of the S.p.A. type of company, that is, the principle according to which only the S.p.A. is held accountable for the company's liabilities through its assets. Indeed, when an S.p.A. is set up, an autonomous entity with rights and obligations comes into being, which accounts for its debts through its present and future assets. In derogation of Article 2740 of the CC, however, the S.p.A. is allowed to create special assets (Article 2447*bis* and following articles), which are reserved for satisfying specific credits and which cannot be touched by creditors with other debt entitlements.

In any event, the shareholders are not accountable for the company's debts, and their sole capital obligation is to pay the contributions. Article 2325 CC establishes an exception to this, however. If the shares of the company belong to just one person, this person will account unlimitedly for the S.p.A.'s debts in the event of insolvency, if the rules applying to S.p.A.s with a sole-shareholder on contributions and advertising have not been observed (*see* §2, VIII).

The liability restricted to the company's assets is offset by a complex set of rules regarding the formation and conservation of the capital, that is, a minimum value that must be contributed when the company is set up and that must continue to exist throughout the company's life so as to guarantee creditors.

The creation of an autonomous legal entity, the exclusive accountability of the company for its debts, and the liability of shareholders limited to the value of the subscribed contribution are not exclusive features of the S.p.A. Among the other types of companies, an S.r.l. (limited liability company) actually has similar characteristics to an S.p.A. but differs from it in terms of broader statutory autonomy in its organization and the nature of its instruments of participation, which do not have the nature of shares, and financing instruments, not allowing the S.r.l. to make recourse to capital markets.

II. Shares and Other Financial Instruments of Participation

131. The second characteristic of the S.p.A., which is highlighted in the name, is provided by the shares. This characteristic is shared by only one other type of company, the S.A.p.A. (limited partnership with share capital), which, however, differs from the S.p.A. in that it does not envisage a limited liability of all the shareholders.

The shares are the instruments that represent the participation of the shareholders in the capital of the company. To facilitate circulation, the share is embodied in a document that circulates according to the rules regulating negotiable instruments. A recent development has led to the so-called dematerialization of shares, which has transformed share certificates into mere electronic records.

As a rule, each share gives the holder an identical set of capital and administrative rights. The creation of various categories of shares is, however, permitted; each category gives holders of the shares specific rights determined by the law or by the by-laws. The result of this is that the position of the shareholder is usually the summation of rights and liabilities arising from his or her shares. Furthermore, the shareholder is allowed to exercise his or her administrative and capital rights (voting, withdrawal, sale, etc.) only over his or her shares.

Following the 2003 Company Law Reform, an S.p.A. is now allowed to issue other financial instruments as well as shares. Such financial instruments may attribute capital or even administrative rights, in accordance with the provisions of the by-laws (Article 2346 CC). Financial instruments of participation other than shares differ from shares in two main respects: (i) they give no right to vote at the shareholders' meeting, and (ii) the contributions resulting from their issue are not ascribed to capital.

III. Closed S.p.A.s and S.p.A.s That Resort to the Risk Capital Market

132. The Italian legal system makes no provision for a specific model of a company reserved exclusively for listed companies or for companies characterized by a widespread ownership of capital. Although regulated with the prospect of its capital being open to widespread ownership, the S.p.A. may be – and indeed is – utilized mainly by firms that have a limited number of shareholders. The existence of very large numbers of shareholders or the listing of the shares on a financial market gives rise to specific requirements, especially as far as protecting minority shareholders is concerned. However, these requirements are not satisfied by the general rules governing the S.p.A. Therefore, in cases in which such prerequisites arise, specific rules will apply to the S.p.A. These rules substantially modify the powers and obligations of shareholders, the system of functioning of the governing bodies, and the obligations and responsibilities of the directors.

To this end, Article 2325*bis CC* defines the framework of application of a kind of S.p.A. sub-model, 'the joint-stock company which resorts to the risk capital market'.

The legislative provision covers two hypotheses: (1) companies with shares listed on a regulated market, and (2) companies with a substantially widespread share ownership. The latter case is specified in Article 111*bis* of the provisions implementing the CC, which, in establishing 'the substantially widespread' share ownership, refers to the contents of Article 116 of Legislative Decree No. 98 of 24 February 1998 (the TUF). In turn, this latter provision refers to the CONSOB regulation on issuers, which defines issuers of financial instruments with a substantially widespread public share ownership according to a series of criteria (i. a minimum number of five hundred shareholders or bondholders that represent at least 5% of the share capital and are not controlling shareholders; ii. net assets of more than EUR 4,400,000, total revenue exceeding EUR 8,800,000 and more than fifty employees so that they cannot draw up the balance sheet in the simplified form under Article 2435*bis* CC) and establishes a number of exceptions.[16]

It follows from this that the rules specifically introduced by the CC as an exception to the general rules governing S.p.A.s apply to joint-stock companies that resort to the risk capital market (as defined above).

Finally, for companies with shares listed on a regulated market, in addition to and, when necessary, in derogation of, the rules of the CC, the provisions contained in the TUF are enforced, and, wherever the TUF makes reference to them, CONSOB regulations apply. These provisions refer not only to the powers of the supervisory authority and the obligations of companies and their governing bodies vis-à-vis CONSOB, but also to many aspects of the company's internal organization, the powers of shareholders, and the manner of functioning of the shareholders' meetings and other governing bodies. Finally, listed companies are under an obligation to comply with the requirements of stock exchange regulations, and they may also adopt Codes of Self-Discipline to further supplement and clarify legal requirements, especially in such areas as: (i) the conduct of the governing and auditing bodies, and (ii) transparency vis-à-vis the shareholders and the market.

Generally speaking, the description of the system of rules applicable to an S.p.A. cannot be set apart from the three frameworks outlined above, that is: (i) the general set of rules regulating joint-stock companies; (ii) the provisions contained in the CC applying to companies that resort to the risk capital market; and (iii) the legislative, regulatory, and self-disciplinary provisions regulating companies with shares listed

16. According to Article 2*bis* of CONSOB Regulation No. 11971/1999, as amended, is qualified as an issuer of financial instruments spread through the public in a significant measure, for the company that: (a) has more than five hundred shareholders, excluding the controlling shareholder, owning as a whole a percentage of share capital of at least 5%; (b) has a net asset, income, and number of employees superior to those provided for in Article 2435*bis* CC. Nevertheless, the CONSOB Regulation excludes: (a) companies in which the preceding limits are overcome without soliciting investments or a public exchange offer (OPS); that have not followed a share placement procedure; in which shares are not negotiated in organized exchanges systems with the consent of the issuer or of its controlling shareholder; (b) banks in which shares are sold or subscribed by its offices. Furthermore, are not qualified as issuer of financial instruments spread through the public in a significant measure the issuer in which shares have limits on the circulation or issuer companies without a lucrative social purpose or with mutual social purpose of enjoyment of goods or services. At last, follow the same qualification the companies with bonds spread through the public in a significant measure having a net asset of at least EUR 5 million and five hundred or more bond holders.

on regulated markets. However, in view of the fact that the general rules prevail, our illustration will follow the general description of the S.p.A. provided in the CC, whereas the rules applying to the aforementioned sub-models will be highlighted when relevant.

IV. The Multiplicity of Organizational Models

133. One of the most significant elements of the 2003 Company Law Reform is the fact that the former single organizational model of the S.p.A. has been superseded by the introduction of three alternative systems of administration and supervision: the ordinary system, the two-tier system, and the single-tier system.

The so-called ordinary system reflects the traditional organizational structure of the S.p.A. This is characterized by a shareholders' meeting vested with the power to appoint the members of the other governing bodies, by a one-person or collegiate administrative body (sole director or board of directors) and by a further body *(collegio sindacale).* The special element is provided by *collegio sindacale,* which is there to monitor the legality of management. In cases in which no external auditing firm is required by law, the *collegio sindacale* may also audit the accounts and, in exceptional circumstances, assume powers in place of the administrative body.

The so-called two-tier board system of administration and supervision draws its inspiration from the German *Aktiengesellschaft* (AG). It is thus characterized by the fact that fewer responsibilities are vested in the shareholders' meeting and that management and watchdog functions are entrusted to two separate bodies. The members of these two bodies are designated and removed in accordance with a pyramidal sequence, with the shareholders' meeting at the base, the supervisory board in the middle, and the board of management at the top.

Finally, the so-called one-tier board system reflects the structure of a British company characterized by just one administrative body, in which, however, there are members vested with management responsibilities and others vested with supervisory responsibilities.

The choice among the three organizational systems, each of which is specifically disciplined by the CC, is left to the preferences of the shareholders, who are free to either specify the preferred model in the by-laws or later modify the company's system of organization. If no specific indication is provided, the provisions pertaining to the ordinary system will apply (Article 2380 CC). As the ordinary system is the one that most resembles the traditional system of the S.p.A. prior to the reform, it is by far the most widespread system, but the two-tier system is beginning to gain a little ground with larger-sized companies.

§2. Formation and Registration

I. Procedures of Formation

134. The procedure by which an S.p.A. is set up consists of two stages.

The first stage includes the signing of the articles of association by the shareholder(s) and the fulfilment of other legal formalities, whereas the second stage consists of registering the articles of association at the *Registro delle imprese* of the place where the company has its registered office.

As a rule, the future shareholders are identified in advance and the articles of association are executed as soon as the necessary conditions have been met: (a) agreement with regard to the content of the articles of association; (b) subscription of the entire capital, which must not be less than EUR 50,000.00; (c) payment by a bank of at least one-quarter of the subscribed capital (or the entire capital if there is a single shareholder), as well as the transfer of non-cash contributions; and (d) administrative authorization for the company's activity, when required (i.e., for financial activities). The CC also provides for a different procedure (the so-called setting up with public subscription), under which, before the articles of association are signed, a group of promoters establishes a program setting out the main provisions of the articles of association of the future company, publishes the program, and collects subscriptions of shares and payments of contributions. This procedure, which is very rarely applied, provides for a meeting of subscribers in which the final version of the articles of association is approved and the first members of the company's governing bodies are appointed.

In both cases, the articles of association must be drawn up by a notary public in the form of a public deed.

The notary public must check that procedural formalities in setting up the company have been complied with and that the articles of association does not infringe upon any mandatory rules laid down by the CC or by the law. He or she must apply for it to be registered at the *Registro delle imprese* within twenty days. If the articles of association contains provisions violating public order or mandatory rules of law, the notary public must refuse to sign the deed. He or she will be subject to administrative penalties if he or she deposits the articles of association for registration in cases for which the legal prerequisites are manifestly lacking (Article *138bis* of Law No. 89/1913, as integrated by Law No. 340/2000). The control over legality previously entrusted to the courts was abolished in the year 2000.

II. Memorandum of Association

135. The memorandum of association usually consists of two documents:

(1) the *atto costitutivo* (articles of association), that is, the act whereby the parties express their intention to set up the company; and (2) the *statuto* (by-laws), that is, the document containing the rules established for the organization and functioning of the company. The *statuto* is an essential part of the memorandum of association and, if it clashes with the *atto costitutivo,* the content of the former will prevail.

The articles of association must provide information on the following basic elements, as listed in the CC:

(a) the name, date, and place of birth or the country of incorporation, domicile, or registered office, and the nationality of the shareholders and the promoters. Both private individuals and legal entities may participate in setting up an S.p.A. The memorandum of association must indicate the number of shares they hold;
(b) the name of the company, along with its main and secondary places of business. The name may be chosen freely, but it must not create confusion with the names or marks of other companies. It must include the words S.p.A.;
(c) the corporate purpose must include a description of the economic activity of the company. It must be possible, clearly defined, and lawful. Charitable activities are not permitted;
(d) the subscribed capital (at least EUR 50,000.00) and the paid in capital (not less than one-quarter of the subscribed capital);
(e) the number and par value of the shares, along with their characteristics and modalities of issue and circulation;
(f) the value of assets and receivables contributed to the company;
(g) the rules regulating the distribution of dividends;
(h) the special rights, if any, reserved for the promoters and the original shareholders;
(i) the system of management, the number of directors along with their powers, and the names of directors with a mandate to represent the company;
(j) the number of members of the *collegio sindacale* ;
(k) the first directors, *sindaci* or members of the *consiglio di sorveglianza*, and, if established, the external auditors;
(l) the cost of setting up the company;
(m) the duration of the company or, if the company does not have a set duration, a period of not more than one year during which the shareholders may not withdraw. Withdrawal is not permitted in the case of listed companies. In this case, the shareholders can easily obtain the same result by selling the shares on the market.

136. In addition to the elements established in Article 2328 CC, the articles of association may be supplemented by other clauses. Important optional clauses of this kind include the arbitration clause, which may be included only in the case of an S.p.A. not admitted to a regulated financia market. References in the arbitration clause must be limited to disputes arising with respect to rights that the parties are allowed to negotiate. The effects of the arbitration clause are also binding on future shareholders and on members of the governing bodies of the company.

III. Registration

137. No more than twenty days after signing, the notary public must deposit the memorandum of association at the *Registro delle imprese* of the province where the company has its registered office, together with documents proving that incorporation formalities have been met. The memorandum may be deposited by means of electronic data transfer, which means that the deposit is virtually simultaneous to signing.

The directors are allowed and required to apply for registration within the time limit that applies to the notary public. Both the notary public and the directors will be liable to pay a fine ranging from EUR 206 to EUR 2,065 if they fail to register the company. Furthermore, any shareholder is allowed to apply for registration within ninety days of incorporation.

The *Registro delle imprese* is kept at the provincial Chamber of Commerce. After a formal check of the documents, the company is registered. If the company has secondary branches ins Italy, a copy of the memorandum of association must be deposited at the local *Registro delle imprese.*

IV. Obligations and Liabilities Before and After Registration

138. It should be stressed that the setting up and the registration of the company give rise to different consequences. Prior to registration, the shareholders are committed by the documents they have signed, and their contributions, which are usually deposited with a bank, are not at the directors' disposal. If the notary public fails to do so, the directors must register the company, but if they or others accept obligations in the name of the company before registration, they will be personally liable. If there are several persons acting in the name of the company, they will be jointly and severally liable.

The share certificates may not be issued prior to registration, nor may a public offer of subscription or acquisition be launched.

If the company is not registered within ninety days of being set up, the memorandum of association will forfeit all legal effects and the shareholders will be entitled to have their contributions returned.

After registration, the company may assume obligations arising from the initiatives of the former directors, but these same directors will continue to account personally for the aforementioned obligations.

Upon registration, the S.p.A. becomes a legal entity distinct from its shareholders. It will have the legal capacity both to enjoy rights and to be bound by obligations (Article 2331 CC).

In the documents and mails the company has to quote the register where it is enrolled, its registration number, and the paid up capital. The CC establishes which information and documents have to be published through registration and through electronic means, if the company has a site of public access.

V. Nullity of the Registered Company

139. Until the company is registered, the nullity of the articles of association will be regulated by the ordinary rules regulating the nullity of a contract contained in Article 1418 and following articles of the CC.

Once the company has been registered, however, a new entity exists by law and the declaration of nullity must, therefore, be coordinated with formalities inherent in liquidating a legal entity having autonomous assets and an autonomous set of rights and obligations. In particular, it is necessary to safeguard the reliance of third parties who have entered into legal relations with the company, while also bearing in mind the fact that the company runs an organized activity, the value of which risks being forfeited, if it is liquidated.

For the above reasons, a declaration of nullity of a company registered at the *Registro delle imprese* has always been limited to a few, pre-established instances. Following the 2003 reform, these instances have been reduced to three. These are as follows: (1) there has been no formal incorporation through a public deed, (2) the corporate purpose is unlawful, and (3) there is no reference in the articles of association to the name of the company, the contributions, the amount of capital, or the corporate purpose (Article 2332, paragraph I, CC). In view of the twofold control applied by the notary public and by the *Registro delle imprese,* the instances of nullity have an extremely limited scope of application.

Furthermore, wherever possible, and in contrast to general legislation, the nullity may be rectified. A court cannot declare the company null and void if the nullity has been eradicated, even if this takes place during the course of the proceedings.

As far as the effects are concerned, the nullity does not give rise to the termination of the legal validity of contracts and legal relations set in place by the company prior to the ruling declaring the nullity, either vis-à-vis the shareholders or vis-à-vis third parties (Article 2332, paragraph II, CC). The declaration of nullity does not immediately extinguish the company, but it marks the start of a phase of liquidation regulated as in other cases of dissolution of the company. To safeguard third parties, the ruling declaring the nullity and appointing the liquidators must be published at the *Registro delle imprese.*

The shareholders may not claim back their contributions, which will continue to guarantee the company's liabilities, until the company's creditors have been paid off (Article 2332, paragraph III, CC).

The provisions concerning the nullity of the company thus have few elements in common with the general institution of nullity of a contract. However, two such elements worthy of note are: (a) the declaration of nullity may be enforced by anyone concerned, including the court ex officio; and (b) the action cannot be barred by limitation.

VI. Founders and Promoters

140. The founders are the persons who sign the articles of association. The promoters, on the other hand, are defined as the persons who, in the rare event of setting up by public subscription, sign the program to set up the company. The promoters may or may not become founders of the company. The by-laws may reserve for the founders and promoters a maximum of 10% of the profits for the first five financial years.

The promoters are jointly and severally liable for any obligations undertaken in the lead up to the company's setting up, but if the company is set up, it will be under an obligation to reimburse any expenses that they have incurred, provided that they are necessary or have been approved by the ordinary shareholders' meeting. The promoters will account to the shareholders and third parties with respect to underwriting the capital, making compulsory payments during the setting up phase, and guaranteeing the truthfulness of the representations published prior to the company's incorporation. They must also guarantee the existence of non-cash contributions, ensuring that they correspond to the certified report.

VII. Shareholders' Agreements

141. It frequently occurs that, either upon setting up the company or thereafter, the shareholders enter into agreements regulating various aspects of the running of the company or the circulation of shares. Such agreements are known as *contratti parasociali* or *patti parasociali,* that is, shareholders' agreements, insofar as they are associated with, and depend on, the company agreement. The *contratti parasociali* may cover a wide range of aspects involving the company, but they tend to focus mainly on such matters as exercising voting rights at the shareholders' meeting and transferring shares.

Until the 2003 reform, the CC made no reference to shareholders' agreements, and consequently there is an abundance of case law debating the legitimacy of restrictions on shareholders' rights. Until the 1990s, the general orientation adopted by the courts was to hold agreements covering voting rights null and void, as they appeared in conflict with the principle according to which the will of the company must be formed in the course of a shareholders' meeting, which means that the shareholders cannot commit themselves to voting in a manner predetermined by third parties.

In the course of the 1990s, case law partly altered its orientation. A number of rulings held shareholders' agreements envisaging obligations simply in terms of exercising the vote (i.e., shareholders' agreements 'giving rise to obliging effects') to be valid, but not shareholders' agreements setting in place mechanisms that make it possible to obtain the concrete result of ensuring that the vote is expressed as agreed (shareholders' agreements 'giving rise to real effects').

A clear affirmation of the general validity of shareholders' agreements can be found in the text of the 1998 TUF for listed companies. The contents of this text have been partially embodied in Articles 2341*bis* and 2341*ter,* which were introduced into the CC by the 2003 reform. Different rules still survive, however, according to the disciplinary framework. Therefore, it must be made a distinction among: (i) rules that are applicable to all joint-stock companies, (ii) provisions applicable to S.p.A.s that resort to the risk capital market, and (iii) specific rules applying to listed S.p.A.s.

142. Article 2341*bis* CC contains a set of general rules for shareholders' agreements aimed at: (i) ensuring a stable share ownership structure and stable percentages of capital held by the shareholders, or (ii) organizing the company's management in advance. Article 2341*bis* makes no provision with regard to agreements that have different purposes, for example, an allocation of profits or losses other than that established in the by-laws. In this framework, agreements covering the extent of profits and losses are legitimate, but a leonine agreement (*societas leonina),* that is, an agreement that totally excludes a shareholder from participating in profits or losses is prohibited (Article 2265 CC).

Furthermore, Article 2341*bis* refers only to agreements designed to achieve the aforementioned aims through three types of obligations: (1) voting obligations, (2) obligations with regard to transferring share, and (3) obligations implying joint control over the company by the shareholders.

Article 2341*bis* implicitly acknowledges the validity of the agreements described above, even if they have been concluded orally, but it contemplates a five-year duration limit. If the agreement is for a longer period, the restriction will be valid for the first five years, but the agreement may be renewed on expiry. If, however, the duration is not established in the agreement, any party to it may withdraw by giving at least 180 days' advance notice.

On the whole, the provisions of Article 2341*bis* aim to protect shareholders from commitments that would alter the nature of their position within the company, thereby jeopardizing the balance among rights, powers, and responsibilities embodied in the company's regulatory framework.

143. As far as companies that resort to the risk capital market are concerned, the further need arises to safeguard third parties, in particular potential shareholders. To this end, a mechanism is envisaged that aims to ensure that shareholders' agreements are disclosed. The agreements must be notified to the company and disclosed during a shareholders' meeting. They must, therefore, be specified in the minutes of the shareholders' meeting and published at the *Registro delle imprese* where the minutes have to be deposited. A shareholder who has failed to declare that he or she is a party to a shareholders' agreement will forfeit the right to vote, and in cases in which his or her vote has already been exercised and was decisive, the resolution passed by the shareholders' meeting may be impugned by anyone wishing to do so.

It should be stressed that no deadline has been established within which the disclosure has to be made. It must, however, be made at a shareholders' meeting. Nondisclosure will not invalidate the agreement, but will simply give rise to termination of the right to vote. Clearly, this way, there is no guarantee of immediate disclosure, and the agreement may remain secret for a long time with no direct or indirect penalty being imposed. Persons planning to purchase shares in an S.p.A. cannot be sure whether or not shareholders' agreements have been reached between or among the other shareholders.

144. The system referred to in Articles 2341*bis* and 2341*ter* CC is not suitable for listed companies, in which the necessity to safeguard potential shareholders and investors must prevail over the confidentiality requirements of shareholders who have signed a shareholders' agreement.

Only for listed companies does Article 122 of the TUF contemplate a much stricter obligation to disclose shareholders' agreements, with serious consequences in the event of non-compliance.

This provision applies both to agreements on how shareholders of the listed company or its holding companies should vote and to agreements with other purposes, that is: (i) agreements committing the shareholders to prior consultation in advance of exercising the vote (with no obligation to exercise it one way or the other), (ii) agreements directly or indirectly involving the transfer of the shares, and (iii) agreements allowing the parties to jointly exert a dominant influence over the listed company or its holding companies.

Although similar, the framework of application of legislative provisions on shareholders' agreements is not quite the same as that of the provisions of the CC. The requirements of the TUF indeed refer to the three aspects considered by the CC (agreements on voting, on transferring shares, and on how the company is to be run) and also extend to types of agreements that only indirectly affect such aspects (prior consultation agreements and agreements on financial instruments giving the right to purchase or sell shares).

Shareholders' agreements relating to listed companies are subject to three disclosure requirements. These are that they must be within five days of being signed: (i) notified to CONSOB, (ii) published in abstract form in the press, and (iii) deposited at the *Registro delle imprese* where the company has its registered office.

If the agreement is not published, it will be null and void, and each of the shareholders may thus disregard it with no risk of penalty. However, in view of the fact that the shareholders may have an interest in not enforcing its nullity, preferring to keep the agreement secret, Article 122 of the TUF provides that any vote exercised by shareholders who are parties to an undisclosed agreement will also be null and void, and that within six months CONSOB may impugn the resolution adopted with the decisive vote of shareholders who, in accordance with the aforementioned provision, are not entitled to exercise the right to vote. The public interest in disclosing shareholders' agreements is thus safeguarded by: (i) harshening the penalty (nullity); and (ii) giving a public authority the power to cancel the effects of the agreement on the company's management.

In the case of listed companies, too, the agreements must have a limited duration (three years). In cases in which they have a longer duration, they will be valid only for the maximum period envisaged by the law, barring renewal.

In the case of open-ended agreements, any shareholder is entitled to withdraw, giving six months' advance notice. In view of the fact that the withdrawal of one or more shareholders from the agreement constitutes a substantial modification of the agreement, this, too, is subject to the disclosure formalities described above.

To prevent shareholders' agreements from becoming a means of excluding the faculty to accept a takeover bid or a public offer of exchange (OPS), Article 123 of the TUF provides that, in these last two events, the agreement will be of no effect, and the shareholders may accept the public offer, thereby withdrawing from the agreement, even without notice.

VIII. The Sole-Shareholder S.p.A.

145. The 2003 reform completed the process of transforming capital companies from contractual types of organizations, that is, organizations based on the intrinsic need for a multiplicity of shareholders, into organizational models of entities owning economic activities that are susceptible to utilization even by just one individual or legal entity. This is the result of the ascertaining of the advisability of extending the benefit of limited liability to economic initiatives carried out by a single party, for at least two reasons. These are: (1) the basic irrelevance of the number of shareholders when it comes to considering the liability vis-à-vis third parties of the entity that owns the enterprise, and (2) the fact that previously, the limited liability of companies with a single shareholder could in fact be achieved by setting up the companies with the participation of fictitious shareholders.

Moreover, a single member company not only lends itself to small-sized personal enterprises, but it also lends itself to the reorganization of large enterprises, thanks to the fact that legal entities can be set up to carry out specific activities or sectors of activities. From this perspective, the single shareholder may even be a legal entity, and it is also possible for an individual or a legal entity to set up, or be the single shareholder of, several companies.

In the wake of the introduction in 1993 of the single member S.r.l., since 2003 Article 2328 CC contemplates incorporation by unilateral deed for the S.p.A., as well as incorporation by contract.

However, in cases in which the S.p.A. model is adopted by a single shareholder, various precautions have to be taken to guarantee the integrity of the assets and safeguard third parties. These precautions imply the adoption of a number of specific measures, in derogation of the general rules regulating the S.p.A.

During the incorporation stage, the single shareholder will account unlimitedly for obligations assumed on behalf of the company prior to registration and must pay the entire contribution, even if it is in cash, and not just 25%, as in the case of multiparty S.p.A.s (Article 2342, paragraph II, CC). Similarly, if, after incorporation, ownership of the shares is concentrated in a single shareholder, that shareholder must arrange to pay the contribution in full within ninety days.

In the case of a single member company, there are also additional disclosure requirements. The articles of association deposited at the *Registro delle imprese* must provide details of the first name(s) and surname (or company name in the case of legal entities), date and place of birth, domicile, and nationality of the single shareholder. In documents and mail, the company's single shareholder status must be specified (Article 2362 CC). Notices to the register must be made by the directors, but the shareholder may also arrange to do this. The name of the company does not, however, have to highlight its one-party status.

In the event of the company's insolvency, violations of the requirement to pay contributions in full and/or to disclose will give rise to the unlimited liability of the single shareholder with respect to any obligations undertaken within the period during which the aforementioned formalities have not been met (Article 2325, paragraph II, CC).

A final precaution was introduced to discourage operations that might lead to an impoverishment of the company's assets to the benefit of those of the shareholder. To be valid vis-à-vis the company's creditors, contracts between the company and the single shareholder or, in any event, deeds implying a benefit for the single shareholder, must in fact be: (i) recorded in the ledger of meetings and resolutions of the board of directors; or (ii) drawn up in writing in a deed with a certain date preceding the attachment (Article 2362, paragraph V, CC). Otherwise, the creditors will be able to sue both the company and the shareholder, as if the operations in favour of the latter had never taken place.

§3. Capital and Assets

I. Functions of the Share Capital

146. An S.p.A. must have a minimum capital of EUR 50,000.00. The minimum capital requirement has always been a feature of the Italian S.p.A. and was confirmed in the second EC directive. The reason for the minimum capital requirement is to provide a guarantee for company creditors insofar as there has to be at least an equivalent net worth. The need for this guarantee is justified for an S.p.A. in view of the fact that, as a rule, neither the shareholders nor the governing bodies account personally for company obligations. The protection provided to creditors by maintaining a minimum capital is achieved through a series of provisions regulating such matters as the valuation of contributions, the utilization of operating results, the balance sheets, and the capital/assets ratio. For the entire life of the company, the net worth of the company may not fall below the level of capital. If this occurs, the capital must be reduced, and if it falls below the minimum legal level, the company must be liquidated. If the company continues to operate when the prerequisites for liquidation arise, this will give rise to the directors' personal, joint, and several liability for any harm caused to the company's creditors. Furthermore, it is envisaged that the company directors will account directly to creditors if obligations with respect to safeguarding the integrity of company assets are violated (Article 2394 CC).

The share capital also performs the function of guaranteeing a minimum contribution required to carry out the company's business, even though there does not have to be any correlation between the amount of the capital and the company's financial requirements. Finally, the share capital plays a role in the company's organization. The shareholders' powers are, in fact, usually commensurate to the amount of their holdings in the share capital. It should, however, be stressed that the 2003 reform extended the possibility of establishing shareholders' powers in the by-laws in a manner not directly correlated to the number of shares they own.

II. Contributions

147. Shareholders' contributions must be made in cash unless the by-laws provides otherwise (Article 2342, paragraph I, CC). The CC favours contributions in cash in view of the certainty in value and the fact that it is possible to obtain payment more easily. Therefore, a partial payment of at least 25% on subscription is permitted only in cases of cash contributions. This possibility does not exist, however, for Sole-Shareholder S.p.A.

If the shareholder makes a partial payment, the directors or the liquidators may request payment of the residual amount at any time, depending on the company's requirements. Besides, according to Article 2346, paragraph 5, contributions must not have a value lower than the overall share capital.

148. Contributions of assets or receivables are also permitted, provided that they are made in full upon subscription of the shares (Article 2342, paragraph III, CC).

The CC makes no provision with regard to contributions based on the granting of know-how or binding relationships involving enjoyment (leases, leasing, or the like), but the prevailing doctrine favours the possibility of atypical contributions, provided that they can be economically valued. The fundamental interest hinges on the fact that both the company and third parties must be able to rely on a value that can be obtained even in the event of the shareholder's default.

Contributions of assets may be based on either ownership or enjoyment. In the former case, legislative provisions covering purchases and sales will apply, and the shareholder, will therefore account to the company for the transfer of ownership and for any defects in the assets. In the latter case, the applicable legislative provisions will be either those pertaining to the real right of enjoyment granted (usufruct) or those pertaining to leases, and the shareholder must guarantee the free and undisturbed enjoyment of the assets by the company. However, it is not possible to contribute assets that do not yet exist or are under construction, because this would mean that the contribution is nothing more than an obligation of the shareholder.

In the event of contributing receivables, if the debtor fails to pay, the shareholder will account to the company for an amount equal to the value of the contribution, plus any interest and expenses sustained by the company in exhausting the debtor's property. Such a liability will not arise, however, in cases in which the failure to pay depends on the company's negligence in acting against the debtor.

In cases of contributions of assets or receivables the problem of valuation arises. The shareholder making the contribution is under a duty to arrange for an expert to be appointed by the court where the company has its registered office to make an appraisal certifying the value of the asset or receivable. The appraisal must specify the criteria adopted in determining this value (Article 2343 CC). The expert must provide an indication of the market value of the asset and will account to the company, shareholders, and third parties for any harm suffered if the appraisal is wrong. He or she risks penal consequences in the event of gross negligence.

The directors must, however, verify the adequacy of the contribution within 180 days of the company's registration, and they may modify the value given in the expert's appraisal, explaining the reasons for this. Until the deadline expires or until such time as the directors issue a positive assessment, the shares may neither be delivered to the shareholders nor be transferred to third parties. If the directors ascertain a difference of over 20%, the shareholder may either pay the difference in cash or withdraw, receiving back the contributed assets, if this is possible. Otherwise, the capital of the company and the number of shares due to the shareholder must be reduced in proportion to the difference in value.

If the shareholder fails to comply with the contribution request, the directors must publish a warning in the *Official Gazette of the Italian Republic*. If the non-compliance continues, they may either file judicial proceedings to levy execution or offer the shares to the other shareholders in proportion to their stakes, at the value of the contribution. If the shareholders do not purchase them, the shares may be sold to third parties by the directors on behalf of the defaulting shareholder through an authorized intermediary. If the shares are not purchased by other shareholders or by third parties, the directors must declare the shareholder disqualified, cancel the shares, and reduce the company's capital accordingly. The directors will nevertheless withhold any sums that have been collected and may sue the defaulting shareholder for damages.

The appointment of an expert by the court is not needed if the shareholder contributes financial instruments: (a) at a price equal or inferior to the average price resulting in the last six months from a regulated financial market; (b) equal to the price resulting from a balance sheet approved by external auditors since no more than one year; or (c) at the price resulting from an expertise made in the last six months by an independent expert.

149. In the cases (a), (b), and (c) the directors, within thirty days from the company's registration, must check if occurred exceptional events causing a significant modification of prices. Within the same period, the directors evaluate the professionalism and the independency of the expert and, if needed, order a new expertise following Article 2343 CC.

The directors have to file by the *Registro delle imprese* a statement concerning a description of assets and receivables contributed by shareholders without an expertise ex Article 2343 CC, their value and evaluation criteria, affirming that their value is at least equal to that one taken in consideration during the company's formation proceeding, that not occurred exceptional events affecting their value and attesting the professionalism and independency of the experts who made the evaluation. Before the filing of this statement the shares may not be transferred.

150. Rules similar to those applying to non-cash contributions are applied if the promoters, founders, shareholders, or directors sell assets or receivables with a value equal to or greater than one-tenth of the share capital to the company during the first two years after its incorporation (Article 2343*bis* CC). Here, too, there is a serious risk of impoverishment of the company's assets, and the authorization of a shareholders' meeting is, therefore, required – following an appraisal of the assets or receivables – certifying that they are not worth less than the consideration paid by the company. If the described procedure is not followed, the vendor and the directors will account to the company for any lesser value of the assets. The appraisal and the authorization by a shareholders' meeting will not be necessary, on the other hand, in cases in which, because of the particular characteristics of the operation, there is no risk of harm to the company's assets (e.g., sale on a regulated market, sale under judicial or administrative control, or sale under normal conditions in the framework of the company's ordinary business).

151. Finally, in the case of an S.p.A., in contrast to that of an S.r.l., contributions of work or services are not permitted. The articles of association may, however, provide that the shareholder should make non-cash contributions, in addition to the proper contribution. In this case, information must be provided on all the elements required to identify the services in question, including the consideration paid for them and the penalties due in the event of failure to pay. In cases in which ancillary services are envisaged, the company will have an interest in the shareholder's personal services. The shares, therefore, have to be registered shares and cannot be transferred without the directors' consent. Clauses relating to ancillary services may only be amended with the consent of all the shareholders, unless the by-laws provide otherwise.

III. Corporate Assets

152. The corporate assets are formed by the sum total of assets and liabilities held by the company and are thus subject to continuous changes, depending on the company's business.

On the balance sheet the statement of assets and liabilities provides a picture of items receivable and payable. Items receivable are divided into the three main items of credits, fixed assets, and floating assets, whereas items payable are divided into the four items of net worth, risk funds, severance indemnities, and debts.

The net worth is formed by the capital, the reserves, and the profits and/or losses. The capital thus appears under liabilities, even though it does not technically constitute a payable. This way, economic balance is attained only when the operating result does not draw upon the capital. This ensures that the company disposes of a minimum assets reserve, represented by the capital, which will enable it to pay off any future creditors.

The corporate assets are, in fact, the sum total of values against which third parties can proceed to satisfy their credits. As a rule, all of the creditors may proceed against the entire assets. Credits are usually satisfied by all the assets, in accordance with the general rules contained in Article 2740 of the CC and in compliance with rightful claims of pre-emption.

IV. Separated Assets

153. The 2003 company reform made it possible to segregate one or more parts of the assets (so-called separated assets) to pursue specific purposes or business initiatives. The reform introduced a series of rules providing for the autonomy (albeit not absolute) of such legal relations with respect to other corporate relations.

By introducing separated assets, the intent was to allow enterprises to avoid costs arising as a result of setting up companies ad hoc for particular businesses, bypassing the complex rules that apply to the groups of companies that are formed in this way. By setting up separated assets, both companies and their creditors will, however, benefit from some of the advantages that come from creating assets and sets of separate relations correlated to specific business initiatives.

As with limited liability companies, the root problem is how to create a set of rules to safeguard third parties, in particular creditors, while differentiating their respective positions. More specifically, when separated assets are set up, there is a need to reconcile the interests of two categories of creditors, which will vary depending on whether or not their credits come within the framework of those inherent in the specific business covered by the separated assets.

154. The CC contemplates two hypotheses: (1) setting up specifically separated assets, specific goods and securities that are already a part of the company's assets; and (2) setting up a loan from third parties for a specific business or a particular activity, envisaging that the loan be repaid wholly or partly out of the proceeds, or some of the proceeds, of this business (Article *2447bis,* paragraph I). The setting up of separated assets as in the former point is subject to a maximum quantity limit (a maximum of

10% of the net worth) and may not involve activities that are reserved by law for entities having specific requisites.

The setting up of the assets must be approved by the governing body with an absolute majority, and the resolution must specify the essential elements of information contained in Article 2447*ter*, which include the business for which the assets are separated, the property and legal relations forming the assets, the economic and financial plan, eventual contributions by third parties and their powers of control and participation, the eventual issuing of financial instruments and the rights acknowledged to their holders, the auditing firm appointed to carry out the audit, and the rules of reporting.

The resolution must be deposited and registered at the companies register so as to safeguard the company's creditors, who have sixty days within which to object. The company may nevertheless proceed with setting up the assets, providing any creditors' guarantees that may have been requested by the court.

If the separated assets include real estate or registered movables, the resolution will take effect only after it has been recorded in the relevant registers.

155. With regard to debts arising from the specific business for which separated assets have been set up, unless the by-laws provide otherwise, the company will account to the extent of such assets, but not for obligations arising from an unlawful act. The creditors of the company with other entitlements may not proceed against the goods forming the separated assets, but only against the portion of income due to the company. If, in the final statement, the separated assets are not sufficient, anyone claiming a credit arising from the specific business referred to above may apply for them to be liquidated in accordance with the standard rules applying to companies. If the company becomes insolvent, the autonomy of the separated assets and of the relations inherent in the specific business will cease to exist, and the limitations applying to the company's creditors will no longer apply.

To ensure that the operations are kept separate, operations relating to the separated assets must specifically indicate the connection with the specific business. Furthermore, the company must keep separate mandatory accounting entries for the business to which the separated assets are intended, prepare a special statement, and provide a report with explanatory notes on the value of the goods and relations included in the separated assets and on the criteria used to identify and quantify them. In the balance sheet's statement of assets and liabilities, if the company has to account for liabilities inherent in the specific business over and beyond the limits of the separated assets, this must be highlighted.

In cases in which the business for which the separated assets have been set up comes to an end or becomes impossible, the directors must prepare a tax statement, which has to be deposited at the companies register together with the reports by the internal and external auditors.

156. In cases in which there is a loan reserved for a specific business, it must be finalized in the form of a contract between the lender and the company, which must be deposited at the *Registro delle imprese*. The minimum contents of the contract are specified in the CC as being the purpose, the time scale, the costs and proceeds of the financed operation, the financial plan, the capital goods, the guarantees provided by the company for the work to be carried out and the total or partial repayment of the loan, the lender's share of proceeds and powers of control, and the time limit for repayment.

The separated assets will consist of the proceeds from the business and of any income on such proceeds, which the company undertakes to collect and itemize separately in accounts. The company's general creditors may not obtain satisfaction from such assets. In addition, the company will account to the lender only to the extent provided for by those assets, unless it has given further guarantees. In the event of insolvency, though, the lender may prove debts in the liabilities to the extent that the credit exceeds the proceeds and the income produced by the financed activity.

157. Separated assets have many elements in common with the phenomenon of securitizing credits. Securitization is, in fact, also a technique whereby an enterprise finances itself by separating off a part of its business, that is, a block of receivables. Securitization is, however, restricted to cases in which there are credits that can be negotiated en bloc, whereas an operation that can be financed with separated assets may have a wide range of characteristics. Furthermore, unlike securitization, it is not necessary to create a company, thereby reducing costs.

V. Modifying the Share Capital

158. Modifying the share capital means amending the by-laws, in which the capital plays a key role. Therefore, the capital can be modified only following a resolution by a shareholders' meeting approved by the majorities envisaged for extraordinary resolutions (*see* §5).

The CC nevertheless contemplates a number of specific provisions on modifications to the share capital, which are based on two principles illustrated earlier: (i) the corporate assets must not be less than a specific percentage of the share capital, and (ii) the capital of the S.p.A. must not be less than EUR 50,000.00. It follows from this that, in certain circumstances, the variation in the share capital is not always the result of a free decision on the part of the shareholders' meeting and that when it falls below the EUR 50,000.00 threshold, the company must be transformed.

Modifying the share capital can affect the percentages of capital held by the shareholders. Consequently, the legislative provisions are designed to ensure that the shareholders maintain a role in the company similar to the role they occupied before the capital was modified, while taking account of the company's interests: (i) in acquiring assets that may be useful for its business; or (ii) in ensuring that certain categories of persons/entities should become shareholders.

Resolutions passed by shareholders' meetings to increase and reduce the capital are subject to a special system of challenge, with reduced deadlines to limit risks for third parties, depending on the extent of subscribed capital. An action for nullity may be filed within 180 days of registration of the resolution at the companies register. If the resolution has been passed without convening the shareholders, who may, therefore, not be aware of it, such an action may be filed until ninety days after the approval of the balance sheets for the year during which the resolution was passed.

As a further safeguard for third parties, in cases of companies that resort to the risk capital market, a ruling of nullity may not be given once the certification attesting that the increase has been fully or partly implemented has been registered at the R*egistro delle imprese*.

A. Capital Increase

159. Increasing the share capital entails that contributions on shares already issued have been paid in full. The directors clearly have to ensure that shareholders pay everything they have undertaken to pay on subscribing the capital before they ask the shareholders or third parties to agree to new commitments.

If the by-laws so permit, the decision to increase the capital passed by the shareholders' meeting may grant a mandate to the directors to carry out the operation. However, in this case, the resolution must: (i) establish the amount of the increase and the period (no more than five years) within which the increase has to be carried out; and (ii) specify whether or not the directors have the power to exclude the right of option for the shareholders. In this case, the directors may decide whether, when, and to what extent the shares should be issued, whether or not to implement the increase in one or more tranches, and whether or not to exclude or limit the right of option. The resolution passed by the shareholders' meeting may, however, further restrict the powers of the directors.

Once the increase has been resolved either by the shareholders' meeting or by the directors, the period begins for subscribing new shares and making payments. The payments must be made to the company in compliance with the rules envisaged for incorporation. If the capital is not subscribed to the predetermined extent, the increase will not be effective and the contributions must be returned. The capital increase resolution may, however, also provide that a partial increase be valid.

The capital increase may be carried into effect without contributions from shareholders, using available reserves existing in the company's accounts (a nominal or free increase). In this case, following the resolution passed by a shareholders' meeting, the increase will be implemented through an accounting operation, that is, by reducing available reserves by the value of the capital increase. The directors must then issue new shares either with the modified nominal capital or only for the value of the increase and distribute them to the shareholders in proportion to the shares they held previously.

The capital increase procedure is finalized by depositing a directors' statement at the *Registro delle imprese* certifying that the capital has been subscribed to the envisaged extent or, if the resolution so permits, to a reduced extent. Once this statement has been deposited, the new capital may be indicated in the company's documents and mail.

If the directors increase the capital with contributions of assets or receivables, they have to file also a statement concerning the evaluation procedure as provided for the formation of the company. The shareholders representing at least *5%* of the capital may obtain a new evaluation by an expert appointed by the court.

160. In case of a capital increase, the shareholders are entitled to a right of option, that is, the right to subscribe new shares in proportion to those already held (Article 2441 CC). Holders of bonds convertible into shares are also entitled to this right. The purpose of the right of option is to allow shareholders to keep the percentage of the capital they hold as it was before, as well as any administrative or capital rights in managing the company.

Under the amendments set out by Law Decree No. 91/2014, converted by Law No. 116/2014, directors must, therefore, deposit the offer of new shares at the companies register and publish it on the company's website, giving shareholders no less than fifteen days to exercise the option. In the case of listed companies, the offer is subject to the requirements regulating prospectuses contained in Legislative Decree No. 58/1998 and in CONSOB regulations.

In case of unlisted companies, shareholders who exercise the right of option may ask to purchase the shares that have not been pre-empted, which will be allocated in proportion to the shares held by those so requesting. In case of listed companies, rights of options that have not been exercised are offered for sale on the stock exchange.

The right of option may conflict with the company's need: (i) to carry out operations requiring allocations of shares to one or more shareholders at a level not proportional to those held; or (ii) to allocate shares to third parties. The CC contemplates four hypotheses of excluding or limiting the right of option, which are regulated differently according to the nature of the interest of the company and of the third parties, giving rise to the following:

(1) The shareholders will not have a right of option in cases in which the capital increase has to be effected in the form of a non-cash contribution. In this case, the reason for the exclusion is the company's need to acquire a non-fungible asset that can be supplied by the new shareholder. The directors must, therefore, draw up a report explaining the reasons for the exclusion and the criteria used to establish the issue price of the shares. The adequacy of the price of the shares must be verified by the *collegio sindacale* and by a court-appointed expert, who will make their reports available to the shareholders at least fifteen days prior to the shareholders' meeting. The meeting will also establish the price, bearing in mind the company's net worth and the stock exchange value of the shares, if they are listed.
(2) The right of option may be excluded or limited in any other cases in which the company's interest so requires. The existence of such an interest must, however, be resolved by the shareholders' meeting with the favourable vote of more than half the share capital. Here, too, the reports prepared by the directors and the *sindaci* explaining the reasons for the exclusion and verifying the adequacy of the issue price must be made available to the shareholders.
(3) Through a resolution passed by the majorities envisaged for extraordinary shareholders' meetings the right of option can be excluded if the new stocks are offered to employees of the company and of its subsidiaries, in pursuance of the encouragement expressed in Article 46 of the Italian Constitution in favour of the participation of workers in managing the enterprise.
(4) Listed companies may wish to increase the quota of capital available on the financial market. To this end, whether the by-laws so permits, it is envisaged that the right of option may be excluded for up to 10% of the preexisting share capital. The price of the new shares must, however, reflect the market price, and this must be certified by an auditing firm. The majority quorum for the above-mentioned

resolutions of the shareholders' meeting is two-thirds of the present capital. Nevertheless, for the validity of such resolution the meeting must be attended as follows: – in the first call at least half of the share capital; – in the second call over a third of the share capital; – in calls following the second at least a fifth of the share capital.

161. The option formalities do not apply in cases in which the shares are purchased by banks or financial intermediaries with an obligation to offer them to shareholders in accordance with the provisions set forth above. To avert disruption to the company's management arising from such a transitory ownership of the shares, it is envisaged that the intermediaries may not exercise the right to vote until the deadline for exercising the option has expired. After this, they may either sell the shares freely on the market or continue to own them, exercising any administrative and capital rights.

B. Capital Reduction

162. There are two main cases in which a reduction in capital may arise, that is, when a shareholders' meeting considers that the capital is excessive in relation to the company's requirements and when losses have occurred. A capital reduction may be also a consequence of the cancellation of treasury shares exceeding the legal limits.

In the former case, the notice convening the shareholders' meeting must specify the reasons and procedures for reducing the capital. The creditors may wish to oppose the reduction because it involves a corresponding reduction of the company's minimal assets. Because of this, the resolution must be registered at the *Registro delle imprese,* and it will only take effect ninety days after registration, if no objections are raised. If the reduction is opposed, the court must then ascertain whether it jeopardizes the creditors and may suspend its implementation unless and until they are given a suitable guarantee.

The reduction may arise as a result of either relinquishing the payment of contributions still due or distributing to shareholders sums of money and property out of company's assets. The shares issued by the company must then be modified. This is done either by replacing them with shares with a lower face value or by transferring to the company shares that are then cancelled. The reduction must not reduce the capital to below the legal minimum or produce violations of other rules inherent in the amount of the capital (e.g., a maximum two-to-one ratio between the value of the bonds and the value of the capital, legal reserve, and available reserves, pursuant to Article 2412 CC or the rules about legal limits of treasury shares).

163. A reduction caused by losses is optional if the losses do not exceed one-third of the capital. Within this limit, therefore, the law says that the capital of an S.p.A. as appearing in the companies' register does not have to correspond to corporate assets of equal value. In such a situation, the directors do not have to convene a shareholders' meeting. If, however, a shareholders' meeting is convened, the capital may either be reduced to adjust it to the residual assets or left unchanged. If, as a result of the losses, the corporate assets have been reduced to less than two-thirds of the capital, the CC requires the governing bodies to take action to put an end to a situation in which the apparent capital is not reflected in adequate assets. As soon as the directors or the board of management acknowledge the losses, they must convene a shareholders' meeting and prepare a report on the company's financial position. The report, together with the observations of the collegio sindacale or of the management control committee, must be made available to the shareholders at least eight days before the shareholders' meeting.

The shareholders' meeting may resolve either to immediately reduce the capital or to carry the losses forward to the following year's accounts. If losses in excess of one-third are confirmed the following year, the shareholders' meeting or the supervisory board must reduce the company's capital when they pass the resolution approving the balance sheets. As this is a mandatory act, the shareholders' meeting must deliberate on the majorities envisaged for ordinary decisions. If the resolution is not passed by the shareholders' meeting, the directors, the *sindaci,* or the supervisory board may apply to the court, which will direct that the capital be reduced in proportion to the losses incurred by the company. The resolution to reduce the capital or the court order must be registered at the *Registro delle imprese*.

If the losses reduce the capital to below the legal minimum of EUR 50,000.00, a special shareholders' meeting must be immediately convened to first reduce the capital and then either increase it to at least the legal minimum or transform the company into a different type of company requiring a minimum capital equal to or less than the residual capital. Without any such resolution, the company will have to be liquidated, and liquidators will have to be appointed either by a shareholders' meeting or by the court.

§4. Shares, Bonds, and Other Financial Instruments

I. Shares

A. Definition and Fundamental Principles

164. Shares are the typical and traditional instrument of participation in an S.p.A. The term *share* no longer has to correspond to a paper document. It refers to a set of rights and obligations that arise as a result of participating in the S.p.A.

The issuing of a document (share certificate) representing participation in the S.p.A. is now optional for any companies that adopt the system of 'dematerialization'. Companies listed on the stock exchange no longer have share certificates.

As a rule, the shares will have a face value corresponding to a fraction of the share capital, but the by-laws may exclude such a specification. In this case, the rules on the face value will refer to the ratio between the number of shares and the total number of shares issued.

Generally speaking, the shareholders will be allocated a number of shares proportional to the capital that they have subscribed. However, the by-laws may also allocate shares non-proportionally, or even without the contribution (or without all the contribution) being reckoned in the share capital. Shares may, in fact, be allocated to shareholders who provide services to employees, but their contributions are not reckoned in the share capital.

This has made it possible to reconcile the S.p.A.'s need to benefit from contributions of services other than those that contribute to the formation of the capital with the need to guarantee third parties with a minimum capital formed in accordance with the rules described above.

165. Usually, the shares are of equal value and attribute rights proportionate to the number of shares held (Article 2348, paragraph I, CC).

The by-laws may, however, envisage the creation of categories of shares with different voting rights and different rights to share in profits or losses. The shares of each category must attribute equal rights to the shareholders. Certain special categories of shareholders are standardized in the CC, but the by-laws may also create non-standard categories.

Unless the by-laws provide otherwise, the shares will attribute the right to participate in the profits and in the liquidation of the company (capital rights). The by-laws may either increase or reduce capital rights, but they may not exclude participation in the profit or in the loss *(pactum leoninum).*

If provided in the by-laws shares may attribute the right to receive profits either: (i) before the profits have been distributed among all; or (ii) to an extent greater than other shares; or (iii) shares that participate in losses only if the loss exceeds the loss absorbed by the other shares. The possibility has also been recently introduced in the creation of categories of shares, the capital rights of which are correlated to the results of a specific sector of the company's business, as provided by the by-laws (correlated shares, Article 2350, paragraph II, CC).

Shares usually give the right to vote at a shareholders' meeting. In the framework of this right, however, the by-laws have ample space to adapt the shares to the requirements of the shareholders; the ban on creating shares with multiple votes has been abolished by the Law Decree No. 91/2014, converted by Law No. 116/2014.

Categories of shares may be created without voting rights or with voting restricted to specific resolutions (distributing profits, extraordinary shareholders' meetings, amendments to the by-laws, etc.) or with voting subject to specific prerequisites, provided that they have been established in advance.

Maximum limits may also be introduced on the number of votes of each shareholder, or variable limits depending on the number of shares, reducing the proportional power of shareholders holding more shares.

Moreover, as far as listed companies are concerned, the by-laws may provide that the shares held by a shareholder for a specified period (anyway, not less than one year) will attribute the right to benefit of an increase up to 10% in the participation in the profits (Article 127*quater* TUF).

The right to receive increased profits may be attributed on behalf of shareholders holding individually not more than 0.5% of the capital. For shareholders having a participation exceeding 0.5%, the right may be granted in the limit of 0.5% of the capital. Anyway, the right may not be attributed to shareholders having a dominant influence in the company.

B. Special Categories of Shares

166. Certain special categories of shares are regulated by the CC and by the TUF (Legislative Decree No. 58/1998).

Shares with a limited vote may not exceed half the share capital. This is to avert creating an excessive imbalance between risk-facing shareholders and shareholders with voting rights.

Shareholders who own special categories of shares will vote at special meetings on resolutions passed at the annual meeting, which might jeopardize the rights attached to the special shares (Article 2376 CC). Any such resolutions passed at the annual meeting must be approved by the majorities envisaged for extraordinary shareholders' meetings, and they may not be deposited at the companies register until they have been approved by a meeting of the special categories of shareholders affected by the resolution.

The rules envisaged for extraordinary shareholders' meetings apply to the special meetings.

1. Shares for Employees

167. The by-laws may allow the shareholders' meeting to allocate to employees of the company or of its subsidiaries shares corresponding to profits earned by the company (Article 2349 CC). The profits must be converted into capital, and the shares issued in the framework of the ensuing capital increase are allocated to the employees on the basis of criteria established by the shareholders' meeting. The by-laws will specify the rights to vote and share in profits and losses, as well as rules regulating the circulation of the shares.

2. Correlated Shares

168. The by-laws may provide for the issuing of shares with a right to share in profits and losses geared to the performance of a specific sector of business (Article 2350 CC). The payment of dividends is subject to the existence of profits in the company's balance sheets. The by-laws must envisage all the elements and criteria required to identify the sector of business, its results, and the manner in which they are itemized in the accounts.

3. Dividend-Right Shares

169. In the event of the shares being refunded, the shareholders may be allocated dividend-right shares, which, unless the by-laws provide otherwise, are bereft of voting rights (Article 2353 CC). The shares will give the right to dividends provided that the ordinary shares have been allocated profits to the extent of the legal limit, and they will give the right to a liquidation quota, once the face value of the ordinary shares has been refunded.

4. Savings Shares

170. Savings shares may be issued by S.p.A.s with ordinary shares listed on Italian-regulated markets or on regulated markets of other EU countries (Article 145 of TUF). They are bereft of voting rights, but attribute capital privileges in accordance with the provisions of the by-laws. The shares must specify the capital rights they attribute and have the denomination of *azioni di risparmio.* Unless otherwise provided, in the event of a capital increase, they attribute a right of option over savings shares and preference shares or, if there are none, over ordinary shares. The ban on exceeding half the share capital also applies to savings shares. If this limit is exceeded, the ratio must be re-established on the terms set forth in Article 145 of the TUF, and, if this is not done, the company must be liquidated.

The by-laws will establish the rights of holders of savings shares in the event of exclusion from trading on regulated markets.

5. Loyalty Shares and Multiple Voting Shares

171. Law Decree No. 91/2014, converted by Law No. 116/2014, introduced both loyalty shares and the dual class system of multiple voting shares. In the international scenario, this kind of stocks is attributed to the founders or to extremely visionary shareholders who make great the company with their ideas and ability. In this way they can keep the control of the corporation while they let fresh capitals in. According to the new text of Article 2351 CC, paragraph 4, non-listed companies have the opportunity to attribute up to three votes each share by a specific clause in the by-laws. Moreover, the issuing of shares with a limited vote (only on particular matters, or up to a certain threshold), or with no vote at all are admitted too. Multiple voting shares are a special class of stocks, and their privileges are transferable. Article 127*sexies* TUF prohibits issuing these shares in listed companies, but they can be approved and issued before the listing and keep their status when the corporation goes public.

172. Article 127*quinquies* introduced in Italy a regulation inspired to the loyalty shares of French law. Under this article it is possible to attribute up to two votes each stock to those shareholders who keep those stocks for more than twenty-four consecutive months. This option has to be expressed in the by-laws and the loyalty shares are subjected to a specific transparency regulation set up by CONSOB. When the stock with the loyalty right is sold, or when in a corporation where loyalty shares represent more than 3% of the share capital a controlling equity share is transferred, the additional vote expires. The by-laws may provide exceptions in case of succession or when new stocks are issued using reserve capital. Loyalty shares are not considered a special category of stocks under Article 2348 CC and the resolution by which they are established (through an amendment of the by-laws) does not provide the right to withdraw from the corporation. Additional votes are included in the calculation for constitution and voting quorum.

C. *How the Shares Circulate*

173. The rules regulating circulation vary according to whether the company issues registered shares, bearer shares, or dematerialized shares, or whether it issues no share certificates.

If issued, the share certificates must indicate the name and address of the company, the date of incorporation, the date and office of registration, the face value (or, if the face value is not envisaged, the number of shares issued and the share capital), the amount of contributions paid in, and the rights and obligations attributed by the certificates.

In the case of unlisted companies, registered shares are usually issued. Theoretically, this means that the effects of the transfer can only occur either once a new shareholder has been registered in the company's register of shareholders and on the certificate or by issuing a new certificate.

This form of transfer requires exhibiting to the company either the certificate or a deed proving the purchase, and it is, therefore, used in cases in which it is not possible to simply endorse the certificate.

However, the signing of the endorsement by the transferor with the signature authenticated by a notary or by another authorized person enables the person specified in it to exercise any rights inherent in the share (Article 2355 CC), even before the transfer is noted in the register of shareholders. The company must, however, update the register of shareholders, which is the instrument used to identify the shareholders.

174. Registration in the register of shareholders is, on the other hand, essential in cases in which the by-laws exclude the issuing of share certificates. This makes the transfer mechanism similar to the transfer mechanism typical of an S.r.l.

In this case, the effects of the transfer will occur only once the transferee has obtained registration in the register of shareholders by exhibiting a deed of purchase of the holding from a registered shareholder.

All financial instruments reserved for trading on regulated markets are subject to the legislative provisions on dematerialization (Legislative Decree No. 213 of 24 June 1998). Like other financial instruments issued by listed companies, shares are, therefore, no longer material certificates, but appear in accounting entries kept by a depositary agent.

The handling of transfers takes place in a centralized manner in the form of a transfer order passed by the transferor to the depositary agent, who cancels the shares from the transferor's account and registers them in the transferee's account. A shareholder who needs to demonstrate ownership of the share so as to exercise his or her rights must obtain a certificate from the depositary agent. In order to exercise corporate rights, registration in the record of shareholders is not necessary.

175. Finally, as a rule, the CC still permits the issuing of bearer shares, but since 1992 special laws require that only registered shares may be issued, with the exception of savings shares and shares issued by variable capital investment companies. The issuing of bearer shares presupposes, however, that the entire contribution has been paid.

The transfer of bearer shares takes effect upon delivery, and exhibition of the certificate is sufficient for corporate rights to be exercised. The provisions on dematerialized shares nevertheless apply to bearer shares traded on regulated markets.

D. Limits on the Circulation of Shares

176. The S.p.A. is a type of company characterized by changing shareholders. These changes are facilitated by the fact that participation is embodied in a certificate. However, especially in the case of unlisted companies, there may be justified reasons for permitting a prior verification of shareholders. For this reason, the CC contemplates a series of limits that may be imposed on the circulation of shares in the by-laws.

This means that:

(a) transferring shares may be prohibited for a maximum period of five years;
(b) transferring may be subject to pre-established conditions;
(c) transferring may be conditional on the approval (which does not have to be justified) of a governing body or of the shareholders, provided that, in the event of refusal, the shareholder is either guaranteed that the shares will be purchased or is given the right to withdraw, with his or her holding being paid at a specific price, bearing in mind the assets of the company, its prospects, and its market value.

Provisions of the by-laws that envisage mere approval without respecting the shareholder's right to monetize his or her shares will be ineffective. Clauses limiting circulation of the shares may be introduced with favourable votes of the majority required for extraordinary resolutions, unless the by-laws require unanimity. Limits on the circulation of bearer shares may not be introduced. In any case, to transfer shares with respect to which contributions have not been fully paid, the vendor is under a duty, jointly and severally with the purchaser, to pay the contributions for three years after the transfer is noted in the register of shareholders.

Usually pre-emption clauses are set out by a contract among shareholders, and the effects of such clauses do not influence legal relations with third parties, nevertheless the Italian Supreme Court held that, when a pre-emption clause is inserted in the article of association, its effects are enforceable against anyone.[17]

E. Usufruct, Pledge, and Attachment of Shares

177. Shares may: (i) be subject to usufruct, (ii) constitute a guarantee in the form of a pledge; or (iii) be attached by judicial order. In all three cases, the problem arises from attributing capital and administrative rights to the shareholder and/or to the party benefiting from the encumbrance. In such circumstances, Article 2352 CC grants the shareholder a right of option, but if he or she fails to promptly pay the amount due, the right of option may be sold to the other shareholders or to third parties. In the event of a capital increase at no cost, the encumbrances will extend to the new shares. The dividends will go to the person who benefits from the usufruct (*usufructuarius*)

17. (Corte di Cassazione, 23 July 2012, n. 12797).

and, unless otherwise agreed, to the pledgee. The right of vote is vested in the *usufructuarius* or in the creditor in the case of a pledge, unless the parties have established otherwise, and it will always be vested in the custodian in the event of attachment.

F. *The Purchasing of Shares by the Issuing Company and by Subsidiaries or Affiliates*

178. There are two fundamental purposes behind the legal limits on the possibility of the shares being owned or on the vote being exercised by the issuing company and by companies that have deals with it that can influence its decisions.

First of all, it is essential that, as a result of operations on shares, the principle according to which the corporate assets must not be less (except at the permitted percentages) than the share capital, should not be eluded. Second, a sound management of the company means that the control exercised over the governing bodies by the shareholders' meeting cannot be influenced by members of the controlled bodies. This has given rise to a series of measures concerning: (i) the subscription and purchasing of treasury shares; and (ii) the purchasing of shares by subsidiaries and affiliates. These need to be examined separately.

1. Subscribing Treasury Shares and Reciprocal Subscriptions

179. The company may not subscribe its own shares (treasury shares). In so doing, the capital would, in fact, remain the same, while the assets would be reduced by the value of the contribution relating to the shares subscribed. If the shares are subscribed by the issuing company, they are allocated by law to the founders or, in the case of a capital increase, to the directors, who are thus obliged to pay the contribution. The reciprocal subscription of shares between two companies is also prohibited, as this would have the same effect as that described above.

2. Purchasing Treasury Shares

180. The purchasing of treasury shares is subject to procedural conditions and restrictions and to quantitative limits. The shares may be purchased only using available profits and reserves and, therefore, only if the corporate assets exceed the capital. The purchase must be authorized by a shareholders' meeting, which establishes the fundamental elements of the operation, bypassing the discretionary power of the directors in this respect (quantity, minimum or maximum price, and a period of purchase not exceeding eighteen months). Finally, treasury shares in the corporation that resort to the risk capital market, including the shares owned by the subsidiaries, may not exceed 20% of the capital. This is to ensure that the balance among shareholders at a shareholders' meeting remains basically the same. The rules covering the purchasing of treasury shares do not apply in such cases as a reduction in capital with redemption of shares, purchase for no consideration, succession, merger/demerger, or action for execution. If the purchase goes ahead in breach of legal procedures and formalities and if, in any event, the treasury shares exceed the legal limits, the shares must be sold within the period of time determined by the law and following the procedures established by a shareholders' meeting and cancelled by the directors with a consequent reduction in capital.

Treasury shares give not the company the right to profit and the right of option; they are attributed proportionally to the other shareholders, and voting rights are suspended. Article 2368 paragraph 3, CC provide that in listed corporations treasury shares are calculated to set up the meeting, but not for the calculation of the majority quorum. Instead in unlisted S.p.A. Article 2357*ter*, paragraph 2, CC set out a discipline under which shares are calculated both to set up the meeting and for the majority quorum.

These mechanisms are aimed at ensuring that there are no repercussions on relations within a shareholders' meeting or on relations between a shareholders' meeting and the directors.

Treasury shares may not be accepted as a guarantee, and the company may not grant credits as a guarantee so as to purchase treasury shares. In principle, the company may not loan money or give warranties to the subscribers or purchasers of its shares or receive shares as a warranty for obligations of third parties.

Only the extraordinary shareholders' meeting may authorize such kind of operations on the basis of a directors' report with a complete legal and economic analysis. In any case, the shares are negotiated at the market average price of the last six months or on the basis of last balance sheet as provided for in Article 2437*ter* CC.

3. Subsidiaries

181. Article 2359 of the CC defines the notions of subsidiary and affiliate. The two notions have been included in the CC as they are subjective prerequisites when it comes to enforcing subsequent provisions on purchases of shares between companies, but they are also used by numerous special laws for other purposes (e.g., by antitrust laws and laws on banks, insurance, and finance). In special legislation, however, we find many different definitions of *subsidiary* or *affiliate,* which are provided for specific purposes and may, therefore, differ from the provisions of Article 2359 of the CC.

A company is a wholly controlled subsidiary in cases in which:

- another company has the majority of voting rights at a shareholders' meeting (internal control by right);
- another company has sufficient votes to exert a dominant influence at an ordinary shareholders' meeting (de facto internal control);
- another company is in a position to exert a dominant influence as a result of contractual ties with the subsidiary (external control).

For the purposes of verifying whether or not there is internal control, account must also be taken of the voting rights the company can exercise through trustees or through other subsidiaries. It should be stressed that it is the voting rights that count, regardless of ownership of the shares, whereas ownership of shares without votes or with non-exercisable votes is immaterial. The vote may be available not just as a result of ownership, but also as a result of a usufruct, a pledge over the shares, or even contractual relations that enable a shareholder to sway the vote of others (shareholders' agreements).

The concept of 'dominant influence' refers to cases in which it is not necessary to reach an absolute majority of votes to influence the decisions of a meeting. This tends to be the case when voting rights are spread among large numbers of shareholders who hold minimal stakes in the capital and who have little interest in taking part in shareholders' meetings.

Traditionally, there have been very few cases of external control in Italy, because so-called domination agreements were prohibited prior to the 2003 reform. Even before the reform, however, there could be agreements on how the company should be run (distribution agreements and patent licensing agreements), which are so important for one of the parties that they allow the counterparty to influence company decisions.

A control relationship for the purposes indicated in Article 2359 CC only arises between the holding company and its subsidiary and not between subsidiaries controlled by the same parent company.

4. Affiliates

182. Article 2359, final paragraph, defines an affiliate as a company over which another company exerts 'a considerable influence'. The concept of considerable influence is not specified, but the provision introduces an implied presumption of affiliation in cases in which a company can exercise at least one-fifth of the votes at the ordinary shareholders' meeting (or one-tenth if the affiliate is a listed company).

The tie of affiliation does not affect the rules relating to the shares so much as the rules relating to the balance sheet (*see* below, §7, III.)

5. Operations on Shares of the Holding Company

183. The rules on treasury shares are generally extended to the shares of the holding company in such a way as to ensure that the bars and limits thus introduced are not eluded:

(a) Shares in the holding company may not be subscribed. Any shares that are in any case subscribed will be allocated to the directors along with all ensuing rights and obligations.
(b) The subsidiary may not purchase shares in the holding company except by using available profits and reserves, with the due authorization of the shareholders' meeting and within a limit of 20% of the capital of holdings that resort to the risk capital market.[18]

The subsidiary is not entitled to vote and must set up a non-available reserve equal to the amount of the shares. Any shares purchased in breach of these rules must either be resold within one year or cancelled, with a reduction in capital. The exceptions envisaged in Article 2359 for treasury shares also apply to subsidiaries.

18. In this percentage has to be included the treasury shares of the controlling company and those owned by the controlled companies.

G. *Holding Stakes in Other Enterprises*

184. The purchasing of shares or stakes in other companies or enterprises is regulated by the CC in general terms, and by the TUF, as far as purchasing stakes in listed companies is concerned.

The rules of the CC are designed to safeguard shareholders and third parties against potential risks inherent in purchasing stakes. Consequently, the Code regulates: (i) purchases of holdings that imply de facto a modification of the corporate purpose; and (ii) purchases involving the assumption of unlimited liability.

Unless specifically contemplated in the by-laws, purchasing stakes is prohibited if this involves changing the corporate purpose because of the size of the stakes or the purpose of the company bought into. Although the CC does not specify the effects of a purchase made in breach of this rule, it is generally thought that the directors will account for any harm caused, that the purchase may not be legally invoked, and that it will, therefore, be declared ineffective vis-à-vis the company.

To purchase stakes involving unlimited liability, on the other hand, the authorization of a shareholders' meeting is required, although this is without prejudice to the liability of the directors to the extent of the diligence expected of them. To ensure that shareholders and third parties are duly informed, the holdings must be included in a supplementary note to the balance sheets.

The special provisions of the TUF on purchasing stakes are not designed to safeguard the purchasing company and its shareholders, but to ensure that the market and the shareholders of listed companies are properly informed.

Purchases of stakes in a listed company that lead to specific thresholds being exceeded (3%, 5%, 10%,15%, 20%, 25%, 30%, 50%, 66.6% and 90%) or sales of stakes leading to the percentage falling below the aforementioned thresholds must be notified to CONSOB by the purchaser within five days.

The purchasing of interwoven stakes in excess of 3% is prohibited. The last company to exceed the threshold, therefore, loses the right to vote for the shares exceeding the limit; if it is not possible to assess which was the last company to exceed the threshold, the vote of both companies is limited.

Finally, the purchasing of shares in a listed company at a level in excess of 30% (25% if it is not a SME and there is not another controlling shareholder) of the capital gives rise to the obligation to launch a takeover bid for all the remaining shares at a price not lower than the average price of the last twelve months or the highest price paid by the purchaser during the same period of time.

The purpose of the takeover bid requirement is to ensure equal treatment for all shareholders by distributing to minority shareholders, too, the so-called majority premium, that is, the higher price that is usually paid to obtain control of the company.

CONSOB may grant an exoneration from the takeover bid requirement on the above conditions if the purchaser has exceeded the 30% threshold following a public offer for at least 60% of the capital. This so-called preventive takeover bid must, however, be approved by the majority of shareholders and launched in compliance with the prerequisites established by the law.

II. Financial Instruments of Participation Other Than Shares

185. The 2003 company law reform introduced the right for S.p.A.s to issue financial instruments of participation other than shares (Article 2346, paragraph V, CC). The typical feature of financial instruments of participation is the existence of a contribution not reckoned in the share capital (unlike shares). In exchange for this contribution, capital rights are attributed that are: (i) linked to the performance of the company; and (ii) in any event subordinate to repayment of the company's debts (unlike bonds).

The CC contains few principles with regard to the issuing of financial instruments of participation and to the capital and administrative rights vested in the holders of such instruments. These principles, therefore, have to be inferred from the general system of S.p.A.s and the by-laws.

186. In the absence of any legislative provision, the decision to issue financial instruments of participation rests with the governing body. Only in cases of an issue for the benefit of employees will the decision rest with an extraordinary shareholders' meeting, which may also establish rules on such matters as exercising rights, stock transfers, and grounds of termination or redemption (Article 2349, paragraph II, CC).

There is some doubt as to whether, in cases of issuing financial instruments of participation, the shareholders have the right of option envisaged when shares are issued (Article 2441 CC). The application of Article 2441 CC by analogy could be justified in cases in which financial instruments of participation attribute rights that impact company management. The right of option may be contemplated in the by-laws for the benefit of both the shareholders and the holders of already issued instruments of participation.

Financial instruments of participation may be issued either in exchange for contributions, as with shares, or in exchange for rendering work and services. This further extends the possibilities S.p.A.s have to acquire useful contributions for their economic activity involving a participation in the business risk.

187. The CC provides no clear definition of the administrative and capital rights vested in the holders of financial instruments of participation. Such rights are established by the by-laws, with certain limits. As far as administrative rights are concerned, the right to vote may not usually be granted. However, the by-laws may envisage the right to vote on specific matters, the right to appoint an independent member of the governing body or of the supervisory body and other rights guaranteeing control and self-protection (e.g., taking part in shareholders' meetings, submitting requests to the governing bodies, and examining corporate books).

The by-laws may provide for holders of financial instruments of participation to take part in special meetings that are held to approve resolutions passed by a shareholders' meeting that might harm them.

Capital rights must imply participating in the business risk. There may, therefore, be: (i) payments correlated to the company's performance, establishing amounts and due dates; or (ii) liquidation of participation quotas, provided that they are subordinate to payment of the company's debts. This is the difference between financial instruments of participation and bonds.

188. Financial instruments of participation may be transferred according to the rules contemplated in the company's by-laws. In addition to the protection provided by the administrative rights acknowledged in the by-laws, owners of financial instruments of participation with repayment linked to the company's economic performance may activate the remedies contemplated for bondholders (*see* below, in the next paragraph), if a shareholders' meeting passes resolutions that might harm them. Financial instruments of participation must be described in a supplementary note to the balance sheet, specifying their number, characteristics, capital, and administrative rights, and any operations affecting them.

189. Law Decree No. 83/2012, converted by Law n. 134/2012, introduced new financial instruments for unlisted S.p.A. (excluding micro enterprises under Commission Recommendation of 6 May 2003 No. 361 and banks) in order to endorse their activity in capital markets, and namely: – 'Financial promissory note', which in the past could be issued by unlisted company after a rating report, now are available for every corporation. It is necessary a sponsor (a bank, a broker, or a financial intermediary); these kind of promissory note must be offered exclusively to professional investors that are not shareholders of the issuer; and the last balance sheet must be certified by a qualified auditor. – 'Subordinate bonds' are bonds with a duration of thirty-six months or more, which provide for a right to participate in profits according to a specific clause passed at the moment of their issuing.

III. Bonds

190. A bond is a type of instrument that enables a company to finance its economic activity without direct participation in the business risk. Bonds are usually characterized by the obligation to return the money paid by the bondholder, with interest, on a set due date, regardless of the company's performance or of the existence of other types of credit.

The distinction among bonds, shares, and financial instruments of participation has gradually become blurred following the emergence of: (i) bonds attributing rights linked to the company's performance; (ii) correlated shares; and (iii) bonds convertible into shares.

The 2003 Company Reform Law has encouraged this development by permitting the issuing of participation bonds and convertible bonds. Furthermore, following the reform, bonds may be issued by S.r.l.s and by *società cooperative,* too, and not only by S.p.A.s, as previously envisaged.

191. Bond issues are resolved by the governing body. The issuing of bonds convertible into shares is an exception to this, as it must be resolved by an extraordinary shareholders' meeting. The minutes must, however, be drawn up by a notary and deposited at the *Registro delle Imprese*.

The bond certificates must contain the information envisaged in Article 2414 CC. This information refers both to the issuing company (name, purpose, registered office, capital, and reserves when the bonds are issued) and to the bonds (issue resolution, total amount, face value of each certificate, rights attributed to the bondholder, and criteria applied in determining the returns, guarantee, and repayment date).

192. The bonds may be issued for up to a maximum value equal to twice the sum of the capital, the legal reserve, and the available reserves. This limit is not enforced to guarantee the company's solvency, but to avert excessively risky management conduct arising from the laxer situation that might arise as a result of having an excess of debt capital in relation to risk capital.

Under Article 2412 CC, the limit may be exceeded in cases in which guarantees or other forms of control make the precaution arising from the bonds/capital ratio superfluous (e.g., bonds guaranteed by a mortgage on the company's real estate for at least two-thirds of the value; bonds reserved for professional investors who are under an obligation to guarantee the company's solvency to those to whom they transfer the bonds; and bonds issued by companies listed on regulated markets and listed bonds, in view of the public supervision and the control exercised by the market). Special exceptions may be contemplated by special laws for specific sectors of activity (e.g., banks).

To maintain the debt/capital ratio, the capital may not be reduced (and the reserves may not be distributed) to less than half the value of the bonds. In the event of a reduction in capital resulting from loss, no distribution of profits will be permitted as long as the capital is below the aforementioned ratio in relation to the bonds in circulation.

The TUF and the TUB contain provisions on issuing and placing bonds that are designed to safeguard the transparency and stability of the financial market.

193. The bondholders may enforce their rights either individually or through an organization (meeting of bondholders) and a joint representative.

The meeting of bondholders will be convened by the joint representative, by the company's directors, or by the holders of at least 5% of the bonds. The participants can deliberate upon matters of common interest, which include, *inter alia,* the appointment of the joint representative, changes to the conditions of the loan, access by the company to temporary receivership, or composition with creditors. Changes to the terms of the loan may not, however, give rise to a transformation of the nature of the relationship (e.g., conversion into capital or waiver of repayment).

The resolutions of the meeting of bondholders are passed by the majority envisaged for extraordinary shareholders' meetings. However, as far as resolutions involving changes to the terms of the loan are concerned, the favourable votes of half of the bondholders are required in second call, too. To challenge resolutions, the requirements envisaged for a shareholders' meeting in Articles 2377 and 2379 CC must be satisfied.

The joint representative will be appointed either by the meeting of bondholders or, in cases when this is not possible, by the court, at the request of a bondholder or of the company's directors. Members of the company's governing bodies or anyone ineligible to be appointed auditor pursuant to Article 2399 CC may not be appointed as joint representative. The joint representative will remain in office for three years and may be re-elected.

The joint representative has the task of safeguarding the bondholders. To this end, he or she takes part in the shareholders' meetings, without the right to vote, enforces the resolutions of the meetings of bondholders, and represents the bondholders in judicial disputes, including insolvency proceedings.

The protection provided by the joint representative does not bar the right of individual bondholders to proceed against the company. Such an action is barred only in cases in which it conflicts with resolutions lawfully adopted by a meeting of bondholders.

IV. Convertible Bonds

194. Convertible bonds perform a hybrid function insofar as, in addition to the financing purpose, they also entitle the bondholder to turn his or her credit into participation in the capital. The rules of the CC thus refer to: (i) modifying the capital as a result of the conversion; and (ii) safeguarding the rights of bondholders in the lead up to the conversion deadline.

The issuing of convertible bonds must be approved in a resolution passed by an extraordinary shareholders' meeting, in view of the fact that the conversion implies modifying the share capital and, therefore, the by-laws. The resolution must specify the conversion ratio and procedures. The bonds may not be issued unless the capital has been fully paid in. The issue does not have to take place immediately after the resolution. Indeed, the directors may be authorized to issue the bonds for a pre-established maximum amount within five years of the resolution. The shareholders have the right of option.

The resolution to increase the capital must be registered at the *Registro delle Imprese* within thirty days. After this, every six months, the directors must issue shares to bondholders who exercise the conversion, after which they will deposit a declaration confirming the capital increase.

Conversion is nothing more than a right, and the bondholders may, therefore, waive exercising this right. To ensure that the bondholders are not harmed in the lead up to the expiry of the conversion deadline, the capital may not be reduced by repaying contributions to the shareholders, and the by-laws may not be amended as far as distributing profits is concerned. Such operations will, however, be possible if the bondholders have been given adequate advance notice such as to allow them to exercise the conversion. For the same reason, in the event of a capital increase with no contribution or a reduction in capital resulting from losses, the conversion ratio must be adjusted.

Holders of convertible bonds are entitled not only to the right to interest and reimbursement, but also to the right of option if shares or further convertible bonds are issued.

Sometimes, the bondholder is granted an autonomous right of option or a warrant to purchase shares in the company or in controlled company. The warrant may either be exercised by paying the sum envisaged for purchasing the shares or else selling to third parties.

§5. Shareholders' Meetings

I. Functions and Types of Shareholders' Meetings

195. The function of shareholders' meetings is to express the will of the company in relation to the most important decisions concerning its organization and administration. The powers of shareholders' meetings vary according to the model of administration adopted. Some of the deliberations vested in shareholders' meetings in companies based on the ordinary model and on the one-tier model are, in fact, vested in the supervisory board in two-tier companies (e.g., approving the balance sheets).

The shareholders' meeting is a collective body. Therefore, its deliberations are not simply the sum of the shareholders' wishes, but they require compliance with procedural rules as far as setting up the meeting and passing resolutions are concerned. When the quorums required by the law or by the by-laws are reached, the decision of the shareholders' meeting will be binding on the company and on all the shareholders, including those who disagree or are absent.

In cases in which the company has issued ordinary shares only, all the shareholders may take part. If there are different categories of shares, on the other hand, the holders of ordinary shares and any other shareholders so entitled may take part in the meeting. The holders of shares other than ordinary shares will participate in special meetings that are held to approve resolutions passed by a shareholders' meeting that may cause them damage. Special meetings are disciplined by the rules that apply to extraordinary shareholders' meetings.

Shareholders' meetings may be either ordinary or extraordinary, depending on the subject matter of the resolution. At extraordinary meetings, stricter rules apply to the quorums required to set them up and to pass resolutions. This is to ensure that the resolutions conform to the wishes of shareholders holding a larger percentage of the capital.

II. Ordinary Shareholders' Meetings

196. The responsibilities of ordinary shareholders' meetings are set forth in Article 2364 CC for companies based on the ordinary or one-tier model, and, in Article 2364*bis,* for two-tier companies.

In the former case, an ordinary shareholders' meeting has the authority to do the following:

- approve the balance sheets;
- appoint and remove directors;
- appoint the *sindaci* and the chairperson of the *collegio sindacale* and, if envisaged, the external auditors;
- establish the remuneration due to directors and *sindaci,* if this is not envisaged in the by-laws;
- resolve to file proceedings against the directors and *sindaci,*

- authorize the directors to perform operations, in cases for which this is envisaged in the by-laws;
- approve the rules of the meeting;
- deliberate on any other matters envisaged by specific provisions of law.

The authorization of a shareholders' meeting does not exonerate the directors from liability but simply meets a condition so that they may perform operations with respect to which the by-laws require a prior positive evaluation on the part of the shareholders.

In the case of two-tier companies, an ordinary shareholders' meeting has the authority to do the following:

- appoint and remove the supervisory directors;
- establish the remuneration of the supervisory directors, if this is not established in the by-laws;
- resolve to file proceedings against the directors and *sindaci;*
- deliberate on the distribution of profits;
- appoint the external auditors; and
- deliberate on any other matters envisaged by specific provisions of law.

III. Extraordinary Shareholders' Meetings

197. The resolutions requiring an extraordinary shareholders' meeting are specified in Article 2365 CC, as well as in the specific provisions contained in other legislative measures.

The resolutions of extraordinary shareholders' meetings contemplated in the CC consist of amending the by-laws and appointing or replacing liquidators. However, the by-laws may empower the governing body, the supervisory board, or the management council to adopt resolutions on such matters as: (i) mergers of companies that are wholly owned or owned 90%; (ii) setting up and closing branches and moving the registered office within national territory; (iii) appointing directors with powers of representation; (iv) reducing the capital following the withdrawal of a shareholder; and (v) adapting the by-laws to legal requirements.

IV. Convocation

198. Authority for convening shareholders' meetings usually rests with the governing body (board of directors, sole director, or management board). If there is a collective body, a resolution and/or a mandate on one or more directors is required. A shareholders' meeting may be convened whenever the body responsible deems fit. The law nevertheless envisages a number of cases in which convocation is compulsory.

First of all, once a year, a shareholders' meeting must be convened within either 120 days of the close of the financial year or any shorter period envisaged in the by-laws. In the cases of companies that have to submit consolidated balance sheets or, for special reasons inherent in the structure or purpose of the activity, the by-laws may envisage a period of up to 180 days.

A shareholders' meeting must also be convened in a series of cases in which decisions have to be passed to enable the company to continue operating (reduction in capital, pursuant to Article 2446 CC; reduction and re-establishment of capital or transformation of the company, pursuant to Article 2447 CC); to enable its governing bodies to operate correctly (appointing directors, pursuant to Article 2386 CC, appointing *sindaci,* pursuant to Article 2401 CC; urgent measures if irregularities are ascertained by the *collegio sindacale,* pursuant to Article 2406 CC); or to appoint liquidators in the event of liquidation.

Finally, a shareholders' meeting must be convened whenever shareholders representing at least one-tenth of the capital or any lower percentage contemplated by the by-laws so request. In the case of companies that resort to the risk capital market, the minimum percentage to request the convocation of a shareholders' meeting is fixed in one-twentieth of the capital. The shareholders' request must specify the matters to be discussed, but it may not refer to decisions requiring proposals or reports by the directors.

If the directors fail to convene the shareholders' meeting, it may be convened by the supervisory body, the *collegio sindacale,* supervisory board or management control committee. If the supervisory body fails to do so, the meeting may be convened by the court at the request of the shareholders, after consulting the members of the governing and supervisory bodies. In this case, the court must designate the chair person of the meeting.

199. The convocation must provide an indication of the place, day, and time of the meeting. A date for a second call may also be specified if the quorum is not reached in the first call. The convocation must contain the agenda, that is, the matters on which the participants in the meeting are asked to deliberate. The sole purpose of the agenda is to enable the shareholders to prepare themselves with respect to the matters on the agenda, which may, therefore, be specified in general terms. In respect to listed companies, Article 126*bis* of the TUF provides that shareholders representing at least one-fortieth of the capital may ask an integration of the agenda, within ten days from the publication of the convocation.

As far as companies that resort to the risk capital market are concerned, the convocation must be published at least fifteen days beforehand in the *Official Gazette* or in a daily newspaper specified in the by-laws. In the case of other S.p.A.s, the by-laws may envisage: (i) other manners of convocation, provided that they ensure proof of receipt (e.g., a registered letter with acknowledgement of receipt); and (ii) a reduced period of advance notice of no less than eight days.

Moreover, in the case of listed companies, Article 125*bis* of the TUF provides that the convocation must be published at least thirty days beforehand in the website of the company.

A shareholders' meeting may also be held without convocation if all the shareholders and the majority of members of the governing bodies take part (a general meeting, pursuant to Article 2366, paragraph IV, CC). The shareholders may, however, object to discussing matters with respect to which they consider that they are not adequately prepared.

Even in cases in which the shareholders' meeting has been duly convened, shareholders representing at least one-third of the capital may declare that they are not sufficiently well prepared to deliberate upon one or more matters on the agenda and obtain a postponement of the meeting of up to five days.

V. Quorum Required to Set Up a Meeting and Quorum Required to Pass Resolutions

200. The CC prescribes the minimum percentage of capital that has to be represented for a meeting to be valid (the quorum required to set up the meeting). The quorum required to set up the meeting serves the purpose of ensuring that the debate involves shareholders who represent a substantial quota of the capital. Failure to reach the quorum means that the meeting cannot be held. The meeting may be convened again (meeting in second call) with the same agenda, on a date already envisaged in the first notice of convocation or, alternatively, a new notice may be fixed. Further convocations may be envisaged in the by-laws, but a third convocation is envisaged by law for listed companies (Article 125 TUF).

Furthermore, the CC prescribes the minimum percentage of capital or of capital represented at the meeting by the shareholders, whose favourable votes are required for the resolution to be valid (the quorum required to pass resolutions).

The quorum required to set up the meeting and the quorum required to pass resolutions may vary. They are higher at meetings that address very important matters (extraordinary meetings) and lower in the case of companies that resort to the risk capital market, pursuant to Article 2325*bis* CC. In such companies, the reason for this is that it is difficult to obtain a high turnout because of their fragmented capital. Finally, the quorums may be either increased or reduced by the by-laws within the limits established by the law.

201. The quorums required to set up the meeting are, therefore, as follows:

- ordinary meeting in first call: 50% of the capital;
- ordinary meeting in second and subsequent call: none;
- extraordinary meeting in first call: none, but for the companies mentioned in Article 2325*bis* CC, 50% of the capital or any higher quorum envisaged in the by-laws;
- extraordinary meeting in second or subsequent calls: one-third, but for the companies mentioned in Article 2325*bis* CC, one-fifth of the capital or any higher quorum envisaged in the by-laws;

Larger majorities may be envisaged in the by-laws for the second and subsequent calls, but not for resolutions approving the balance sheets and resolutions designating or revoking company appointments of the governing bodies.

202. The quorums required to pass resolutions are as follows:

- ordinary meeting in first call: the majority of the capital, unless the by-laws require a higher quorum;[19]
- ordinary meeting in second and subsequent call: the majority of the capital attending the meeting;
- extraordinary meeting in first call: 50% of the capital, unless the by-laws require a higher quorum, but for the companies referred to in Article 2325*bis* CC, two-thirds of the capital represented by the shareholders at the meeting;
- extraordinary meeting in second or subsequent call: two-thirds of the capital represented by the shareholders at the meeting. For other companies, on the other hand, one-third of the capital is required in any case for the resolutions of particular importance listed in Article 2369, paragraph V.

As for the quorums required to set up the meetings, larger majorities to pass resolutions may be envisaged in the by-laws for the second and subsequent calls, but not for resolutions approving the balance sheets or resolutions designating or revoking company appointments of the governing bodies.

For the companies referred to in Article 2325*bis* CC, the by-laws may establish a single convocation, excluding meetings in second call and further convocations. In this case, the quorums required to set up meeting are as follows:

- ordinary meeting: none;
- extraordinary meeting: one-fifth of the capital.

The quorums required to pass resolutions are as follows:

- ordinary meeting: the majority of the capital;
- extraordinary meeting: two-thirds of the capital.

VI. The Right to Take Part in a Meeting and the Right to Vote

203. Shareholders and other people who have the right to vote may take part in shareholders' meetings (Article 2370 CC). Current legislation has thus provided a negative answer to past doubts as to whether holders of shares without voting rights may or may not take part. As a rule, therefore, persons other than holders of the right to vote and members of the governing bodies are not admitted, but, in the case of listed companies, CONSOB has recommended that financial analysts and specialized journalists be admitted to ensure that the information provided in the course of the meeting is made available to the market.

The by-laws may require the shareholder to deposit shares at the company or at selected banks within a deadline, which, in the case of the companies referred to in Article 2325*bis,* may not be more than two days. If the shares are dematerialized, the deposit procedure is replaced by a notice by the intermediary in whose files the shares are entered.

---

19. For the appointment of company's bodies, the by-laws may provide for voting systems not based on the majority principle.

If registered shares are deposited, the holders must be registered in the stock ledger.

204. If there is a conflict between the interest of a shareholder and that of the company, this may either invalidate the right to vote or make the resolutions voidable. The former case arises when a shareholder who is also a director votes on resolutions concerning his or her own liability and when a shareholder who is also a member of the board of management votes on resolutions concerning the appointment, removal, and liability of the supervisory directors.

In any other cases in which a shareholder has an interest for himself or herself or for others in conflict with that of the company, he or she is not deprived of the right to vote. However, if his or her vote plays a decisive role in approving the resolution, it may be voided pursuant to the provisions of Article 2377 CC, if it is such as to harm the company.

205. If the by-laws so permit, a shareholder may take part in a shareholders' meeting either by correspondence, by electronic systems, or by telecommunications. In the case of listed companies, voting by correspondence and by electronic systems is regulated by CONSOB.[20] Shareholders voting by correspondence are held to be in attendance for the purposes of verifying the quorum.

A shareholder may take part in the shareholders' meeting through a representative unless this is prohibited by the by-laws. However, representation is strictly regulated by the CC and is subject to limits so as to prevent: (i) the shareholder depriving himself of herself from exercising his or her vote without fully understanding what this might imply; and (ii) the representative pursuing his or her own interests, which may be in conflict with those of the persons whom he or she is representing.

First of all, the power of representation must be granted in a written document specifying the name of the representative, which must be preserved by the company. If the representative is a legal entity, only an employee or a delegated person of the company may take part in the meeting. To avert conflicts of interest, in unlisted companies, members of the governing or auditing bodies and employees of the company or its subsidiaries may not be appointed as representatives.

206. As far as listed companies are concerned, Article 135*decies* of the TUF envisages the possibility for the shareholder to designate a representative who is in a 'conflict of interest' position, provided that the representative gives written communications of the conflict to the shareholder and the shareholder gives the representative specific voting instructions. Conflict of interest subsists in every case in which the representative has an interest in the deliberation, due to his position in the organs, his participation in the capital and other cases regulated by the TUF.

Moreover, listed companies – at each shareholder meeting – may appoint a person to whom shareholders can confer proxies with voting instructions. By-laws, however, may exclude this possibility. After all, for listed companies Article 136 of the TUF admits the solicitation of proxies, concerning specific decisions and including voting recommendation, directed to more than two hundred shareholders. Scope and procedures of the solicitation are regulated by the TUF and CONSOB regulations.

In the case of the companies referred to in Article 2325*bis* CC, the power of attorney may only be granted for one meeting at a time, so as to prevent proxies from

20. CONSOB Deliberation No. 11971 from 14 May 1999 and its amendments.

acquiring durable positions that could influence the meeting, without having to face the risks of underwriting the capital. For similar reasons, in unlisted companies, no more than 20 shareholders (companies not envisaged in Article 2325*bis)* or 50, 100, or 200 shareholders, depending on the capital of the company (up to EUR 5 million, up to EUR 25 million, more than EUR 25 million, respectively), may be represented.

207. For listed companies, the TUF contains specific provisions aimed at encouraging shareholders to take part in shareholders' meetings through two instruments: soliciting proxies and collecting proxies (Articles 136 to 144 of the TUF).

The soliciting of proxies may be carried out only by authorized intermediaries acting on behalf of a principal, who must be a permanent (more than six months), and not a marginal shareholder (at least *1%* of the capital). The soliciting is subject to the supervision of CONSOB, which disciplines, among other things, the procedures and contents of the prospectus and the proxy form. The vote by proxy thus obtained is expressed either by the principal or by the intermediary.

Collecting proxies, on the other hand, may be carried out only by associations of at least fifty small-member shareholders (who individually own less than 1% of the capital). The legal representatives of the associations will vote according to the instructions of the members, which means that they may vote in one way for certain of those that they represent and differently for others. As things stand, little use has been made of soliciting and collecting proxies for the following reasons: (i) the high level of concentration of capital in Italian-listed companies, which means that the votes of small shareholders are not important; and (ii) the fact that the proxies have to be collected for each meeting, which discourages the formation of stable groups of shareholders.

VII. The Chairperson of the Shareholders' Meeting, the Secretary, and the Minutes of Resolutions

208. The chairperson of the shareholders' meeting is designated either by the by-laws or by the majority of shareholders in attendance. The chairperson plays a key role at the meeting in terms of ensuring that it is held correctly and produces positive results. The chairperson therefore has to verify the existence of the quorum required to set up the meeting and the right to vote of those attending, guide the debate and the votes, and check the results, which must be quoted in the minutes. The chairperson is assisted by a secretary, also designated by the by-laws or the participants of the meeting, who draws up the minutes. At extraordinary meetings and in other cases in which a notary is present, the duties of the secretary will be performed by the notary.

The minutes must specify the date, the names of shareholders in attendance or represented by proxy and the capital they own, as well as the procedures and results of votes, indicating the shareholders voting for and against or those who have abstained. The minutes must be: (i) drawn up immediately and copied out in the ledger of sessions and resolutions of shareholders' meetings, (ii) signed by the chairperson and the secretary, and (iii) deposited at the *Registro delle imprese* if the law so requires. The minutes of extraordinary meetings must be drawn up by a notary.

VIII. Nullity and Voidability of the Resolutions

209. The aim of rules on defects in meeting resolutions is to limit disputes, thereby ensuring stable company management and safeguarding third parties who have relied on the resolutions passed at the meetings. Various instruments are used to this end: (i) defects are restricted to cases of nullity and voidability; (ii) the possibility exists of rectifying defects; (iii) there are short periods of termination in filing a claim; (iv) there are legitimization requisites inherent in the quota of capital; and (v) an action for damages is available in certain cases instead of challenging.

Furthermore, there are no organized rules regulating the nullity and voidability of resolutions like those regulating the nullity and voidability of contracts. In particular, the nullity of resolutions may be rectified, and an action to ascertain nullity usually has to be filed within a period of limitation.

Cases of nullity or voidability are limited: the most serious hypothesis of nullity is that of a resolution modifying the corporate purpose, which envisages unlawful or impossible activities. In such a case, there is no deadline within which the proceedings have to be filed, and they may even be filed ex officio.

Resolutions that are adopted without a meeting having been properly convened or without drawing up minutes are held to be null and void, as are resolutions passed in cases in which the subject matter is impossible or unlawful. In such cases, within three years of the resolution being registered at the *Registro delle imprese* or copied in the corporate book, its nullity may be ascertained by the court ex officio and the claim may be filed by anyone so concerned. The convocation will, however, not be null and void in cases in which it has been sent by a member of a governing body and it is such as to enable those entitled to participate to know the date of the meeting.

Similarly, the deliberation may be null and void for lack of the minutes, but this is not the case if the minutes specify at least the date and subject matter of the resolutions and are signed by the chairperson of the shareholders' meeting, the chairperson of the board of directors, or the supervisory board and by either the secretary or a notary.

210. The particular interest that a capital increase, reduction in capital, or bonds issue resolution may have for the company or for third parties justifies even stricter limits on challenges. Proceedings may not be filed more than 180 days after registration at the *Registro delle imprese* or, if there is no convocation, after the approval of the balance sheets of the year during which the resolution was carried into effect, even if only partially. In the case of the companies referred to in Article 2325*bis,* there is even a bar on challenge once the capital increase has been even only partially carried into effect and once it has been certified at the register, or once the reduction in capital or bonds issue have been implemented. In such cases, the safeguarding of the third parties who have subscribed the shares or obtained the bonds or the results produced by the reduction in capital will prevail over any interest the shareholders or third parties may have for the resolution to be declared null and void. Any such shareholders or third parties may, however, claim and obtain damages for any harm they have suffered.

211. As a rule, the nullity of a resolution resulting from a lack of minutes may be rectified by drawing up file minutes afterwards, provided that this takes place before the next shareholders' meeting. The resolution will come into force with effect from the date of the meeting, although this is without prejudice to the rights of third parties who, bona fide, have not been informed.

If there was no convocation, on the other hand, anyone who may have agreed, even subsequently, to the meeting being held will be barred from filing proceedings.

The resolution may not be declared null and void, however, if it has been replaced by another resolution that complies with the law and the by-laws, although this is without prejudice to the right to damages and any rights meanwhile acquired by third parties.

212. In addition to the cases of nullity described above, violations of the law or the by-laws will also give rise to the voidability of resolutions. The voidability of a resolution may, therefore, depend on: (i) defects in convocation or voting procedures; or (ii) file subject matter of the resolution. However, in view of the fact that such defects are less serious than those giving rise to the nullity of the resolution, the challenge of voidable resolutions is subject to a number of prerequisites that have been created to avoid disrupting the company's management.

First of all, there are some defects that do not give rise to the possibility of the resolution being annulled because they are not such as to determine the decision or produce a detriment to shareholders or third parties. This applies in cases in which persons not entitled to do so have participated in the meeting or voted (or in cases of errors in counting votes), whenever this has not played a key role in reaching the quorum required to set up the meeting or the quorum required to pass the resolution (*see* Chapter 5, paragraph 171 above). The same also applies to defects in the minutes, provided that they are not such as to make it impossible to verify the content, effects, or validity of the resolution.

Second, the challenge may be filed only by shareholders who own, either individually or collectively, at least 5% of the capital. This percentage is reduced to one per thousand in the case of companies referred to in Article 2325*bis,* but the by-laws may either lower both thresholds or exclude the requisite for a minimum percentage. The shareholders who are unable to reach the threshold may claim damages for the harm they have suffered as a result of a resolution that does not comply with the law or the by-laws.

Third, an action for annulment, as indeed an action claiming damages, must be filed within ninety days of the resolution or, if envisaged, from the time the resolution is deposited or registered at the *Registro delle imprese.*

213. Furthermore, if the resolution is replaced by another resolution that conforms to the law, there is no longer any need for it to be annulled. In such a case, therefore, the proceedings may not be filed. If, however, the proceedings have already been filed, they become a non-suit, although this is without prejudice to the reimbursement of legal costs and the eventual claim for damages.

Finally, the annulment must not jeopardize third parties who in good faith have relied on the validity of the resolution and have acquired rights under deeds by which it is carried into effect. The annulment will, however, be effective vis-à-vis the shareholders and obliges the governing bodies to act accordingly.

IX. Challenging Resolutions

214. Proceedings to challenge resolutions must be filed by suing the company before the court of the place where it has its registered office, or before an arbitral court, if so provided in the by-laws of unlisted companies. If more than one claim is filed, the actions must be consolidated and decided in a single ruling.

The proceedings occur in two stages. The first stage, which is not necessary but very common, seeks to have the effects of the resolution suspended for the duration of the proceedings. The second stage is to obtain a ruling on whether or not the contested defects in the resolution and its effects exist.

215. During the preliminary stage, the shareholders who have filed the proceedings must prove that they have the minimum quantity of shares to qualify to proceed. This prerequisite to proceed must exist both when the proceedings are filed and throughout their duration. If the prerequisite lapses as a result of shares being sold to persons who do not wish to take part in the proceedings or for other reasons, the court cannot annul the resolution but only rule on the claim for damages, if filed. This is one of the most important provisions designed to limit litigation, because only long-term shareholders who intend to preserve their ownership of the shares for the entire duration of the proceedings may obtain an annulment ruling and are, therefore, interested in filing the proceedings.

On filing the annulment petition, the shareholder may ask the court to suspend the effects of the resolution with immediate effect until the outcome of the proceedings. The decision with regard to the suspension will be made by the court after allowing the company to submit its defence arguments, but in very urgent cases, it may be made in the form of a properly motivated measure *inaudita altera parte.* In this latter case, though, the suspension measure must fix a hearing to allow the company to submit its defence arguments, following which the court may then confirm, modify, or revoke the suspension measure. The decision must be made bearing in mind the gravity of the alleged defects and weighing the harm the plaintiffs or the company could suffer if the resolution were or were not suspended. The court may thus make the suspension subject to the shareholders' paying a guarantee to indemnify any harm that might be caused to the company by such a measure.

In the course of the proceedings, the judge may attempt to settle the dispute or recommend modifications, which, in his or her opinion, should be made to the resolution so as to allow the company, prior to the ruling, to adopt a substitute resolution that will, as already explained, make a non-suit of the proceedings to have the defective resolution annulled.

The measures suspending the resolutions and the rulings on the invalidity of such measures must be registered at the *Registro delle imprese* so that they are available to anyone concerned.

§6. Company Administration and Supervision

I. The Three Systems of Administration and Supervision

216. Three alternative systems of administration and supervision exist for S.p.A. These alternatives stem from the need to give S.p.A.s flexible organizational structures. An S.p.A. is, in fact, the type of company chosen not only by the major listed companies or by companies with large numbers of shareholders, but also by medium-to-large-sized companies with small numbers of shareholders. The three systems differ mainly in terms of the duties of the governing and supervisory bodies and the manner in which they are regulated, but this also implies a different role for the shareholders' meetings. The three models of internal organization are alternatives and may be used by closed companies, by companies that resort to the capital market pursuant to Article 2325*bis* of the CC, and by listed companies.

217. The ordinary system is characterized by the presence of a governing body (board of directors or sole director) and a *collegio sindacale,* both appointed by the shareholders' meeting, which is entrusted with the functions indicated in Article 2364 CC. This type of model is currently the most widely used.

218. The two-tier model is characterized by the presence of two bodies that must be collective: supervisory board, which not only watches over management but also performs some of the functions entrusted to shareholders' meetings in the ordinary system and the management board, which is appointed by the supervisory board and is responsible for running the company and its business'. In the two-tier system a shareholders' meeting, therefore, has the reduced functions mentioned in Article 2364*bis CC.* This magnifies the distinction between: (i) the role of the governing and supervisory bodies, which are responsible for properly performing their functions; and (ii) the position of the shareholders who benefit or suffer from the effects of management.

219. In the one-tier system, on the other hand, we find a collective governing body (the board of directors) and a supervisory body (the management supervision committee) formed by non-executive directors members of the board of directors. The role of shareholders' meetings is identical to that envisaged in Article 2364 CC for the ordinary system.

220. Furthermore, in all three models, the auditing of accounts is entrusted to an external auditor. In the case of S.p.A.s in the ordinary system that do not come within the sphere of application of Article 2325*bis CC,* the by-laws may, however, provide that the *collegio sindacale* be entrusted also with auditing the accounts, thereby averting the need to appoint an external auditor and the ensuing cost.

221. Although the three models of organization and supervision are alternative, the CC attributes a priority role to the ordinary system. Three paragraphs are, in fact, dedicated to the requirements concerning the directors, the *collegio sindacale,* and the auditing of accounts in this system, whereas the rules governing the one-tier system and the two-tier system are contained in just one paragraph for each model. This is because many of the provisions relating to the ordinary system are explicitly incorporated in the other systems and also because, unless otherwise provided, the rules relating to directors and *sindaci* in the ordinary system apply respectively to the members of the management board and the supervisory board in the two-tier system and to the members of the board of directors and the management supervision committee in the one-tier system (Article 2380, paragraph III, CC, and Article 223 of the provisions implementing the CC).

Furthermore, the rules on the ordinary system will apply in all cases in which the by-laws do not provide otherwise. Unlike the rules governing the ordinary system, this means that there has to be a specific reference in the by-laws if the rules governing the two-tier or one-tier system are to apply.

222. It is always possible to change the system of administration and supervision. Changes to the by-laws must be resolved by an extraordinary shareholders' meeting.

II. The Ordinary System

A. The Governing Body

1. The Appointment of Directors and Their Termination of Office

223. Generally speaking, the directors are appointed at a shareholders' meeting, which will establish the number of directors unless it is envisaged in the by-laws. Usually, the shareholders' meeting passes a resolution covering the entire list of board members, in such a way that appointed directors are all representative of the shareholders who hold the majority of the capital. The by-laws may, however, provide that the directors be elected according to criteria that allow the minority shareholders to appoint one or more directors. For example, the by-laws may envisage that two or more lists of directors be formed and that a certain number of directorships be reserved for the minority list or for the minority list that has received the most votes. In the case of listed companies, the list vote is compulsory. This means that at least one directorship must be reserved for the list most voted for by shareholders who have no ties with the list that obtained the majority of votes (Article 147*ter* TUF).

224. In exceptional cases, the directors may not be appointed at a shareholders' meeting. This may occur when the directors are designated: (a) in the deed of incorporation; (b) by holders of financial instruments (other than shares) to whom the by-laws give the power to appoint some of the directors (Article 2351, paragraph V, CC); (c) by the other members of the board of directors when one or more directors forfeit office, provided that the majority of directors appointed at the shareholders' meeting have remained in office and that the by-laws do not envisage the termination of all directors when one of them forfeits office (the *simul stabunt simul cadent* clause); and, finally, (d) in cases in which the law or the by-laws provide that one or more directors be appointed by the State or by a State-controlled agency (Articles 2449 CC).

225. Traditionally, only natural persons may be appointed as directors, and they do not have to be shareholders. Nevertheless, some recent court decisions allowed for companies to be appointed as directors.[21] Company employees may even be directors. Disqualification, bankruptcy, ban from public office, and incapacity to hold executive office following a criminal sentence (Article 2382 CC) are grounds for ineligibility.

21. Trib. Milan, 27.2.2012 in *Giur. it.* 2012, p. 2585 e Trib. Milan, 27.3.2017, n. 3545.

Specific requisites on the part of the directors may be envisaged in special laws or in the by-laws. In this context, reference may be made to codes of conduct introduced by trade associations. The requisites established in the so-called Preda Code are particularly important. This is the Code of Self-Discipline prepared for listed companies by the company that manages the Italian Stock Exchange *(Borsa Italiana* S.p.A.).

The subsequent emergence of grounds for ineligibility pursuant to the law or the by-laws in the course of the directorship will give rise to termination.

226. The position of board director is incompatible with: (a) the performance of certain public duties (e.g., CONSOB Commissioner), especially if it implies powers of management; and (b) conducting specific activities.

227. In listed companies, at least one director – or two if the board consists of more than seven members – must have the requisites of independence envisaged for the *sindaci* and also, if the by-laws so envisage, any further requisites established either by the company that manages the financial market or by trade organizations (so-called independent directors, Article 147*ter* TUF).

228. Self-regulatory sources also include the Code of Self-Discipline for listed companies, which devotes a chapter to describing the principles and criteria to be applied in establishing the independence of the directors. The basic principle is extremely general: independent directors are held to be those 'who have no dealings, and who have not recently had dealings, either directly or indirectly, with the issuer or with persons associated with the issuer, that is, dealings that are likely to currently influence their autonomy of judgment'. The criteria describe the sphere of application of the principle in a series of examples that are not mandatory because: (a) they are not comprehensive; and (b) the envisaged hypotheses do not necessarily mean that the requisite does not exist. This is because the board of directors, under the supervision of the *sindaci,* may consider that, in particular cases, the factors considered are not likely to jeopardize the autonomous judgment of the director.[22]

The presence of independent directors is now a well-established practice. Their number is proportionally higher in companies with a higher degree of capitalization and with larger governing bodies.[23]

229. The appointment must be registered in the *Registro delle imprese* within thirty days by the designated director himself or herself. The *Registro delle imprese* must be provided with such information as personal details (first name(s), surname, date of birth, domicile, and nationality), the duration of the appointment, any powers of representation, and whether or not such powers are to be exercised with joint signature with other directors or separately.

---

22. In addition to the cases envisaged in the TUF and the CC, the Code of Self-Discipline highlights such matters as (a) additional fees; (b) the presence of the director and of an executive director in the board of directors of several companies; (c) the lasting duration of the directorship; (d) the capacity of shareholder or director in a company coming within the network of the auditing firm. See 2015 *Code of Self-discipline,* Article 3. *Independent directors, 14 and following pages, in* <www.borsaitaliana.it>.

23. The data provided by Assonime in *Corporate governance in Italy: self-regulation, remuneration and comply or explain principle (Year 2016),* <www.assonime.it>, Table 11, indicates the distribution and the qualifications of independent directors in market segments FTSE Mib, FTSE Mid cap and FTSE Mid small cap, as in the total number of issuers.

230. The directors will remain in office for the time envisaged in the by-laws, which may, however, not be more than three years. Directors who are co-opted by the other directors will forfeit their office with the directors who co-opted them.

Directors may be re-elected, unless this is forbidden by the by-laws.

231. The directors will forfeit their position on the expiry of their mandate, which is normally for three financial years. In this case, they forfeit their position as of the date on which the shareholders' meeting is convened to approve the balance sheets for the third year. The severance will, however, only come into effect once the new board of directors has been appointed. This is to avoid periods of inactivity in the company's management.

Severance from office may also come about as a result of: (a) a director forfeiting the requisites required by law or by the by-laws in exercising the directorship; (b) the director's resignation; or (c) his or her removal by the person who appointed him or her. Removal without cause ('*giusta causa*') will give rise to the company's obligation to indemnify damage suffered as a result of not receiving fees for the remaining period, along with any other ancillary benefits.

The severance must be registered at the *Registro delle imprese* following the same procedure as that followed for the appointment.

2. The Board of Directors and the Sole Director

232. The board of directors is responsible for running the company and managing its economic activity with a view to achieving the corporate purpose. After the 2003 reform, this duty cannot be reserved, not even partially, for a shareholders' meeting, nor can it be delegated to a shareholders' meeting by the board of directors. Therefore, even in cases in which a shareholders' meeting authorizes a particular choice of the board of directors, the board will assume sole liability for the action taken.

An S.p.A. may also be run by just one person (the sole director), but usually, the by-laws envisage that several directors should form the board of directors. If the by-laws do not establish the number of directors, it will be established at a shareholders' meeting.

233. If there is a board of directors, a shareholders' meeting will elect the chairperson. If the shareholders' meeting does not elect the chairperson, the board itself will arrange to do so. The chairperson of the board of directors does not necessarily have powers of management and representation. On the other hand, his or her duty will be to deal with running the governing body. The chairperson will convene meetings, prepare the agenda, and ensure that the directors are provided with the information they need to assess whether or not resolutions are appropriate. He or she will also chair board meetings (Article 2381, paragraph I, CC).

234. Within the board of directors, it often occurs that one or more members are appointed to deal with everyday management, whereas the board deliberates upon the most important matters and periodically verifies the progress of the company's operations and its management. The CC, therefore, envisages that, if the by-laws or the shareholders' meetings so permit, the board may appoint one or more directors (chief executive officers) or an executive committee, formed by two or more directors, who are entrusted with certain operating duties. However, to ensure the collective participation of the directors and in depth reflection, certain decisions may not be delegated (i.e., issuing bonds or increasing the capital as instructed by a shareholders' meeting; drafting the balance sheet; reducing the share capital; projects of mergers or demergers). Furthermore, the board of directors is responsible for evaluating the company's organization and any strategic plans concerning both the company's business and financial aspects. The delegated authority does not imply a definitive transfer of duties, which means that the board can issue directives and withdraw the authority at any time, making decisions regarding any aspect of management.

To ensure the board's control, at the frequency envisaged in the by-laws and at least every six months, the chief executive officer(s) must report on the general state of progress, on foreseeable developments, and on the most important operations. All the directors may ask for information on operations, and they will be called to account if they either make, or fail to make, decisions without acquiring the information needed to this end. The chief executive officer(s) is under an obligation to reply to any requests for information that he or she receives at the board meeting.

235. The decisions of the board of directors are taken in the course of meetings at which at least either the majority of directors or the quorum established in the by-laws must be in attendance. The appointment of proxies to participate in board meetings is not permitted, but if the by-laws so envisage, the meetings may be held by teleconferences or by videoconferences. Resolutions must be passed by a majority of those attending. Resolutions that are against the law or against the by-laws may be challenged either by absent or dissenting directors, or by members of the *collegio sindacale,* within ninety days. The shareholders may also challenge resolutions, but only if these jeopardize their individual rights.

3. The Power of Representation

236. Upon the appointment of one or more directors, the authority to represent the company may be delegated either: (i) separately, that is, to each one individually; or (ii) jointly, that is, requiring the will of all the representatives. The power of representation must be specified in the *Registro delle imprese.* The resolution delegating the power of representation may envisage limits (e.g., by establishing the maximum values of operations that can be carried into effect by each director), which will not, however, jeopardize the validity of operations implemented with third parties unless it is proven that such third parties have acted deliberately to damage the company. If the limits imposed on the power of representation are breached, the director(s) will be called to account for any damage caused to the company.

4. The Remuneration of the Directors

237. Article 2389 CC gives shareholders' meetings the power to establish the fees of the directors and of the members of the executive committee. In the ordinary system, the remuneration of directors entrusted with special assignments envisaged in the by-laws is, on the other hand, left to the decision of the board of directors after consulting the *collegio sindacale,* but the by-laws may reserve for the shareholders' meeting decisions with regard to the total amount of fees, including those of directors with special assignments. The system thus seeks to protect the company against self-referential choices on the part of the governing body or against less-than-optimal solutions arising from the relationships that frequently exist between a select group of majority shareholders and the directors, or at least the executive directors. The opinion of the supervisory body is, in fact, required to avert, or at any rate, to bring to light, disproportionate fees or fees established according to criteria that are incompatible with the company's best interests.

The remuneration may acquire various forms in terms of both its nature (remuneration for employment as a senior manager or remuneration simply associated with the assignment) and its entity (fixed or variable). The remuneration may be either on a once-only basis or periodical.

The director will benefit from a full payment, even if the company withdraws his appointment without cause. This may be very expensive and thus constitutes a serious disincentive against replacing the director if his or her conduct, while not meeting the requirements of dismissal on cause, is not satisfactory.

Mixed or variable fees may come in many forms. Article 2389 CC envisages that the fees may consist, 'either in full or in part, of shares in profits or of granting the right to subscribe shares to be issued in future at a predetermined price', thereby explicitly legitimizing the phenomenon of stock options. The possibility of giving directors the right to subscribe new shares is, however, subject to the shareholders waiving the right of option. Consequently, there has to be a duly motivated proposal submitted for the approval of the *collegio sindacale* and a resolution passed at an extraordinary shareholders' meeting.

238. In the case of listed companies, the rules are stricter because of legal requirements, the measures imposed by CONSOB, and the principles of conduct envisaged in non-mandatory sources, such as the aforementioned Code of Self-Discipline.

The procedure by which the fees of directors with special assignments are determined has been examined by the Code of Self-Discipline, which provides for a special internal committee, the remuneration committee, to be set up. The purpose of this committee is to draft proposals and opinions and ensure information and transparency on fees and the criteria by which they are determined. The creation of a remuneration committee is now a consolidated practice followed by a vast majority of the most highly capitalized companies and by a substantial percentage of listed companies. The committee usually consists of three members, two of whom are independent, while the third one is usually non-executive.

The Article 114*bis* of the TUF gives the shareholders' meeting power in approving remuneration plans in the form of stock options, in derogation of the aforementioned Article 2389 CC, which continues to apply only to fixed or variable fees other than stock options.

Information for the market is guaranteed by making it compulsory for the issuing company to provide CONSOB and the market – prior to implementing remuneration plans – with a detailed series of elements that make it possible to assess the impact of the initiative on the progress of the company and the performance of its shares.

5. Directors' Obligations and Preclusions

239. The directors have a duty to use diligence in fulfilling their task of honestly running the company (Article 2392 CC). The duty of honest administration takes the form of a series of fulfillments specifically envisaged by the law. However, it actually goes even further than this. The general principle of the duty to use diligence, in fact, encompasses anything the directors do in terms of organizing and running the firm and preserving its assets. The diligence criterion is adopted in its stricter conception of 'professional diligence' (Article 1176 CC), based on the assumption that anyone who accepts an assignment to run a company cannot justify negligent behaviour resulting from their ignorance or inexperience. Since, however, the economic activity is intrinsically risky for, the fact that they take risks and that there may be negative results is not necessarily a factor justifying liability. The directors do, in fact, have a duty to acquire all the information that is required, and if they do not have the required competency, they must avail themselves of advisors so that they can come to the right decisions. If, however, they use diligence in meeting this preliminary requirement, they are free to make any management decisions (including high-risk decisions) without incurring any liability if the initiative produces a negative result (the business judgment rule). In assessing diligence, therefore, we should not consider whether or not the decision was right in light of the elements acquired and the company's economic situation, but we should ascertain whether the directors have made all the technical and economic inquiries that are required to make an informed decision on the risks and the potential benefits. In spite of this, there are some case law precedents that also envisage liability in cases in which the decision appears to be unreasonable, even though there were adequate prior inquiries.

240. Although the diligence criterion applies to all the directors, its application varies according to the director's role and specific duties. More specifically, we need to distinguish between executive directors and non-executive directors. The former must be fully informed of the elements that they use to make the decisions with which they are entrusted, while the non-executive directors are expected to supervise the work of the executive directors, asking for information and making decisions on the basis of the information provided by the company's executive directors or senior managers. The non-executive directors will not, therefore, be liable if they make decisions on the basis of erroneous or insufficient information provided by the executive directors and they have not been able to check it.

The diligence criterion may also be applied differently, according to the director's specific competencies, which will aggravate his or her liability if he or she lacks the necessary ability. All the directors, however, have a duty to acquire appropriate information and, if the information is technical, to make up for their lack of knowledge by using experts. Liability resulting from negligence may also be attributed to a de facto director or to anyone who performs management duties without receiving an assignment from the competent body.

241. There are numerous director obligations specifically envisaged by the law. Such obligations refer to such matters as the business carried out by the company and protecting company assets on behalf of shareholders and third parties. They also extend to the company's organization, and if the company's shares are listed, to relations with the financial market.

One of the most important obligations of directors is to prepare draft balance sheets for the year and draft consolidated statements, to be annually submitted to a shareholders' meeting. The balance sheet must provide a truthful and accurate portrayal of the company's economic situation and its assets.

The directors are also under an obligation to protect the company's assets and ensure that their value does not fall below that of the share capital. As we have already seen (§3. V), in cases in which the assets/capital ratio envisaged by law lapses, the directors must adopt the initiatives contemplated by Articles 2446 and 2447 of the CC. If circumstances requiring the company's dissolution arise, the directors will be under an obligation to run the company with the sole aim of preserving the company assets and maintaining their value, and they will account for any damage caused to the company, shareholders, and third parties as a result of breaching this obligation (Article 2486 CC).

242. The directors are precluded from carrying out activities in competition with those of the company, whether they do so in their own right or as shareholders with unlimited liability or as directors/general managers of competing companies. If they breach this preclusion, they may be removed and obliged to pay damages (Article 2390 CC).

243. The directors are under a specific disclosure obligation in cases in which they have a personal interest or an interest on behalf of third parties in a specific operation, even if the interest in question does not conflict with that of the company. In this case, the director has a duty to notify the directors and the *collegio sindacale* of this interest, providing any elements that may be useful to evaluate it. In listed companies, the directors must inform the *collegio sindacale* every three months of any interests that might affect the company's operations.

Usually, the fact that a director has such an interest does not mean that he or she cannot take part in decisions inherent in the operation. In such a case, however, a procedure has to be followed confirming the fact that this has been taken into account and providing the reasons for the decisions. If there is a sole director, the existence of the interest must be disclosed to the first shareholders' meeting. If, on the other hand, the interest affects the chief executive officer, he or she must refrain from closing the operation and submit this fact to the board of directors, highlighting the existence of his or her interest. The board of directors will then explain the reasons for the decision and its utility for the company.

244. To protect the company against potential damage arising from decisions affected by the interests of one or more directors, the directors and the *sindaci* may proceed judicially to have such decisions cancelled. The judicial suit may be filed in cases in which: (i) the director has failed to disclose his or her interest; (ii) the decisions have not been motivated specifically explaining the convenience for the company; or (iii) the decisions have been adopted with the decisive vote of the director who has an interest in the operation. The suit may not be filed by the directors who approved the decision if they knew of the existence of the other director's interest.

245. The directors will account for any damage the company suffers following breaches of the obligations mentioned above and for any damage resulting from the gains made by the director concerned or by third parties as a result of using data or information acquired in the course of their activities.

Any dealings carried out with third parties in good faith while implementing operations approved under resolutions invalidated as a result of breaches of the aforementioned obligations will, however, continue to be valid and effective.

246. In the companies that resort to the risk capital market ex Article 2325*bis* CC, the directors will be bound by more important disclosure obligations in the framework of operations involving a particular risk for the company's assets. CONSOB has, in fact, introduced specific rules concerning information for the market and the procedure to be followed in operations involving related parties,[24] and Article 2391*bis* CC provides that directors are under an obligation to guarantee both the transparency and the essential and procedural propriety of such operations, illustrating them in the report on operations. Any such operations must be submitted to the company's supervisory body, which will provide the shareholders' meeting with its own assessments.

247. If the directors breach their obligations or preclusions, they will be liable to indemnify the damage and, if the circumstances arise, they will incur penal liability. The liability to indemnify damage is defined as a contractual liability, that is, it is subject to the general principles that apply in cases of breaches of contractual obligations. Consequently, the party acting judicially has to prove the breach of an obligation or a preclusion, the damage suffered, and the causal links between the breach and the damage. The damage must be an immediate and direct consequence of the breach. The liability also implies intention or negligence on the part of the director. This means that a director who has used the diligence required by his or her role and competency will not be liable.

Generally speaking, the liability is joint and several, which means that all the directors will account individually for the entire damage vis-à-vis the party who has suffered it (Article 2392, paragraph II, CC). The burden of indemnification rests with the directors in equal measure, unless a different degree of liability is proven (Article 1298 CC).

However, the difference between the roles of executive directors (chief executive officers and members of the executive committee) and non-executive directors means that the latter cannot be held responsible for breaches committed by the former in performing the duties entrusted to them. All the directors will, however, be liable if they fail to do everything in their power to prevent detrimental acts of which they are aware or if they fail to act to eliminate or reduce the damage.

Directors who have not personally breached obligations and preclusions may avoid liability if they arrange to register their disagreement with the board's decisions in the ledger of meetings and resolutions, immediately notifying the *collegio sindacale* to this effect (Article 2392, paragraph III, CC).

Furthermore, directors will account for breaching the general principle of *neminem ledere* (Article 2043 CC) in the framework of damage, caused during the course of performing management duties, which is not the result of breaching specific obligations inherent in their role.

24. CONSOB regulation No. 17221 of 12 Mar. 2010 modified by CONSOB regulation No. 1789 of 23 Jun 2010.

6. Lawsuits Against Directors

248. Three types of lawsuit may be filed against the directors: a corporate lawsuit, a creditors' lawsuit, and an individual lawsuit by a shareholder or a third party.

249. The aim of a corporate lawsuit is to sentence the director responsible to indemnify the damage caused to the company. The lawsuit may be filed by the company, the shareholders, or else the receiver, liquidator, or special liquidator, in the respective events of bankruptcy, compulsory administrative liquidation, and extraordinary administration.[25] The lawsuit may be filed within five years of the time the director leaves office.

250. The company may file the lawsuit after a resolution by a shareholders' meeting or a resolution by file collegio sindacale passed by a majority of two-thirds of the members. On the majorities envisaged for an ordinary shareholders' meeting (§5, II), the shareholders' meeting may resolve to file the lawsuit upon approving the balance sheets of the year during which the breaches are assumed to have been committed, even if the matter is not on the agenda. If shareholders representing at least one-fifth of the share capital vote in favour, the lawsuit will give rise to the automatic removal of the director and his or her replacement. The shareholders' meeting may resolve by a majority to waive or settle the lawsuit. The waiver or settlement will, however, not be possible if it is vetoed by shareholders representing at least one-fifth of the capital or any different percentage required for shareholders to file the lawsuit. In the case of the companies referred to in Article 2325*bis* (§1, III), this percentage is reduced to one-twentieth or to any lesser percentage envisaged in the by-laws for shareholders to file the lawsuit.

251. Shareholders who hold at least one-fifth of the share capital or the different percentage, not exceeding one-third, envisaged in the by-laws, may file a derivative action on behalf of the company. In the case of the companies referred to in Article 2325*bis* (§1, III), this percentage is reduced to one-fortieth or to the lower percentage established in the by-laws.

The purpose of the action is to re-establish the company assets that have been damaged by the conduct of the director. This means that the shareholders cannot obtain compensation for themselves through such an action. They actually act in lieu of the company, which must, however, be summoned to appear in court. The action is filed through one or more joint representatives appointed by a majority of shareholders wishing to act, so that they can coordinate the shareholders' and the judicial initiatives.

If the lawsuit is won, the damages are awarded to the company, but the shareholders are entitled to reimbursement, by the company, of costs that have not been debited to the directors under the ruling or have not been paid by them.

---

25. Compulsory administrative liquidation is one of the insolvency procedures envisaged in the bankruptcy law (Royal Decree No. 267 of 16 Mar. 1942 as amended lastly by Legislative Decree No. 5/2006), which applies in the event of crisis, or irregularities, in managing State-controlled enterprises or enterprises subjected to administrative supervision. The latter companies may include banking and insurance companies, stock-brokering firms, companies managing investment funds, and auditing firms. Extraordinary administration is an administrative procedure envisaged for major commercial firms in crisis, the aim of which is to preserve productive assets through resumption, reactivation and reconversion pursuant to Legislative Decree No. 270/1999.

In the same way, if the lawsuit is waived or settled, any amounts owing must be awarded to the company. The shareholders' meeting may resolve also to waive and settle derivative actions filed by shareholders, provided that the shareholders in question do not exercise the right of veto described above.

252. A creditors' lawsuit may be filed only in cases in which the directors have breached obligations inherent in preserving the company assets. Furthermore, the creditors may act only in cases in which the company's assets are insufficient to satisfy them. The creditors' action, therefore, has more specific prerequisites than those of the corporate derivative action. In the event of bankruptcy, such an action can be filed only by the receiver.

If the company has filed a derivative action and has been awarded damages following breaches of the directors' obligations in the framework of preserving company assets, the creditors' action cannot be filed because the directors cannot be sentenced to indemnify the same damage twice. In such a case, the creditors may act against the company and obtain satisfaction from the assets re-established with the damages paid by the directors.

If, however, the company waives the action, this will not prevent the creditors' lawsuit. If the company agrees to settle, the creditors may act with a view to having the settlement declared ineffective as far as they are concerned, provided that the prerequisites of the Paulian action arise (Article 2901 CC).

253. An individual shareholder or a third party may also act to obtain compensation for the damage that he or she has suffered following breaches committed by the directors. Such a lawsuit may, however, be filed only if the shareholder or third party has suffered direct damage or damage that is not a consequence of the damage suffered by the company's assets. Cases of this kind include cases in which the shareholder or third party has been induced to subscribe (or sell) shares in unfavourable conditions or when a bank has granted financing on the basis of balance sheets that do not provide a true portrayal of the company's economic situation and its assets.

7. The General Manager and the Executive in Charge of Drafting Accounting Documents

254. The CC provides no definition of the duties of the general manager. Frequently, however, the largest companies appoint a general manager as head of the company's employees. In some companies, the duties of the general manager are established in the by-laws. The main task of the general manager is usually to implement the decisions passed by the governing body and to report to it on the work carried out by the company's administrative structure.

The Law No. 262 from 8 December 2005 has introduced for the listed companies the function of the executive in charge of drafting accounting documents. The nomination of this executive is mandatory according to the modalities established in the articles of association.

This executive, that may or may not be a member of the governing body, is responsible to draft the balance sheet, the consolidated balance sheet and all the others accounting documents. He must also, together with the general manager, attest in a written document the truthfulness of all the communications realized to the market.

The rules on liability envisaged for directors apply to general managers appointed by a shareholders' meeting or pursuant to the by-laws and to the executive in charge of drafting accounting documents, but only with respect to the duties assigned to them.

B. *The Collegio Sindacale ('Board of Auditors')*

1. The Function of the Collegio Sindacale

255. The collegio sindacale is the supervisory body by which Italian S.p.A.s have been characterized ever since the 1882 Code of Commerce. In the 1942 Code, even after the 2003 reform of company law, its main function consists of watching over the legality and propriety of the company's administration. Prior to the 2003 reform, the collegio sindacale also supervised the company accounts. Today, this control is entrusted to an external auditor. Only the closed S.p.A.s that do not fall within the definition given in Article 2325*bis* (§1, III) and that are not obliged to publish consolidated balance sheets can still appoint the collegio sindacale to watch over the company accounts and not appoint an external auditor.

The mechanisms that are applied to appoint the members of the collegio sindacale are strictly linked to the function of supervising the company's administration. By designating one or more members of the collegio sindacale stakeholders who may belong or not to the group of majority shareholders can, in fact, monitor the company's management and discover eventual irregularities.

The role played by the *collegio sindacale* is such that its members have to meet specific requisites of independence and competency, which are even more rigorous in cases in which companies perform complex activities (banking, insurance, financial brokerage, etc.).

In exceptional cases, the *collegio sindacale* also acts as a substitute for the board of directors (sections 3 and 4).

2. Appointment and Remuneration

256. The *collegio sindacale* is formed by three to five members who are initially appointed in the articles of incorporation and after this by a shareholders' meeting. Two substitutes *sindaci* must also be appointed. In listed companies, there may be more than five *sindaci,* and the minorities are entitled to designate at least one or two *sindaci* depending on whether the board consists of three or more members (Article 148 TUF). The chairperson of the *collegio sindacale* is appointed by the shareholders' meeting, but in listed companies, one of the *sindaci* elected by the minority must be elected chairperson. The reason why certain *sindaci* have to be appointed by the minority is, at least in the case of listed companies, to ensure greater independence from the group of controlling shareholders and the directors and thereby reinforce the effectiveness of control over management.

257. The *sindaci* must satisfy personal requisites of independence, respectability, and professionalism.

To guarantee independence, the following persons cannot be appointed *sindaci:* (a) the spouses or relatives of the directors of the company or another group company;

(b) persons who are directly employed by the company or who have a consultancy engagement that might influence what they do. Even a shareholder may be appointed *sindaco,* unless this is banned by the by-laws. The by-laws may, in fact, envisage further grounds for ineligibility or incompatibility and impose limits on combining mandates.

Persons who are in any of the situations envisaged in Article 2382 CC (i.e., persons who are bankrupt, disqualified, sentenced for crimes involving debarment from public or executive office, etc.) may not be elected.

At least one member of the *collegio sindacale* must be registered on the roll of accounting auditors. If the other *sindaci* do not satisfy this requisite, they must be either professionals registered on the lists specified by the Ministry of Justice[26] or university professors of legal or economic subjects.

The Minister of Economy envisages further requisites of professionalism and respectability for listed companies. Special further requisites are also envisaged by the relevant supervisory authorities for companies operating in such areas as banking, insurance, and finance.

258. The *sindaci* will be remunerated either pursuant to the by-laws or in accordance with the annual resolutions passed by the shareholders' meeting. When professionals are involved, the remuneration is often gauged to their tariffs.

3. Termination and Replacement

259. The appointment of a sindaco has a three-year duration and comes to an end when the shareholders' meeting called to approve the first balance sheets after this period is held. Sindaci may be re-elected.

The appointment may also come to an end as a result of death, relinquishment, termination, or removal. Termination arises in cases in which the eligibility requisites have lapsed. Removal can be resolved only by a shareholders' meeting on just grounds and must be approved by the court (Article 2400, paragraph n, CC). Unlike the directors, therefore, the members of the *collegio sindacale* cannot be removed at the discretion of a shareholders' meeting. This is to ensure that the risk of removal does not jeopardize their independence.

The need for an effective supervisory body to exist throughout the life of the company is further highlighted in the mechanism by which *sindaci* are replaced. If a *sindaco* leaves office, by law, he or she must be replaced by the most senior alternate *sindaco,* who will remain in office until the next shareholders' meeting, which must then arrange for him or her to be definitively replaced. If there are not enough substitutes *sindaci,* a shareholders' meeting must be immediately convened to appoint the new *sindaci.*

4. Powers and Duties

260. The task of the *sindaci* is generally defined by the CC as ensuring that the operations of the company, its governing bodies, and employees comply with both the law and the requirements of the by-laws (Article 2403 CC). In addition to specific

26. Ministerial Decree No. 320 of 29 Dec. 2004.

legal requirements, the *sindaci* must ensure that the company's administration is based on principles of fairness and transparency and that the organizational structure is adequate. Furthermore, in listed companies, the *sindaci* must also check that the group leader issues appropriate instructions to subsidiaries, so that they can provide the necessary information to the public.

261. The *sindaci* must meet either at least once every three months or at any more frequent intervals contemplated in the by-laws. The meeting may also be held at a distance using telecommunications systems, but the minutes recording the checks carried out and comments for the directors must be copied in a special book. The meeting can be held if the majority of *sindaci* in office are in attendance. If the *sindaco* fails to participate in two meetings in the course of a financial year without providing justification, he or she will forfeit his or her office. Decisions are passed by a majority of attending *sindaci,* and dissenting *sindaci* may arrange for their disagreement to be recorded in the minutes so that they can evade liability arising as a result of the resolutions passed by the majority.

262. Each year, the *collegio sindacale* prepares a report that must be deposited at least fifteen days before the shareholders' meeting convened to approve the balance sheets. In this report, the *collegio sindacale* gives its comments on the progress of the company, spotlights any irregularities in management, and advances proposals with respect to approving or modifying the balance sheets.

263. The *sindaci* may, individually if need be, inspect the company and the documentation regarding its activities. Information may also be acquired by submitting requests to the governing bodies of the company and to the governing and supervisory bodies of subsidiaries. Inspections may also be carried out with the aid of assistants paid by the *sindaci,* but the governing body may refuse to give confidential information to persons who are not *sindaci.* The inspection and control operations must be recorded in the ledger of meetings and resolutions of the *collegio sindacale.*

264. The *sindaci* will receive complaints from shareholders with respect to facts that are open to objection. If the complaints are submitted by shareholders representing at least 5% of the share capital (2% for the companies mentioned in Article 2325*bis)* or the lower percentages envisaged in the by-laws, the *sindaci* must immediately carry out the necessary checks. Once they have completed their inquiries, they must send a report to a shareholders' meeting concerning the facts reported. If serious irregularities in management emerge, the *sindaci* must convene a shareholders' meeting so that it can adopt the necessary measures. A similar power may also be exercised by the *sindaci* if the directors fail to convene the shareholders' meeting as required by law or if they do so unjustifiably late. The work of the *sindaci* is, therefore, not simply to supervise passively, but it also includes taking steps to ensure that situations of inactivity or irregularities in the company's management can be overcome. This power includes the power of the *sindaci,* as indeed of the other persons specified in Article 2409 CC (*see* below in §6, n, C), to file a statement with the court concerning any founded suspicion of serious irregularities in management that might damage the company or other group companies. Such a judicial initiative would appear to be an extreme remedy, which is available in cases in which the other powers of the *sindaci* do not permit them to eliminate irregularities in management.

5. Liability

265. The *sindaci* must fulfil their duties diligently and professionally (Article 2407 CC). The commitment expected of the *sindaci* varies according to the size of the company, the structure of the governing body, and the state of relations between the shareholders and the directors. Special attention is required in the cases set forth in the principles of conduct drawn up by the National Counsel of Business Consultants and Chartered Accountants, such as the existence of wide-ranging delegated authorities within the governing body or cases in which a directorship is filled by a shareholder. In listed companies, the commitment expected of *sindaci* increases considerably as a result of disclosure obligations vis-à-vis CONSOB and obligations with respect to disclosures for the shareholders' meeting established by CONSOB concerning intragroup operations or operations with related parties. Although the *sindaci* do not necessarily have to be registered on professional rolls, a high standard of diligence and skill is expected of them as they perform their duties, similar to that expected of professionals, thereby increasing their responsibility. In any event, the commitment expected of the *sindaci* is defined as a commitment geared to means, that is, they are expected to apply any appropriate controls. If they have fulfilled their duties properly, they will not be called to account for eventual failure in averting damage caused by acts of management adopted in conflict with the law or with the requirements of the by-laws.

266. The *sindaci* will be exclusively liable for failing to meet their own obligations and concurrently liable in the framework of controls over management in the event of non-compliance by the directors. Instances of exclusive liability include, for instance, breaches of secrecy obligations concerning information and facts that they have acquired in the course of conducting their activities and failing to issue statements, or making false statements, which might jeopardize the company or mislead shareholders or third parties.

The claims of liability inherent in inadequate controls over management are much more serious. In such cases, the *sindaci's* liability stems from their own acts and not from the acts of other persons, even though this implies the existence of defaults or irregularities in management.

If the *sindaci* are to be called to account for damage caused to the company, shareholders, or third parties by the company's management, evidence must be provided not only that they have breached their obligation to act with diligence and professionalism in supervising, but also that, if the controls had been carried out properly, this would have prevented the damage from arising. The courts, therefore, have to make a probability assessment of the impact of proper supervision, as far as causing the damage is concerned.

267. The liability of the *sindaci* will be personal in cases in which the violation is committed by an individual auditor, which is usually the case in hypotheses of direct liability. Their liability will be joint and several in cases in which it concerns collectively exercised duties. The *sindaci* are, moreover, jointly and severally liable with the directors for damage caused to the company's management in cases in which proper supervision could have averted such damage. The liability will, however, be joint and several vis-à-vis third parties who have been damaged, while internally, it will be allocated according to the contribution made by the directors and *sindaci* through their acts or omissions.

268. The rules concerning the liability of directors will apply to actions filed against the *sindaci.*

C. Lawsuit in Court in case of suspected management malpractice

269. Article 2409 CC contemplates the possibility of filing a lawsuit concerning suspected serious malpractice in management with the court in whose district the company has its registered office. This applies only to malpractice that have been committed by directors in breach of their duties arising under the law or the by-laws and that may damage the company or its subsidiaries. Since the persons who are allowed to file the statement are not usually entitled to access the company's documents, they do not have to prove the existence of the malpractice. It is sufficient for them to produce elements substantiating a justified suspicion.

270. The statement may be filed by shareholders holding at least one-tenth of the capital or, for the companies mentioned in Article 2325*bis* CC (*see* above), at least one-twentieth of the capital. The statement is usually filed by minority shareholders, and it is one of the main tools of defence against management abuses. The statement may, however, also be filed by the majority of shareholders, who may utilize it if they are in conflict with the directors. The statement may also be filed by the *collegio sindacale,* the supervisory board in two-tier companies, the management supervision committee in one-tier companies, or the public prosecutor for the companies mentioned in Article 2325*bis* CC. Shareholders who are unable to reach the aforementioned thresholds can, therefore, report management malpractice either to the supervisory bodies or to the public prosecutor so that the statement can be filed.

271. The statement usually focuses on malpractice in management and on the activities of bodies entrusted with management. Only in the case of listed companies may CONSOB (Article 152 TUF) file a statement to the court concerning malpractice committed by the supervisory bodies *(collegio sindacale,* supervisory board, or management supervision committee, depending on the type of organizational model adopted).

272. The proceeding starts with a petition and falls within the procedure of rulings decided in chambers. Such rulings are characterized by: (i) the fact that there does not necessarily have to be a conflict between the parties' positions; (ii) the judge's increased powers of investigation; and (iii) the nature of the ruling, which may be revoked or amended at any time. The petition must be reported to the company, the directors, and the *sindaci,* who will also be questioned by the court. Only in exceptionally urgent cases the court may adopt decisions *inaudita altera parte,* following which it may either confirm or revoke the measure after questioning the directors and the *sindaci.* The company may arrange to suspend the proceeding, if a shareholders' meeting removes the directors and the *sindaci,* appointing persons with the required professionalism who take active steps to identify and eliminate the irregularities.

The court may order an inspection, adopt any appropriate temporary measures, and convene a shareholders' meeting. The inspector's powers of investigation are established by the court and, whenever necessary, he or she may avail himself or herself of technical advisors.

In the most serious cases – more frequently after the inspection – the court may remove the directors and *sindaci* and appoint a judicial administrator for a specific period of time. The judicial administrator thus assumes the position of a public officer entrusted with the company's everyday management and with carrying out any further acts, including acts of an extraordinary nature, indicated by the Court. The judicial administrator may also file a derivative action against the directors and *sindaci*. On completing his or her assignment, the judicial administrator will submit a report and statement and he or she will chair the shareholders' meeting at which the company's new directors and *sindaci* are appointed or at which the company is either placed in liquidation or placed under insolvency proceedings. The administrator is entitled to receive a fee established by the court.

273. The costs of the lawsuit will be sustained by the persons filing the statement, if they are shareholders. In other cases, the costs will be sustained by the company.

III. The Two-Tier System

A. The Supervisory Board

1. Appointment and Termination of Office

274. The members of the supervisory board are first appointed in the articles of association and after this by a shareholders' meeting. By analogy with the rules provided for members of the board of directors, an exception to this is provided by cases of appointment by holders of financial instruments of participation, who may be entitled to appoint an independent member of the board (Article 2351 CC), or by the State or public bodies (Article 2449 CC). In the case of listed companies, at least one member of the supervisory board must be appointed – in accordance with the procedures established by CONSOB – by the minority shareholders (Article 148, paragraph 4*bis*, TUF). There must be at least three members of the supervisory body.

275. The delicate duties of the supervisory directors call for requisites that combine in part those required of both board directors and *sindaci*. The members of the supervisory board must, in fact, have the requisites envisaged in Article 2382 CC for board directors. If they do not have them, they cannot be elected. If these requisites are forfeited while in office, the directors will lapse from office. Furthermore, with the same effects, they may not occupy positions as members of the management board or have links of direct employment or collaboration or any other type of economic relationship with the company or with holding companies/subsidiaries such as to compromise their independence. In the case of listed companies, the supervisory directors must have the same requisites of independence as those envisaged for internal auditors (Article 148, paragraphs II and III, TUF), and their assignments are subject to the combination limits contemplated by CONSOB (Article 148*bis* TUF). The by-laws may envisage further grounds for ineligibility or termination of office, limits on combining positions, or incompatibilities. At least one of the supervisory directors must be enrolled on the Register of Accounting Auditors. Further requisites of respectability, professionalism, and independence are required by law for companies engaged in particular activities or, alternatively, they may be established in the by-laws.

276. Like the *sindaci,* the supervisory directors must notify the shareholders' meeting at the time of their appointment of any positions they hold in other companies, and their appointment or termination from office must be promptly registered at the *Registro delle imprese* (Articles 2400 and 2409*quaterdecies* CC).

The position will have a duration of three years, but the board will only lapse with effect from the date of the meeting of shareholders called to approve the balance sheet of the third financial year. There are no limits as far as the re-election of directors is concerned.

A shareholders' meeting may remove the supervisory directors at any time. If they are removed without cause, however, the company will be obliged to indemnify the damage brought about by the removal. In this case, therefore, a rule similar to that contemplated for the board of directors applies, which is different from that which applies to the *sindaci.* This is envisaged precisely to facilitate changing the governing bodies in cases in which the shareholders' meeting expresses a different wish (after changes in the majority shareholders, for instance).

In all events, if one or more members of the supervisory body lapse during their term of office, the shareholders' meeting must promptly appoint substitutes.

277. The chairperson of the supervisory board is elected by a shareholders' meeting (Article 2409*duodecies,* paragraph VIII, CC). He or she cannot be dismissed by the board, but only by a shareholders' meeting. He or she, therefore, enjoys a position of autonomy compared to the other directors and, although the law does not so envisage, it is thought that he or she can exercise powers similar to those envisaged for the chairperson of the board of directors.

The remuneration of the supervisory directors is regulated in the same manner as that of the *collegio sindacale* (Articles 2402 CC).

2. Powers and Duties

278. The supervisory board combines some of the duties assigned in the ordinary system to either a shareholders' meeting or the *collegio sindacale,* with some of its own duties. Certain powers of the board may vary according to the provisions of the by-laws, by either curbing or extending the duties of shareholders' meetings. The by-laws may, therefore, give rise to a corporate model in which the role of the supervisory board and that of the management board are characterized by a high degree of autonomy, or alternatively, they may give the shareholders' meeting an albeit modest power to intervene in management choices.

279. Like a shareholders' meeting in the ordinary system, the supervisory board appoints and removes the members of the governing body (the management board) and establishes its remuneration. The by-laws may, however, reserve this function for a shareholders' meeting. The supervisory board, moreover, approves the financial year's balance sheet, and the consolidated balance sheet, if one is produced. Here, too, the by-laws may, however, envisage that liability for approving the balance sheets will switch to a shareholders' meeting: (a) if the balance sheets are not approved by the supervisory board; or (b) at the request of one-third of the members of the management board or the supervisory board. Furthermore, the supervisory board may be vested by the by-laws with the power to pass the resolutions referred to in Article 2365, paragraph 2, CC, on merging; setting up or closing branches; assigning powers of representation; reducing the capital if a shareholder withdraws; adapting the by-laws to the law; or transferring the registered office within Italy.

280. Many duties of the supervisory board are those entrusted to the *collegio sindacale* in the ordinary model of S.p.a.s. First and foremost, the supervisory board monitors compliance with the law, with the by-laws and with principles of sound corporate management, makes sure that the company adopts an appropriate administrative and accounting model, and checks its functioning (Articles 2403 and 2409*quaterdecies* CC). Unlike the *collegio sindacale,* the supervisory board may never be engaged in auditing activities, which, in two-tier companies, is always entrusted either to an external auditor or to an audit company. The latter are nevertheless obliged to provide information to the supervisory body.

Like the *collegio sindacale,* the supervisory board is kept informed by the shareholders of any malpractice in management and, if the prerequisites set forth in Article 2408 CC arise, it must make a prompt inquiry and report on its findings to a shareholders' meeting. Furthermore, if the management board is responsible for an omission and there is need of urgent decisions the supervisory board must convene a shareholders' meeting (Articles 2367, 2406, paragraph 2, and 2409*quaterdecies* CC). The supervisory board is obliged to report to the court if it has justifiable reason to suspect serious malpractice in management in cases in which they are such as to cause harm to the company or its subsidiaries. Furthermore, if the conditions arise, it may challenge the resolutions of the management board or file liability lawsuits against the management directors on behalf of the company (Articles 2409*undecies* and 2409*terdecies* CC).

The supervisory board may also challenge resolutions passed by a shareholders' meeting in breach of the law.

281. To carry out their supervisory work in the best possible way, the members of the supervisory board must attend meetings of the shareholders and of the management board.

The supervisory board must meet at least once every ninety days, in accordance with the procedures established in the by-laws. The minutes of its meetings must be recorded in a special ledger (Articles 2404 and 2421 CC).

As far as majorities, voting procedures, challenging resolutions, and effects vis-à-vis third parties are concerned, the resolutions passed by the supervisory board are governed by the same rules as those envisaged for resolutions passed by the board of directors (Articles 2388 and 2409*quaterdecies* CC). The resolution of the supervisory board approving the balance sheet may also be challenged by the shareholders. As far as proceedings filed to ascertain its invalidity are concerned, the rules envisaged for resolutions of the shareholders' meeting in this respect will apply (Articles 2434*bis* and 2409*quaterdecies* CC).

At least once a year, the supervisory board must submit a report on its activities to a shareholders' meeting, highlighting any omissions or irregularities it may have ascertained.

282. Should the by-laws so envisage, the supervisory duties may also include approving any strategic operations or industrial and financial plans prepared by the company. This ensures prior control over a number of fundamental management choices, but it does not exonerate the management board from liability for what it has done.

In the case of listed companies, there are specific provisions establishing that the supervisory directors may: (i) proceed, separately if need be, with inspections and controls; and (ii) ask the management board for information, if necessary by calling a meeting thereof. Two or more directors may proceed to convene a shareholders' meeting (Article 151*bis* TUF).

3. Liability

283. Article 2409*terdecies* CC establishes that the supervisory directors must operate with the diligence implicit in the nature of their appointment. In view of the importance and complexity of the supervisory function, a professional level of diligence is thus required, similar to that required of other governing bodies.

284. Liability for damage caused to the company or to third parties is, however, subject to a number of conditions being met. It is, in fact, not sufficient to show that the damage has been caused by malpractice in management and that the supervisory directors have failed to carry out their supervisory work or have done so negligently. The supervisory directors will account for the damage only if it is proven that – if the supervisory work had been carried out properly – the malpractice, and, therefore, the damage, could have been avoided. Providing evidence of this kind is not easy, but case law will probably adapt to the approach they adopted in the framework of the liability of members of the *collegio sindacale.*

B. The Management Board

1. Appointment and Termination of Office

285. The members of the management board are first appointed in the articles of incorporation and after this by the supervisory board. By analogy with the system envisaged for members of the board of directors, an exception to this is provided by cases of appointment by holders of financial instruments of participation (Article 2351 CC) and by the State or public bodies (Article 2449 CC). There must be at least two members of the management board.

As far as the grounds for ineligibility/termination and the requisites of professionalism, respectability, and independence are concerned, the rules relating to board of directors will apply (Articles 2380*bis,* 2387 and 2409*undecies* CC, *see* above). Persons holding the position of supervisory director may not be appointed. Shareholder status is not required for persons acting as management directors.

The rules relating to advertising appointments and lapsing, powers of representation, and the effects vis-à-vis third parties of defects in the appointment resolution and of limits on the power of representation also apply to the management directors (Articles 2383, 2384, 2385, and 2409*undecies* CC).

The position has a duration of three years, but the board will only lapse with effect from the date of the meeting of the supervisory board called to approve the balance sheet of the third financial year. There are no limits as far as the re-election of directors is concerned.

Unless the by-laws provide otherwise, the supervisory board may remove the management directors at any time. If they are removed without cause, however, the company will be obliged to indemnify the damage brought about by the removal. In all events, if one or more members of the board lapse during their term of office, the supervisory board must promptly appoint substitutes.

The remuneration is established by the supervisory board, unless the by-laws entrust this function to a shareholders' meeting.

2. Powers and Duties

286. Like the board of directors in the ordinary system, the management board is obliged to run the enterprise and carry out any activities that may be necessary to achieve the corporate purpose.

The by-laws may extend the duties of the management board by entrusting it with decisions usually vested in a shareholders' meeting, pursuant to Article 2365, paragraph 2, CC, on merging; setting up, or closing branches; assigning powers of representation; reducing the capital if a shareholder withdraws; adapting the by-laws to the law; or transferring the registered office within Italy.

Generally speaking, management decisions must be made by the board, but, to the extent of the limits and following the modalities envisaged for the board of directors, certain powers may be delegated to one or more directors. Article 2409*novies* CC, in fact, refers to the provisions on delegating authorities referred to in Article 2381 CC (*see* above). Contrary to the rules applying to the board of directors, though, the CC does not provide that a special clause in the by-laws is needed to delegate authorities within the management board. In addition, the possibility of setting up an executive committee within the management board is not envisaged.

287. Like the board of directors, the management board elects its chairperson internally. The chairperson is responsible for guaranteeing the body's functioning, as he or she arranges to call meetings, establish the agenda, regulate meetings by putting resolutions to a vote, and proclaim resolutions that are approved. The chairperson may be removed by the board.

The resolutions of the management board are passed by a majority unless the by-laws envisage larger quorums. As far as any further aspects regarding the manner in which meetings are held and the validity of resolutions are concerned, including cases of conflict of interest, the provisions relating to the board of directors will apply (Article 2409*undecies* CC, which refers to Articles 2388 and 2391 CC). Resolutions that fail to comply with the law or the by-laws may be challenged in court within a period of ninety days by absent or dissenting management directors, by the supervisory board, and by shareholders (but only with respect to resolutions jeopardizing their rights).

288. Rules relating to the board of directors on non-competition, disclosure obligations and abstention requirements with respect to operations in which the directors have an interest – whether acting in their own right or on behalf of third parties – apply in full to the management board, as do – in the case of listed companies or companies with securities widely held by the public, pursuant to Article 2325*bis CC* – transparency and accuracy obligations relating to transactions with third parties (*see* above, in relation to Articles 2390, 2391, and 2391*bis,* referred to in Article 2409*undecies* CC).

3. Liability

289. The members of the management board are obliged to perform the duties vested in them by the law or by the by-laws with the diligence implicit in the nature of the appointment as far as their duties are concerned. With regard to establishing standards of diligence, criteria applied in assessing conduct and responsibilities vis-à-vis the company, company creditors, shareholders, and third parties (*see* the rules relating to the board of directors) (Article 2409*undecies,* in fact, refers to Articles 2392, 2394, 2394*bis,* and 2395 CC).

A number of specific provisions are, on the other hand, contained in Article 2409*decies* of the CC as far as filing corporate liability proceedings is concerned. Proceedings to ascertain the liability of the management board and assess compensation for damage suffered by the company may be filed, as for the board of directors, either through a resolution passed by a shareholders'meeting or at the initiative of minority shareholders who reach the percentages of capital established in Article 2393*bis CC* (*see* above with reference to the liability of the board of directors). Furthermore, proceedings may be filed following a resolution passed by the supervisory board. In view of the fact that the supervisory board has the authority to remove the management directors, the supervisory body will usually first proceed with the removal and then with the liability proceedings. It is envisaged that removal will come about by right (with consequent, immediate replacement), however, in cases in which the resolution passed by the supervisory board is approved by a majority of at least two-thirds of the directors. The same effects will be produced if a shareholders' meeting resolves to file liability proceedings by the votes of at least one-fifth of the share capital.

The supervisory board also has the authority to approve by a majority settlements in the framework of rulings on the liability of the management directors, provided that they do not object shareholders holding at least one-fifth of the share capital or, in the case of listed companies or companies with widely held shares, pursuant to Article 2325*bis* CC, at least one-twentieth or any other percentage envisaged in the by-laws for shareholders to file liability proceedings (Article 2393 CC).

Therefore, a shareholders' meeting and minority shareholders with substantial percentages have the power to ensure that eventual agreements between members of the management and supervisory boards do not give rise to the company forfeiting its possibility of obtaining indemnification for damage caused by *mala gestio.*

In all events, a settlement between the company and the management directors does not affect creditors, shareholders, or third parties.

As with the board of directors, the proceedings must be filed within five years of a management director's termination of office.

C. References to the Ordinary System

290. Upon examining the specific provisions relating to the supervisory board and the management board, we find numerous references to the rules set in place for the governing and supervisory bodies in the ordinary model of S.p.A.s (*see*, specifically, Article 2409*undecies*, Article 2409*quaterdecies*, and Article 2409*quinquiesdecies* CC). There is also a general provision in addition to the aforementioned rules. As far as any aspects not specifically covered are concerned, unless otherwise provided, the provisions relating to members of the board of directors will also apply to members of the management board (Article 2380, paragraph 3, CC). It thus clearly emerges that the ordinary model of administration and supervision of

S.p.A.s is the main model. This is partly because it had already been contemplated before the 2003 reform and is still the one most widely used. The two-tier system and the one-tier system are, therefore, regulated only with respect to their differential elements, and any legal vacuums can be filled by either extending or analogically applying the provisions of the ordinary system.

IV. The One-Tier System

A. The Board of Directors

1. Appointment and Termination of Office

291. The appointment and termination of office of directors in S.p.A.s based on the one-tier system of administration have few special features compared to the provisions applying to S.p.A.s based on the ordinary system of administration. The most significant difference consists of the fact that, in the case of one-tier S.p.A.s, several directors have to be appointed who then form a board of directors, which means that there cannot be a sole director. This is clearly a result of the fact that the supervisory body (the management supervision committee) is 'within' the governing body. This means that the governing body has to consist of: (i) directors entrusted only with management functions; and (ii) directors also entrusted with supervisory functions.

On the question of who is responsible for the appointment, there are no differences compared to the ordinary system. The appointment rests with a shareholders' meeting, apart from the exceptions previously described concerning appointments by holders of financial instruments of participation, by the State or public bodies, and by minority shareholders in the case of listed companies (Articles 2351, 2449 CC and Article *147ter* TUF).

Furthermore, the provisions relating to companies based on the ordinary system of administration also apply to the subjective requisites of directors (respectability, professionalism, and independence, as indicated in Article 2387 CC) and the grounds for ineligibility and termination of office indicated in Article 2382 CC. However, in view of the fact that the directors forming the committee responsible for supervising management have to be selected from within the board of directors, some of the directors must also have the requisites needed to perform supervisory functions.

Therefore, in addition to the above requisites, at least one-third of the board directors must also have the even stricter requisites of independence envisaged in the ordinary system for members of the *collegio sindacale*. The following persons may, therefore, not be appointed: (a) spouses, relatives, or relatives-in-law of directors of the company or of another group company; and (b) persons who have direct employment or consultancy links with the company or a group company such as to influence their work (Articles 2409*septiesdecies* and 2399 CC). The by-laws may establish further requisites of independence, referring specifically to the codes of conduct of trade associations or of the companies that run regulated markets. In the case of listed companies, the board directors must have the respectability requisites contemplated by ministerial decree, and the member designated by the minority list must meet the stricter independence requisites envisaged for members of supervisory bodies (Articles 147*ter* and 148 TUF). Furthermore, CONSOB has established a set of rules imposing limits on combining administrative and supervisory functions, and the supervisory authority will itself oblige anyone who exceeds such limits to leave (Article 148*bis* TUF). In the case of all companies, whether listed or unlisted, the directors are obliged to inform a shareholders' meeting that they have accepted the appointment, specifying the administrative and supervisory positions that they hold in other companies.

As far as any other aspects concerning duration, remuneration, and termination of office are concerned, the rules envisaged for the board of directors of S.p.A.s based on the ordinary system will apply.

2. Powers and Duties

292. Apart from the specific duties inherent in the appointment, responsibilities, and functioning of the management supervision committee (*see* below, section B), the board directors of one-tier companies have the same powers and duties as directors of companies based on the ordinary system.

In the one-tier system, though, the distinction between executive directors and non-executive directors is greater. This distinction, in fact, plays a key role when it comes to selecting the members of the supervisory body (i.e., the management supervision committee), who may only be selected from among the non-executive directors. In this respect, the executive directors are held to be: (i) the members of the executive committee, if one is set up; and (ii) any directors who are entrusted with delegated authorities in managing the enterprise or who, de facto, carry out management functions.

3. Liability

293. Apart from specific aspects inherent in the appointment, responsibilities, and functioning of the management supervision committee (*see* below, section B), the liability of board directors in one-tier companies is regulated in the same way as in companies based on the ordinary system.

Generally speaking, liability will be joint and several, that is, all the directors will account individually for the entire damage vis-à-vis the person who has suffered it (Article 2392, paragraph II, CC), and the indemnification will be split between the directors in equal measure, unless a different degree of liability is proven (Article 1298 CC).

However, the division of roles between executive and non-executive directors, which is necessary in the board of directors of one-tier companies, means that the latter cannot be made to answer for violations committed by the former in exercising the duties assigned to them. All the directors will, however, be liable if they fail to do everything in their power to prevent prejudicial acts of which they are aware or if they fail to act to eliminate or reduce the damage. In this respect, the liability of members of the management supervision committee is even greater, as they have greater powers to ascertain, prevent, and combat practices contrary to the law or the by-laws.

B. The Management Supervision Committee

1. Appointment and Termination of Office

294. The board of directors appoints the members of the management supervision committee from among its members. Article *2409octiesdecies* CC nevertheless envisages that the by-laws may provide otherwise. In the absence of specific legal guidelines, it is thought that the by-laws may reserve the appointment of members of the management supervision committee either for a shareholders' meeting or for holders of financial instruments of participation, or for the State or public authorities, in any cases in which they can appoint one or more members of the board of directors. It follows from this that board directors appointed by persons other than the majority shareholders should perform a supervisory, rather than a management, function.

The number of members of the committee is established by the board of directors, unless the by-laws provide differently, in all cases of companies, defined by Article 2325*bis* CC, there must be at least three members.

The appointment requires specific requisites of professionalism, respectability, and independence. The professionalism and respectability requisites are established in the by-laws, which may also envisage requisites above and beyond those required for the position of board director, pursuant to Article 2387 CC. As far as the independence requirement is concerned, first of all, the directors must not have executive functions – whether de facto or by delegated authority – either in the company itself or in its holding companies or subsidiaries. Furthermore, the members of the management supervision committee may not: (a) be spouses, relatives, or relatives-in-law of directors of the company or of another group company; or (b) be tied to the company by direct employment or consultancy links such as to influence their work. The by-laws may establish further requisites of independence, referring to the codes of conduct of trade associations or to the rules of the companies that run regulated markets. At least one member must be enrolled on the Register of Accounting Auditors.

There are no specific rules as far as removal is concerned. It is, therefore, thought that the power of removal is entrusted to those who appointed the committee (usually the board of directors). In accordance with general principles, the removal may take place even without grounds, but in this case, there will be an obligation to indemnify the damage.

In case of death, relinquishment, or any other cause of termination of office, the board of directors is obliged to promptly appoint a substitute from among its members who has the aforementioned requisites or, if this is not possible, it must do so by co-opting a person from outside the board of directors, provided that he or she has the requisites required for the position.

2. Powers and Duties

295. The management supervision committee has much more limited functions than those of the supervisory bodies that we find in the ordinary and the two-tier systems. Its main task is to ensure that the organizational, administrative, and accounting structure of the company is such as to provide a true portrayal of the company's operations. The supervisory committee will carry out any further supervisory activities entrusted to it by the board of directors. The committee does not carry out the accounts auditing activities, which, in the one-tier system, are always entrusted either to an external auditor or to an audit company. The supervisory committee may consult the external auditors and the internal supervisory bodies to obtain information and ensure that operations are faithfully portrayed in the accounts.

In the case of listed companies, the management supervision committee monitors compliance with: (i) the corporate governance rules envisaged in codes of conduct that the company has decided to adopt; and (ii) the instructions given by holding companies with regard to information disclosures; and it must notify CONSOB of any irregularities ascertained, providing it with any relevant documents.

In the one-tier system, the supervisory body does not have the power to appoint or remove the management board, challenge resolutions, or file liability proceedings (which power is vested in the supervisory board in two-tier companies), nor does it have the substitute powers, pursuant to Article 2406 CC, vested in the *collegio sindacale* in companies based on the ordinary model. The power to report to the court on the suspicion of serious malpractice is not specifically mentioned in the CC, but it is envisaged for listed companies (Article 152 TUF).

In addition, the members of the committee are also members of the board of directors. They have access to information regarding operations during board meetings, and they combine the powers arising from their twofold status. Furthermore, they attend the meetings of the executive committee and can thus acquire further information on operations (Articles 2409*octiesdecies* and 2404 CC).

In the case of listed companies, Article 151*ter* TUF envisages that the committee may delegate members of its own to carry out inspections, while any member may request information from the executive directors and from the internal supervisory bodies of the company and of companies controlled by the company. Furthermore, they may convene either the board of directors or the executive committee, specifying the matters to be discussed.

If malpractice in management is raised by the shareholders and if the prerequisites referred to in Article 2408 CC arise, like the *collegio sindacale,* the members of the committee must promptly investigate and report on their findings to a shareholders' meeting.

As far as the body's functioning is concerned, the committee appoints the chairperson from among its members and must meet at least every three months or at any greater frequency envisaged in the by-laws. Like the *collegio sindacale,* the committee is a collegiate body that is legally formed if the majority of its members are in attendance, and its resolutions are valid if they are passed by the majority of those attending. Members may arrange to have the fact that they disagree with the resolutions recorded, and, by so doing, they will remain extraneous to any consequent responsibilities.

3. Liability

296. The rules relating to the management supervision committee do not envisage specific responsibilities. Therefore, the general principles on the liability of members of the board of directors vis-à-vis the company, shareholders, creditors, and third parties will apply (*see* above in section A. 5 and A. 6, relating to companies based on the ordinary system of administration). More specifically, in the event of breach of legal obligations or of requirements of the by-laws concerning deeds of management delegated to the executive committee or to one or more chief executive officers, responsibility will rest primarily with those who have implemented them or failed to act when required to do so (Article 2392, paragraph I, CC). In addition, the supervisory function provided by the management supervision committee implies that its members may also be held to account for such violations in cases in which they have not done everything in their power to prevent or avert the ensuing damage (Article 2392, paragraph 2, CC).

C. References to the Ordinary System

297. On examining the specific provisions relating to the board of directors and the management supervision committee, we find numerous references to the rules established for the governing bodies and, in some cases, to those relating to the supervisory bodies in the ordinary model of S.p.A.s (*see*, respectively, Article 2409*noviesdecies,* Article 2409*septiesdecies,* paragraph 2, and Article 2409*octiesdecies,* paragraph 6, CC). There is also a general provision in addition to the aforementioned rules. As far as any aspects not specifically covered are concerned, unless otherwise provided, the provisions relating to members of the board of directors in the ordinary system will also apply to members of the board of directors in the one-tier system (Article 2380, paragraph 3, CC).

As far as auditing accounts is concerned, too, the rules on the one-tier system in almost every respect apply to the *sindaci* in the ordinary system (Article 2409*noviesdecies,* paragraph 2, CC).

It is thus confirmed that, as we have already stressed, the ordinary model of administration and supervision of an S.p.A. is the main model, provided by the legislator and is still the one most widely used. The two-tier system and the one-tier system are, therefore, regulated only with respect to their differential elements, while any legal vacuums can be filled by extending or analogically applying the provisions of the ordinary system.

§7. Company Books, Books of Account, Balance Sheet, and Auditors

I. Company Books

298. Companies must keep the company books as listed in Articles 2412 and 2447*sexies* CC, that is:

(a) the register of shareholders must specify the number of shares for each category, the first name(s) and surname(s) of holders of registered shares, transfers, restrictions on shares, and payments made;
(b) the register of bonds must specify the value of bonds issued and bonds redeemed, the first name(s) and surname(s) of holders, transfers, and restrictions affecting them;
(c) the register of financial instruments issued in the framework of assets separated for a specific business, providing details of the characteristics of the securities, the value of instruments issued and instruments redeemed, the first name(s) and surname(s) of holders, transfers, and restrictions affecting them;
(d) the register of meetings and resolutions of shareholders' meetings;
(e) the register of meetings and resolutions of either the board of directors or the management board, depending on whether the company adopts the traditional, one-tier or two-tier system of administration;
(f) the register of meetings and resolutions of the *collegio sindacale,* the supervisory board, or the management supervision committee, depending on whether the company adopts the traditional, one-tier or two-tier system of administration;
(g) the register of meetings and resolutions of the executive committee;
(h) the register of meetings and resolutions of meetings of bondholders;
(i) the register of meetings and resolutions of holders of financial instruments and bondholders.

299. The shareholders, bondholders, and owners of financial instruments referred to in Article 2447*sexies* may inspect the registers pertaining to their respective meetings. The shareholders may also inspect the register of shareholders. The joint representative of the bondholders may inspect the register of bondholders and the register of shareholders' meetings.

II. The Books of Account

300. Commercial enterprises must keep the journal book, the inventory book, and the other entries required, depending on the type and size of the enterprises (Article 2214 CC). The journal book and the inventory book must be progressively numbered and kept in order with no cancellations, white spaces, or line spaces. The journal book records the daily operations carried into effect by the enterprise. The inventory book is drawn up each year and provides details of assets and liabilities. Following Legislative

Decree No. 82 of 7 March 2005, the accounts entries may be created and kept using information-technology systems. Enterprises must keep the original copies of all letters, telegrams, and invoices received and copies of all letters, telegrams, and invoices sent. All such documents must be preserved for ten years.

Enterprises also have to keep a register of fiscal books and an employee register.

III. The Balance Sheet

A. The Purpose of the Balance Sheet

301. The balance sheet is the main instrument providing information on the economic and financial situation of the company and its assets. The people who benefit from the information contained in the balance sheet are, first of all, the shareholders, who need to know the results of company operations so that they can: (i) decide whether or not to distribute profits or balance losses; and (ii) assess the value of their holdings. In view of the fact that the balance sheet must be made public by depositing it at the *Registro delle imprese,* the information it provides also benefits creditors and third parties generally, who can in this way make an assessment of the company's reliability. The balance sheet is also useful for anyone intending to invest in the company, because through it they can assess the advisability of investment and the value of the holding. Finally, the balance sheet figures are of relevance to any administrative and jurisdictional authorities that may be called upon to verify the state of the company's operations. The balance sheet thus provides a set of information required by various economic operators who can base their choices on it. However, it has to be drawn up in compliance with strict rules, which ensure that it is intelligible and that it accurately reflects the state of operations. The main principles governing the manner in which balance sheets are drawn up are contained in Articles 2423 to 2435 of the CC, which apply to S.p.A.s. These rules are nevertheless reiterated to a great extent in the rules applying to S.a.a.s (Article 2454 CC), to S.r.l.s (Article 2478*bis* CC), to *società cooperative* (Article 2519 CC), and, less so, to any entities that carry out business as a commercial enterprise (Article 2217 CC).

B. Principles in Drawing up the Balance Sheet

302. There are three principles governing the manner in which the balance sheet is drawn up: clarity, truth, and accuracy.

The principle of clarity takes the form of a series of measures designed to make it easier to understand the company's assets and its economic and financial situation, and the criteria by which the balance sheet is drawn up. To this end, the structure of the balance sheet plays a key role in that it is compulsory and ensures that balance sheets are uniform. Furthermore, the clarity requirement means that the directors are obliged to provide information in the supplementary note on the choices of, and reasons for, the valuations contained in the balance sheet and on any exceptions to the ordinary valuation criteria.

The principle of truthful and accurate portrayal means that any facts that are susceptible to affecting management must be portrayed in the balance sheet and that its items are entered in accounts according to the criteria envisaged in accounting techniques and incorporated in the CC. Nevertheless, Article 2423 paragraph 4 allows derogations when their effects are not significant for the truthful and accurate portrayal. In any case the duty to correctly keep company books up to date cannot be waived.

303. Article 2423*bis* CC lists the principles to be applied in drawing up the balance sheet.

First of all, the balance sheet must be drawn up on a prudent basis. It is often the case that balance sheet items do not have a certain value or that their value is susceptible to variation if uncertain events occur. The prudence criterion, therefore, requires that the balance sheet takes account of the risk of costs or of factors that might have a negative impact on the values of individual items.

The valuations must be expressed bearing in mind the future economic function of the assets and the continuation of the business. The valuations must consider how the assets are to be used, distinguishing, for instance, between assets that are allocated to remain at the company's disposal (fixed assets) and assets that are addressed to be sold (investments), applying the various criteria established in the CC for the various hypotheses.

To avert surreptitious reductions of corporate assets, profits may only be distributed after they have been effectively earned at the end of the financial year.

The balance sheet must be drawn up on an accrual basis. This means that proceeds and costs must be entered when the rights or obligations arise and not at the time of their collection or payment. Similarly, account must be taken of risks and losses, even if they are known only after the close of the financial year.

The valuation criteria cannot be modified. This is to ensure that the values and the results of the balance sheets can be directly compared. If, exceptionally, this were to give rise to a violation of the principle of truthfulness and accuracy of the balance sheet, the criteria may be altered. Any such choice must be explained and justified in the supplementary note.

C. The Structure of the Balance Sheet

304. In the framework outlined by Directive 2013/34/EU, Legislative Decree No. 139/2015 amended Article 2423 CC defining the balance sheet as composed of: (i) The statement of assets and liabilities (ii) The profit and loss account (iii) The financial statement (iv) The supplementary note. In addition to those elements there are three annexes: (1). The report of directors; (2). The report of statutory auditors (*collegio sindacale*); (3). The report of auditors or of the audit company.

305. The CC distinguishes among three types of companies according to the kind of balance sheet they have to draft:

(1) large companies that are subject to the ordinary provisions;
(2) small companies, which are requested to draft a balance sheet in abbreviated form (Article 2435*bis* CC);

(3) micro companies, which benefit from a simplified balance sheet (Article 2435*ter* CC).According to the accounting definition, small companies are those that during the first year of business or for two consecutive years, do not exceed two of the following limits: – EUR 4,400,000 of assets in the statement of assets and liabilities, – EUR 8,800,000 of proceeds on sales and services; and – an average of fifty employees. For the purpose of the account discipline, micro companies are those firms that during the fiscal year had a maximum of: – EUR 175,000 total assets; – EUR 350,000 total income; – five employees (on average).

1. The Statement of Assets and Liabilities

306. The statement of assets and liabilities portrays the assets and liabilities of the company as of the date on which the balance sheet closes. The assets are divided into three categories of items: shareholders' receivables, fixed assets, and current assets. The liabilities are divided into five categories of items: net equity, risks and charges fund, employees' severance benefits fund, and accrued expenses/deferred income. The statement of assets and liabilities and the profit and loss account are divided into 'categories of items' (shown in capital letters) and subdivided into 'items' (shown in Roman numerals), which in turn are subdivided into 'sub-items' (shown in Arabic numerals). The order and subdivision are mandatory. Unifications or setoffs are not permitted, and alongside each item, the corresponding value appearing in the previous balance sheet must be provided.

Articles 2424*bis* and 2426 CC establish the criteria to be followed in drawing up and valuating items.

2. The Profit and Loss Account

307. The profit and loss account portrays the state of operations in the course of each financial year and is divided into five categories of items: value of output, production costs, financial proceeds, and charges, value adjustments of financial assets, and liabilities. The algebraic sum of the four elements already mentioned gives the fifth category: the result for the financial year before taxation. After deducting tax, the profit and loss account concludes by highlighting the year's profit or loss.

Articles *2425* and 2426 CC establish the criteria to be followed in drawing up and valuating items.

Legislative Decree 139/2015 amended the discipline of the balance sheet by harmonizing the Italian CC with international standards, so that Article 2357*ter*, paragraph 3, now provide that treasury shares are considered a passive item of net assets.

3. The Financial Statement

308. The financial statement regulated by Article 2425*ter* CC, shows the difference and the composition of liquidity in the current fiscal year and in the former one with details concerning financial flows coming from business, investments, financing and operations with members.

4. The Supplementary Note

309. In the supplementary note the directors are obliged to provide a series of further elements of information specified in Articles 2427 and 2427*bis* CC. This information covers such matters as valuation criteria, changes to and the breakdown of certain items, the reasons for accounting choices, and a range of further information relating to operations that appear neither in the statement of assets and liabilities nor in the profit and loss account. A specific disclosure must be provided concerning the financial instruments held and their valuation based (or not based) on the fair value criterion.

5. The Balance Sheet in Abbreviated Form

310. Drawing up the balance sheet on the basis of the standard structure may prove to be costly for small-to-medium-sized businesses and unnecessary in terms of providing adequate information on the state of their operations. Therefore, companies that, during the first year of business or for two consecutive years, do not exceed two of the following limits are allowed to draw up their balance sheets in abbreviated form: EUR 4,400,000 of assets in the statement of assets and liabilities, EUR 8,800,000 of proceeds on sales and services, and fifty employees.

The balance sheet in abbreviated form is characterized by the absence of a number of sub-items and the unification of certain items in the statement of assets and liabilities and in the profit and loss account, together with the possibility of omitting certain information in the supplementary note, in accordance with the specific provisions of Article 2435*bis* CC. The financial statement is not mandatory for corporations that draft the balance sheet in abbreviated form.

D. Approving the Balance Sheet and Distributing Profits

311. In the case of S.p.A.s based on the traditional or one-tier system, the balance sheet is drawn up by the board of directors, which assumes responsibility for complying with the legal principles governing its formation. Once the balance sheet has been approved, this does not, however, release the directors from liability. The balance sheet must be drawn up and submitted for the approval of a shareholders' meeting within four months of the close of the financial year, or within six months in the case of group-leading companies.

The balance sheet must be sent to the *collegio sindacale* and to the external auditor at least thirty days before the shareholders' meeting called to approve it, and it must be deposited at the registered office at least fifteen days before that date so that the shareholders can examine it. Together with the balance sheet, a report on operations prepared by the directors, including an analysis of the company's situation, progress, and operating results must be deposited. The report must, moreover, contain a series of elements specified in Article 2428 CC, including research and development activities, treasury shares and those of group companies, and significant events that have occurred after the close of the financial year, as well as foreseeable developments in operations. Within the same deadline, the report of the external auditor and, in the case of companies with traditional system, the report of the *collegio sindacale,* must be deposited at the registered office. In its report, the *collegio sindacale* reports on the audit activity carried out, making observations and recommendations on the balance sheet and, in particular, on any exceptions to the accounting standards adopted by the directors.

312. The balance sheet is then approved by an ordinary meeting of shareholders. Within thirty days, the balance sheet, along with the attached reports and the approval resolution, must be deposited at the *Registro delle imprese.* In the case of companies that do not have shares listed on regulated markets, the list of shareholders and of persons with voting rights must also be deposited, specifying the shares they hold and any transfers that have occurred since the close of the previous balance sheet.

313. Once the balance sheet has been approved, a shareholders' meeting may resolve to distribute the profit.

A 5% quota of the profit has to be set aside by law until such time as a legal reserve corresponding to 20% of the capital is set up. The shareholders' meeting may by a majority resolve either to distribute the residual profit or to set it aside in optional reserves. If the shareholders' meeting does not decide to distribute the profit, the shareholders are not entitled to receive dividends. However, if dividends are distributed and collected in good faith by the shareholders, they are not obliged to return them even if the resolution approving the balance sheet is annulled.

Prior to the approval of the balance sheet, advances on dividends can be distributed only by companies subject to an accounting audit by auditors registered on the special register, provided that specific conditions set forth in Article 2433*bis* CC are met.

314. In the case of S.p.A.s based on the two-tier system, the balance sheet is drawn up by the management board, deposited within the deadline indicated above together with the report on operations and the auditor's report at the registered office, and submitted for the approval of the supervisory board. The resolution on distributing profits is not, however, adopted by the supervisory board, but by a shareholders' meeting.

E. Challenge of the Resolution Approving the Balance Sheet

315. The resolution approving the balance sheet is subject to the general rules on challenging contained in Articles 2377 and 2379 CC. In the case of S.p.A.s based on the two-tier system, the resolution of the supervisory board may be challenged, pursuant to Article 2377, by absent or dissenting members of the supervisory board and by the shareholders. In the hypotheses of nullity, the resolutions of the shareholders' meeting or of the supervisory board may be challenged by anyone with an interest, and the invalidity may be ascertained ex officio by the judge. Within the hypotheses of nullity the courts also include cases in which a balance sheet that fails to comply with the mandatory accounting rules is approved.

316. To limit litigation, the CC nevertheless envisages subjective prerequisites and conditions for filing and continuing proceedings. First and foremost, if the balance sheet has been passed with no comments on the part of the auditor, the challenge can be filed only by shareholders who own at least 5% of the capital. Furthermore, if the balance sheet for the subsequent financial year has been approved, the challenge may not be filed, or if it has already been filed, the proceeding cannot go ahead unless the resolution approving the new balance sheet is also challenged.

In the case of listed companies, the challenge may also be filed by CONSOB within six months of the time when the approval resolution was deposited.

The ruling may not alter the balance sheet but simply deprive it of effects, thereby obliging the governing bodies concerned to draft and approve a new balance sheet.

F. The Consolidated Balance Sheet

317. The consolidated balance sheet is regulated by Legislative Decree No. 127/ 1991, as amended by Legislative Decree No. 139/2015.

The purpose of the consolidated balance sheet is to provide a portrayal of the economic and financial situation – with the same characteristics as those of the financial year's balance sheet – of companies coming under unitary control as if they were one enterprise. The consolidated balance sheet provides the shareholders with information on the existence of a group relationship and its overall progress. The fact that a consolidated balance sheet is prepared constitutes a presumption as far as the application of rules regulating groups (Article 2497*sexies* CC) is concerned.

318. The consolidated balance sheet is mandatory for any joint-stock companies that control an enterprise and for any cooperatives, mutual insurers, and public economic entities that control a joint-stock company, as indeed for S.n.c.s and S.a.s.s, if all their shareholders are joint-stock companies. Moreover it is also mandatory for *Enti di Interesse Pubblico* under Article 16 of Law Decree No. 39/2010 (*see* below).

The obligation arises whenever we find a situation of control exercised through: (a) the majority of votes at an ordinary shareholders' meeting, even if this is based on a shareholders' agreement; or (b) a contract or clause in the by-laws attributing the right to exercise a dominant influence.

The obligation does not arise, however, if on aggregate the enterprises do not exceed the thresholds established in Article 27 of Legislative Decree No. 127/1991 (two of the following requites: EUR 20 million asset; EUR 40 million income; 250 employees) or if the controlling enterprise is in its turn 95% controlled by a company that has to draw up a consolidated balance sheet, provided that the intermediary controlling company is not listed on the stock exchange or unless 5% of its shareholders so request.

If the above prerequisites are not met, several companies belonging to the same group will draw up consolidated balance sheets only for the enterprises they control.

319. The structure of the consolidated balance sheet is the same as that of the balance sheet for the financial year, with each item giving the aggregate value for the consolidated enterprises. The possibility exists of not consolidating the accounts figures of subsidiaries in cases in which: (i) they are economically irrelevant; (ii) the rights of the holding company are restricted; (iii) the figures are not promptly available; or (iv) the securities are not held to exercise control but to sell them to third parties. The figures of subsidiaries must not be consolidated in exceptional cases in which this might provide a misleading picture of the group's overall situation.

The consolidation applies to the entire value of the items appearing in the subsidiaries' balance sheets, regardless of the percentage of capital held by the holding company.

In cases in which there are situations of credit or debt between group companies, the relevant value is eliminated and deducted from that of the relevant balance sheet items. Shares in the holding company owned by subsidiaries are entered under an item known as treasury shares.

Companies listed on regulated markets draw up their consolidated balance sheet in accordance with international accounting principles even if this is in derogation of Italian law.

320. The consolidated balance sheet is approved by the shareholders' meeting or, in the case of S.p.A.s based on the two-tier system, by the supervisory board of the holding company. As far as auditors' obligations and challenging are concerned, the rules envisaged for the financial year's balance sheet apply.

IV. Auditors

A. The Role of the Auditors

321. Under the organization of S.p.A.s established in the 1942 CC, the auditing of accounts was entrusted to the *collegio sindacale,* which based its supervisory function over management on the three parameters of legality, compliance with the by-laws, and rules of accounting. The position of *sindaco* did not, therefore, require accounting skills. For this reason, supervision over accounts has – first for listed companies and then more generally – been gradually wrested from the *sindaci* and entrusted to duly qualified parties such as an external auditor or an auditing firm, in compliance with the provisions of Directive 84/253/EEC (eight corporate directive) and more recently by Directive 2006/43/EEC.

322. Today, the auditing of accounts must in all events be entrusted to external auditors or to an auditing firm. For the so-called *enti di interesse pubblico* (entities of public interest) as defined by Article 16 of Legislative Decree No. 39/2010, including listed companies, banks, insurances, financial intermediaries and companies that resort to the risk capital market, stricter rules are imposed concerning independence, competence, transparency and supervision of the auditing firms by CONSOB.

B. The Qualifications Required of External Auditors

323. The auditing of accounts must be entrusted to an external auditor or to an auditing firm registered on a register set up at the Ministry of Economy and Finance (MEF). Registration is regulated by Legislative Decree No. 39/2010, which envisages such prerequisites as respectability, adequate qualification, at least three years of training, and successful results in a qualifying examination. As far as auditing firms are concerned, the firm must have its registered office in an EU Member State, the directors must satisfy the prerequisites of respectability, the majority of them must be registered in an EU Member State, there must be a prevalence of shareholders enrolled on the register (in terms of number of shares as far as partnerships are concerned, and in terms of voting rights at the shareholders' meeting in the case of joint-stock companies), the shares must indicate the name of the shareholder and may not be transferred and, finally, the persons in charge of the auditing must be enrolled in the register.

324. In the case of companies that do not resort to the risk capital market, pursuant to Article 2325*bis,* that do not have to draw up consolidated balance sheets, and that adopt the ordinary system of administration, the accounts may be audited by the *collegio sindacale.* In this case, though, all members of the *collegio sindacale* must be enrolled on the register.

C. Appointment and Termination of Office

325. The external auditor and the auditing firm are appointed by a shareholders' meeting after receiving the opinion of the supervisory body. To carry out their activities properly, they need to have special requisites, such as adequate technical and accounting competency, honesty, and independence of assessment. This means that, to start with, only persons who are enrolled on the aforementioned register may be appointed auditors. Furthermore, persons may not be appointed auditor if they have received the sentences listed in Article 2399 CC, which exclude appointment as auditor, and the same also applies if they have the personal or work relations listed in this article with the company or with its shareholders or directors. The company's by-laws may establish further grounds for ineligibility and incompatibility or else establish stricter professional requisites than those laid down by the law. As with the *sindaci,* if the requisites required for the assignment are terminated in the course of fulfilling the assignment, the external auditor will terminate by law his or her office.

326. The duration, which is established by law for the assignment as three years, cannot be modified by the by-laws or by the deed of appointment. Although the CC makes no provision in this respect, the appointment is thought to be renewable. The shareholders' meeting is also responsible for establishing the fees due to the auditors, which must, however, be calculated according to the criteria established in a set of principles provided by Legislative Decree No. 39/2010.

327. The external auditors may relinquish their office and they may be removed by a shareholders' meeting on just grounds after consulting the supervisory body. Diversity of opinions about auditing procedures or evaluations of the accounts does not integrate a just ground of removal. The auditors remain in office until a new auditor or auditing firm is in charge, but in any case for no more than six months since termination. The auditors, the auditing firms, and the audited company have to notify to the MEF and the CONSOB the grounds of removal, dismissal or termination by agreement of the auditing contract.

D. Powers and Duties

328. The external auditor and the auditing firm have three main tasks: (i) to check at least every three months that the accounts are kept properly and that they faithfully reflect the company's progress; (ii) to check that the balance sheets for the year and the consolidated balance sheets, if any, correspond to the data set forth in the accounts and are in compliance with law; and (iii) to prepare a report with an assessment of the year's balance sheets and the consolidated balance sheets, which must be made available to the shareholders at least fifteen days prior to the shareholders' meeting called to approve the balance sheets. To this end, the external auditor is entitled to obtain documents pertaining to the company's management and can arrange for inspections to be carried out. The work carried out must be set out in a special book. The external auditor has a duty to maintain secrecy and exchange with the supervisory body any information that may be useful for their respective tasks.

329. The external auditor's assessment of the balance sheets bears upon the shareholders' right of challenging. If the external auditor issues no comments on the balance sheets, the statements are presumed to be in order. Consequently, only shareholders who dispose of at least 5% of the capital are entitled to challenge them. This is to avert challenging aimed simply at creating a conflict within the company. The 5% requisite is, however, not necessary in cases in which the external auditors issue comments on the balance sheets, express a negative assessment, or refuse to give an assessment.

E. Liability

330. The external auditors' liability is regulated by the same principles established for the *sindaci.* The external auditors will, therefore, be liable vis-à-vis the company, shareholders, and third parties for damage caused as a result of breaching their obligations and for failing to comply with their duty of diligence in supervising. As with the *sindaci,* their obligation to indemnify is based primarily on the fact that they have failed to ascertain malpractice in management. This implies proving that the damage could have been prevented or reduced if the supervision had been carried out properly. The evidence is based on an assessment of probability, which makes it possible to confirm a causal link between the auditor's default and the damage. Unlike the *sindaci,* however, their liability can arise only in cases in which the malpractice in management gives rise to breaches of accounting rules. As a parameter of the external auditor's diligence, reference may be made to the auditing standards prepared by the National Councils of Business Consultants and Chartered Accountants.

If the assignment is conferred on an auditing firm, its liability will be joint and several with the company and with the persons who have carried out the activities on behalf of the company.

The action is time-barred five years after the auditors' termination of office.

F. The Auditors of Listed Companies and Companies Qualified as Enti di Interesse Pubblico (Entities of Public Interest)

331. In the case of listed companies, companies that resort to the risk capital market and the other companies qualified by Legislative Decree No. 39/2010 as *Enti di Interesse Pubblico,* the provisions of the CC are supplemented and partially derogated by Articles 155 and following articles of the TUF, and by Article 16 and followings of Legislative Decree No. 39/2010, which envisage stricter rules geared to protecting public savings and interests. CONSOB exercises a supervisory role over both the auditing firms and the relationship between these firms and the listed companies.

CONSOB watches over the independence, technical capacity, and due execution of assignments, and in this framework, it may ask for deeds and documents, carry out inspections, and recommend auditing principles and criteria. CONSOB also disposes of powers of sanction of varying gravity, which even include cancellation from the special register.

The assignment is granted by a company's shareholders' meeting for a nine-year period for auditing firms and seven-year period for auditors, which may be renewed only after three years since the termination of the previous. The resolution must be notified to CONSOB. This Authority must also be duly informed of removal resolutions, which must indicate the just grounds and specify the new firm entrusted with auditing.

Furthermore, Article 155 of the TUF specifies for listed companies that the auditors must inform without delay CONSOB of any irregularity they discover during the auditing activities.

On the issue of assessments of the balance sheets, the TUF is more detailed inasmuch as it envisages the possibility for the auditing firm to express a positive assessment with no comments, a positive assessment with comments, a negative assessment, or a declaration stating that it cannot issue an assessment. In the latter three cases, reasons must be given. The auditing firm must promptly inform CONSOB in cases in which it expresses a negative assessment or when it declares that it cannot issue an assessment.

On the matter of resolutions passed by shareholders' meetings approving the year's balance sheets and the consolidated balance sheet, the now generally accepted principle established in Article 2434*bis* CC applies, under which, if the auditing firm gives a positive assessment, the challenge can be filed only by shareholders who dispose of 5% of the capital.

In any event, CONSOB may challenge the year's balance sheets or the consolidated balance sheet within six months of the time they are filed at the *Registro delle Imprese*.

§8. Amending the Articles of Association

I. Types of Amendments and Procedures

332. Amendments to the articles of association and the by-laws may be required for a variety of reasons, ranging from simply adapting to new legislation to radically transforming the company. The bodies responsible and the procedural rules will, therefore, clearly vary from case to case. The existence of a corporate organization and the company's need to adapt mean that the general contractual principle requiring the consent of all the contracting parties will not apply. In the case of joint-stock companies, the consent of all the shareholders is, in fact, never required, but instruments have been set in place to safeguard dissenting shareholders in the most radical hypotheses of change.

Furthermore, the rules on amendments are designed to safeguard the interests of third parties and the mandatory principles of company law. Consequently, it is envisaged that amendments be made public in the same way as the articles of association and that their validity be checked either by a notary or by the court.

In addition to the rules governing the approval and registration of the amendment at the *Registro delle imprese,* there are also specific provisions covering: (i) changes to the share capital; and (ii) transformations and mergers/demergers. In both cases, please refer to the specific paragraphs (for changes to capital *see* §3. V. of this chapter; for transformations and mergers/demergers, *see* Part III, Chapter 2).

333. As far as certain amendments not thought to jeopardize the minority shareholders are concerned (mergers of fully owned or 90%-owned companies, modifying powers of representation, setting up or closing secondary offices, changing directors with power of representation, reducing the capital following withdrawal, adapting the by-laws to legal requirements, and transferring the registered office inside Italy), the by-laws may vest decisional power in the governing body or, in the case of two-tier companies, in the supervisory board or the management board.

334. In all other cases, the decision must be made by a shareholders' meeting with the majorities envisaged for extraordinary shareholders' meetings (*see* §5, paragraph III). Larger majorities (more than one-third of the share capital) are envisaged for companies that do not resort to the capital market pursuant to Article 2325*bis* of the CC in cases of amendments involving the corporate purpose, early dissolution or continuance of the company, resuming the regular business of the company under liquidation, transferring the registered office abroad, and issuing shares without voting rights or with limited or restricted votes.

Finally, specific majorities are envisaged with respect to barring or reducing the right of option in such events as: (i) capital increase (*see* §3. V); (ii) heterogeneous transformation; or (iii) transformation of the company into a different type of organizational model (*see* Part III, Chapter 2).

335. The minutes of the extraordinary shareholders' meeting approving an amendment to the by-laws must be drawn up by a notary. The same notary has to check that the resolution and the new by-laws comply with the law. If this is so, he or she must then proceed within thirty days to deposit them at the *Registro delle imprese.* Otherwise, within the same thirty-day period, he or she must inform the directors of the legal violation that he or she has ascertained. The directors may then convene a shareholders' meeting for it to either confirm the amendment or modify the resolution. If the shareholders' meeting confirms the amendment to the by-laws within the next thirty days, the directors must then submit it to the court for registration or verification of its compliance with the law. If the directors fail to submit the resolution to the court, or if the court does not issue the registration order, the amendment resolution will forfeit its effectiveness. Amendments to the by-laws are, therefore, devoid of effect unless they pass a legal compliance check on the part of the notary or the court. Once the legal compliance check has gone through, the resolution and the amended text of the by-laws must be deposited at the office of the *Registro delle imprese,* which then formally checks that the documentation is complete.

II. Shareholders' Withdrawal

336. The right of withdrawal is acknowledged to shareholders in the cases envisaged by the law or by the by-laws. The hypotheses envisaged by law refer to resolutions or events that radically alter the economic or organizational prospects of the shareholding in the company. More specifically, Article 2437 CC envisages the right of withdrawal in the following cases: changes to the corporate purpose that radically affect the company's activity, transformation, transferring the registered office abroad, revoking the liquidation, removing the grounds for withdrawal envisaged in the by-laws, changing the criteria used to value shares in the event of withdrawal, and changing voting or holding rights. The shareholder is also entitled to withdraw if the estimate of contributions in kind is changed (Article 2343 CC), if the company is made subject to the directives of another company or if this situation changes (Article 2497*quater* CC, *see* Part III, Chapter 1, §6), and in the event of delisting.

Furthermore, if an unlisted company does not have a specific duration, the shareholder may withdraw on 180 days' advance notice or on any longer period of notice established in the by-laws, provided that this is not more than one year.

In all the hypotheses described, the by-laws may not exclude the right of withdrawal, and any clauses to the contrary are null and void.

337. The shareholder is also entitled to withdraw if the duration of the company is extended or if limits on transferring shares are either added to or removed from the by-laws. The by-laws may, however, exclude these two hypotheses of withdrawal.

In the by-laws of unlisted companies, other grounds for withdrawal may be envisaged. This does not apply to listed companies in which there is less need to safeguard the shareholder's interest in selling his or her investment, as this result can be easily achieved by selling on the stock exchange.

338. The shareholder may withdraw by sending a registered letter to the company either within fifteen days of the resolution's registration at the companies register or within thirty days of when he or she came to know of the event justifying withdrawal. The shareholder may also withdraw with respect to only a part of his or her shares, but upon making the withdrawal declaration, he or she must deposit the shares at the registered office and may no longer sell them.

To balance the shareholder's right with those of the company and the majority shareholders, it is envisaged that the withdrawal will forfeit its effectiveness if the resolution justifying it is revoked or if the company is placed in liquidation. In the former case, there are no longer any grounds for withdrawal, and in the latter case, the shareholder in any case obtains liquidation, although this is subject to the different procedure of a company liquidation in which all holders of shares are in the same position.

339. In the event of withdrawal, the value of the shares is established by the following criteria provided by law. In the case of listed companies it is the average market price over the six months immediately preceding the calling of the shareholders' meeting that approved the amendments that gave rise to the right to withdraw. In the case of unlisted companies, on the other hand, it is the value of the corresponding quota of equity, bearing in mind both the income prospects and the market price, if ascertainable. In the latter case, the by-laws may establish different criteria.

The liquidation value in the event of withdrawal must be notified to the shareholders at least fifteen days prior to the shareholders'meeting called to resolve an amendment justifying withdrawal.

A shareholder who does not agree with this valuation may ask the court to appoint an expert appraiser, who will issue his or her assessment within ninety days.

340. Once the liquidation value of the shares has been established, for at least thirty days, the directors must make them available for purchase by the other shareholders in proportion to the number of shares they hold. If the other shareholders do not purchase all or some of the shares, the directors may sell them to third parties. If the shares are not purchased by third parties within 180 days, they will be purchased by the company either by using the available reserves, or, once a resolution has been passed, by an extraordinary shareholders' meeting, by using a part of the legal reserve or capital with a consequent, proportional reduction of capital.

§9. Mergers and Takeovers

I. Mergers

341. The Italian legal system provides the same merger rules for all models of companies and envisages no specific rules for S.p.A.s. Please refer, therefore, to the part dedicated to the common rules (Part III, Chapter 2, §2).

II. Takeovers

A. Takeovers of Unlisted Companies

342. Acquiring a position of control over the management of an S.p.A. either by purchasing shares or by other legal instruments assigning voting rights entails the application of a specific set of rules for companies listed on regulated markets. For unlisted S.p.A.s and for all other types of companies, on the other hand, the CC contains common rules regulating the specific legal obligations and consequences that arise in cases in which a company is managed and coordinated by another company or entity.

In this section, we shall, therefore, examine the rules relating to takeovers of listed companies, whereas the rules common to unlisted S.p.A.s and other models of companies will be covered in Part III, Chapter 1.

B. Takeovers of Listed Companies

343. Acquiring control over the management of a listed S.p.A. usually takes place by purchasing shares or other securities that assign voting rights in a sufficient quantity for it to be possible to appoint the members, or majority of members, of the governing bodies. Control may thus be acquired either by just one person or entity or else by several persons or entities linked by an agreement as far as the S.p.A.'s management is concerned.

The shares may be purchased by anyone so entitled either through a series of autonomous operations or through a takeover bid such as a public offer of purchase *(offerta pubblica di acquisto)* (OPA) or an offer of exchange *(offerta pubblica di scambio)* (OPS).

To ensure fair treatment for holders of listed shares, protect minority shareholders, and at the same time favour an efficient functioning of the so-called market for corporate control, the Italian legal system envisages highly detailed rules for OPA or OPS in general and also, more specifically, for mandatory OPA.

The legislation currently in force is contained in the TUF of 1998, which has been amended several times, especially when Italy transposed the Directive 25/2004/EC into law and finally by Law Decree 91 of 24 June 2014. These sources are supplemented by the set of rules issued by CONSOB on issuers (adopted under Resolution 11971 of 14 May 1999, and later amended several times). CONSOB is, in fact, the authority entrusted with monitoring the efficiency and transparency of the market for corporate control set in place to protect investors, and, therefore, regulates and monitors the information provided and the regularity of the procedure, as well as compliance with obligations incumbent upon both the offerors and the target company. As far as sharing responsibilities with other supervisory authorities of EU countries is concerned, it is envisaged that CONSOB will monitor public offers covering securities issued by companies: (a) registered in Italy and listed on a regulated Italian market; (b) registered in a different EU State but listed exclusively on an Italian market; or (c) registered in a different EU State and listed on markets other than those of the State where it is registered, if this is requested by the issuer and if the securities were initially admitted to listing in Italy.

344. The rules contained in the TUF can be split into two parts: a first general part (Articles 102–104*ter*) applicable to all types of OPAs and OPSs, and a second part (Articles 105–112) applicable to mandatory OPAs and cases of mandatory purchases of shares.

The terms OPA and OPS are held to mean any offer, invitation to offer, or promotional message, however made, directed towards either the purchase or the exchange of financial products (apart from securities issued by the central banks of EU States), targeting the public.

The public offer will, therefore, be an OPA if the consideration offered is formed only by money, an OPS if the consideration is formed by other securities or by both securities and money.

345. In brief, the main phases of an OPA or an OPS are as follows.

(a) The offeror sends CONSOB the offer document to be published, which contains the information that enables recipients to decide whether or not to accept the offer. The offeror must offer the same conditions to all owners of securities of the same kind but, unless there are legal restrictions, it may indicate a maximum quantity of securities that are intended to be purchased. The offer will be irrevocable, and any clause to the contrary will be null and void. The offeror may not make the offer subject to conditions dependent on the will of the offeror. Within fifteen days (thirty days in special cases), CONSOB may ask the offeror for supplementary information and request particular modalities of publishing the offer document and guarantees to be supplemented. Once this deadline has passed, the offer document is held as having been approved and may be published. Article 102 of the TUF provides that the offeror – with respect to OPS related to bonds and other debt securities – may require to CONSOB that the offer is subject to the rules relating to Initial Public Offering (IPO). CONSOB will respond to the request within fifteen days.

(b) The company issuing the securities to which the offer refers must disseminate a statement, the content of which is established in the aforementioned CONSOB rules. In it, the company has to provide any elements that will make possible to appreciate the offer, along with a substantiated evaluation by the directors, while also providing information on any events of significance justifying the OPA. The statement must be sent to CONSOB at least two days prior to the date envisaged for its dissemination, and CONSOB may ask for it to be supplemented.

(c) After the publishing of the prospectus, the period for acceptances starts to run. Acceptances are received at care of the offeror, designated intermediaries, and depositories authorized to provide investment services, after signing the acceptance form. The period of acceptance, that is, the time in which it is possible to sign the acceptance form, may last from a minimum of twenty-five to a maximum of forty days in the case of an OPA for the target entire capital or a preventive OPA, and from a minimum of fifteen to a maximum of twenty-five days in other cases of offers, barring extensions authorized by CONSOB. During this phase, all the parties involved (the offeror, the issuer, the controlling and controlled entities, the shareholders of the offeror, and the issuer) must behave in compliance with the rules on transparency and honesty laid down by the law. The transparency obligations apply for the entire period of time between notification of the offer to CONSOB and the date by which the consideration has to be paid. Furthermore, CONSOB may ask for news and documents to be published to ensure that the public is fully informed. It may also request further documents, carry out inspections, and acquire information from company representatives.

(d) Article 104 of TUF envisages, for target companies, the obligation to refrain from acts or operations that are in conflict with the objectives of the offer, even if they have been decided before the offer, unless a specific authorization has been resolved by either an ordinary shareholders' meeting or an extraordinary shareholders' meeting (the 'passivity rule'). The authorization must be adopted at least eighteen months prior to notifying the offer.

Furthermore, under the so-called neutralization rule, during the offer acceptance period, restrictions on transferring securities contemplated in the by-laws will be of no effect vis-à-vis the offeror, and this will also apply to restrictions on the right to vote in cases in which shareholders' meetings deliberate upon the passivity rule. Also multiple voting shares fall under the discipline of the neutralization rule, and in this period such shares will attribute one vote each. And, if the offeror reaches at least 75% of the capital, at the first shareholders' meeting called to amend the by-laws and appoint either the directors or the members of the management or supervisory board, any special rights or restrictions on voting rights contemplated in the by-laws or in shareholders' agreements will be of no effect, including multiple vote. If the offer is successful, the offeror must pay fair indemnification for the loss of rights caused by the neutralization rule. This indemnification will be equal to the difference in the price of the securities before and after the offer. Both the passivity rule and the neutralization rule are applicable subject to a condition of reciprocity, that is, only if similar rules also apply to the offeror company.

The passivity rule and the neutralization rule have been amended several times. During the international crisis, in order to protect Italian companies, the Law Decree 185 of 29 November 2008 had envisaged the right to introduce the two rules into the by-laws. Afterwards, the Legislative Decree 146 of 25 September 2009 provided for the passivity rule to be the default rule applicable to all listed companies. Anyway, the passivity rule may be waived by means of introducing a specific provision in the by-laws. On the other hand, Article 104*bis* of the TUF provides the neutralization rule to be applicable only if it has been introduced in the by-laws.

(e) During the acceptance period, competing offers may be proposed, and the original offer may be modified (e.g., by increasing the price or increasing the quantity of shares to be purchased), but the conditions cannot be made less favourable.

1. Takeover Bids for the Entire Capital

346. An OPA for all securities admitted to trading in a regulated market is mandatory under Articles 105 and 106 TUF for anyone who comes into possession of a stake of more than 30%. The threshold is 25% in large enterprises where there are not shareholders who hold a higher share, while the by-laws of a listed SME may provide for, in lieu of 30%, a tailored threshold between the 25% and the 40% of the share capital or the voting rights. In fact, the stake refers to the quota of voting rights represented by securities admitted to trading on a regulated market, held either directly or indirectly through trustees or third parties (this is the case of a so-called indirect purchase). After the introduction of multiple voting shares in the Italian system, the threshold may be referred to voting rights and do not necessarily represent an equal value of the share capital, since a shareholder can be entitled a certain level of voting rights without buying the corresponding amount of share capital as before the reform.

347. The requirement of launching an OPA for the entire capital extends to cases in which the threshold is exceeded by parties who have signed a shareholders' agreement, by controlled and controlling companies or companies subject to joint control, by a company and the members of its administrative or supervisory boards or the general managers and, finally, by persons who liaise to obtain control of the company that has issued the securities. Therefore, any persons who, acting by mutual agreement, have purchased a corporate holding in excess of the aforementioned threshold are under a joint and several obligation to launch the OPA.

An OPA for the entire capital is also mandatory in the case of so-called consolidation of the holding. In this case, persons who already hold more than 30% of the ordinary shares of a listed company but who do not dispose of the majority of voting rights at the ordinary shareholders' meeting are obliged to launch the public offer after purchasing, even indirectly, more than 5% of the capital represented by ordinary shares.

An OPA for the entire capital is, however, not mandatory in cases in which there are one or more shareholders, other than those who hold more than 30%, who control the company, and also in a series of cases regulated by CONSOB (regulation n. 11971/1999 and following amendments) in which there is a prevailing interest (i.e., saving companies in crisis) or in which there is no effective change in the company's control.

The by-laws of an SME may exclude the application of an OPA discipline until the fifth balance sheet after the listing has passed (Article 106, paragraph 3*quater*, TUF).

Finally, an OPA for the entire capital is not mandatory in cases in which the threshold is exceeded following an earlier OPA or an OPS targeting all the shareholders (who have, therefore, already had a chance to sell the shares on uniform conditions) or following a preventive OPA (*see* No. 2).

348. The purpose of an OPA for the entire capital is to allow the remaining shareholders to leave the company following the formation of a new group controlling it, by obtaining a price equal to that paid so as to obtain control of the company. The purchase must, therefore, be offered at the highest price paid by the offeror for the same securities in the previous year or, if there are no such purchases, at the average market price during the same period. The consideration may be formed partly or totally by financial instruments in place of cash.

The price may be set by CONSOB at a higher or lower level if this is justified by particular circumstances.

2. Preventive Takeover Bid

349. To facilitate smooth functioning of the market for corporate control, the TUF envisages the possibility of acquiring control of a listed company without having to launch an OPA for the entire capital, which is rather costly and thus discourages takeover attempts.

Article 107 of the TUF, in fact, allows anyone who is not obliged to launch an OPA for the entire capital to voluntarily launch an OPA or an OPS for at least 60% of the ordinary shares, if he or she – or the persons with whom the offeror is working in liaison – has not purchased more than 1% the year before. In such a case, the offer price is free, and the offer may be subject to reaching a minimum threshold of acceptances set by the offeror, provided that this is equal to the majority of securities'calculated net of those already held by the offeror and by the majority shareholder, if he or she holds more than 10%, and by persons linked to them by agreements.

This way, if sufficient acceptances are reached, the offeror can acquire control of the company, and at the same time, any shareholders who accept the offer receive the same price.

However, this procedure does not always allow the offeror to bypass the OPA for the entire capital requirement. This obligation will arise in any case, if in the year after the close of the preventive OPA: (a) either the offeror or the persons with whom the offeror is working in liaison have made purchases of holdings in excess of 1%; or

(b) the shareholders' meeting of the issuing company has resolved merger and/or demerger operations.

3. Obligation to Purchase and Squeeze-Out Right

350. To enable minority shareholders to sell their securities when the market is not sufficiently liquid, two cases of mandatory purchase are envisaged.

Pursuant to Article 108 of the TUF, an offeror who, after launching an OPA for the entire capital, comes into possession of a stake of at least 95% of the capital represented by securities, is under an obligation to purchase the remaining securities of shareholders who so request. If the corporation issued different categories of securities, the obligation to purchase is limited to categories for which threshold of 95% has been reached.

Furthermore, anyone who has a holding, however obtained, in excess of 90% of the share capital represented by securities admitted to trading on a regulated market, is under an obligation to purchase the remaining securities from whomsoever so asks, unless he or she recreates – in the next ninety days – a floating stake sufficient to ensure the regular course of trading.

The price will either be the price offered in earlier public offers, if they were full offers, or else the price established by CONSOB, bearing in mind the average market price in the last six months and the price indicated in any public offers.

351. Finally, anyone who acquires at least 95% of securities with voting rights after launching an OPA for the entire capital acquires the right to purchase the residual securities at the price indicated in the OPA within three months of the offer closing, provided that he or she has previously declared that he or she wishes to avail himself or herself of this right.

§10. Dissolution and Liquidation

352. The dissolution and liquidation of S.p.A.s are regulated by the CC in rules common to all corporations. Please refer, therefore, to Part III, Chapter 3, §1.

Chapter 2. The Società a Responsabilità Limitata (S.r.l.) ('Limited Liability Company')

§1. Characteristics

I. Characteristics of the S.r.l.

353. The S.r.l. is characterized by its internal flexibility in terms of organization and control and is, therefore, suited to small and medium-sized Italian enterprises and to international companies when they set up their subsidiaries in Italy. In particular, an S.r.l. is used to set up single member companies, although the 2003 Company Law Reform also introduced the single shareholder S.p.A. .

Prior to the Company Law Reform, an S.r.l. was considered a kind of 'S.p.A. without shares', because many of the rules governing an S.p.A. also applied to an S.r.l.

Through the reform, the legislature set in place a new and autonomous set of rules, stressing the importance of personal financing by members and increasing their control, while reducing the power of creditors.

Thanks to this, the S.r.l. has now become a business association combining the characteristics of an S.p.A. (limited liability of members) with those of a partnership (flexibility of structure).

In particular, the legislature has given the members broader discretionary power, leaving them free to draft the articles of association according to their requirements and to be less formal in establishing rules for the administration of the company. By means of further interventions, the legislator has amended Article 2463 paragraphs 4 and 5 cc, and it is now possible to set up an S.r.l. with a lower capital share, but with some restriction in terms of reserve capital. In addition, it has been introduced Article 2463*bis* CC, by which takes shape the S.r.l.simp. (S.r.l.s.): a peculiar corporation tailored on necessities of start-up and young entrepreneurs.

§2. Formation and Registration

I. Formation Procedure

354. The incorporation of an S.r.l. is regulated by Article 2463 CC, pursuant to which the contract (or a unilateral deed in the case of single member companies) must be drawn up by a public notary and registered by him or her within twenty days at the Registro delle imprese. Any deed drawn up differently will be void and cannot be registered.

355. As an exception, an S.r.l.s., which is regulated by Article 2463*bis* CC, can be only set up by natural persons.

II. Essential Elements of the Articles of Association

356. Unlike an S.p.A., in the case of an S.r.l., the deed by which the company is set up and the clauses concerning its organization may be produced in a single document containing the essential elements specified in Article 2463 CC.

357. For S.r.l.simp. the content of the article of association is fix and determined by a ministerial decree that provides for a specific form, which is mandatory under Article 2463*bis*, paragraph 3 CC. Founding members can only implement the standard model by adding articles that cannot be contrary to the provisions already set out by the decree and the general discipline of S.r.l. The law initially limited the use of the S.r.l.simp. to persons under 35 years, but this provision has been already abolished.

358. The members of an S.r.l. may pay their contributions in the form of cash, assets, or services, provided that the contribution can be economically valued. The capital must be fully subscribed, and the members must deposit at least 25% of their contribution in cash with a bank or an insurance policy or a bank guarantee for the same amount, or they can pay directly to those officers mentioned in the article of association. Contributions of assets or of credits must be made in full at the moment of the incorporation. If there is a single member, he or she must deposit the full amount of his or her contribution immediately. Contributions of services must be accompanied by an insurance policy or a bank guarantee of an amount equal to their value.

359. The share capital of an ordinary S.r.l. is at least EUR 10,000.00. If the by-laws provide for a lower capital, and precisely included between EUR 1 and EUR 9,999.00, shall be fully paid in cash at the time of the incorporation.

The S.r.l.simp. must have a share capital under the ordinary threshold of EUR 10,000.00.

360. If the company is set up by natural persons, their nationality must be specified in the article of association, as well as any other relevant personal data (i.e., name, date of birth, and residence). If it is set up by legal persons must be indicated the name, the country of incorporation and the registered seat. The S.r.l. cannot subscribe its own shares. There is no limit on the number of members.

361. The by-laws must provide for the municipality where the registered office and the branches of the S.r.l. are located. As a result, the S.r.l. will be allowed to change its registered office in the same municipality without having to hold an extraordinary members' meeting. Changing the municipality is not treated as an amendment to the articles of association and may be implemented by a board resolution, unless otherwise provided. It will, in fact, only be necessary to specify the change in the documents to be registered at the Registro delle imprese.

362. S.r.l.simp. shall disclose its legal status of simplified and not regular s.r.l. in mail, documents and electronic accounts linked with the public administration, together with the amount of the share capital, the seat and the Registro delle imprese where it is registered.

363. The company name does not have to be connected with the members and may contain the name of a person or place, provided that this does not mislead third parties with respect to the quality or place of origin of the products and services provided by the company. Generally speaking, the company name must not contain false representations of the company's true activities.

364. As far as the corporate purpose is concerned, the articles of association must provide an indication of the envisaged, albeit potential, business activities, but it is not compulsory to specify each one of them.

365. Shares are usually proportional to contributions (Article 2468 CC), but the articles of association may envisage differently, specifying each member's contribution and rights. Some members may be acknowledged special rights in terms of voting powers or dividends, which – unless otherwise provided – cannot be modified without the unanimous consent of the members. In any case, the quota assigned to each member will be established in the articles of association.

366. The articles of association must give information on the company's management, including the names of the persons vested with powers of management (usually one or more members), that is, the legal representatives. Any limitations on the powers of the legal representatives will be unenforceable against third parties, even if they have been published in the Registro delle imprese, unless there is evidence that they acted wilfully to damage the interests of the corporation (Article 2475*bis* CC).

367. The description of the corporate governance of the company must include an eventual body entrusted with internal supervision. A collegio sindacale (a traditional Italian internal supervisory body required for an S.p.A., *see* Chapter 1) is required only if the capital of the company is equal to or greater than the minimum established for an S.p.A. (EUR 50,000.00) or if the S.r.l. exceeds for two years at least two of the following limits: assets totalling EUR 4,400,000, income totalling EUR 8,800,000, and fifty employees.

368. An S.r.l. may be set up without an expiry date. In such a case, any member may withdraw at any time giving six months prior notice. This period of notice may be extended to as much as one year if the articles of association explicitly specify this.

III. Registration

369. The registration of an S.r.l. follows the general rules established for an S.p.A. Therefore, no more than twenty days after it is signed, the notary public must deposit the memorandum of association at the Registro delle imprese by the Chamber of Commerce where the company has its registered office, together with documents proving that incorporation formalities have been met. Either the directors or the members may register the company at its expense, within ninety days of incorporation.

If the company has branches in Italy, a copy of the memorandum of association must be deposited at the local Registro delle imprese. After a formal check of the documents, the company is registered and, under the Italian system, acquires legal status.

370. Prior to registration, the members are committed by the documents they have signed, and their contributions, which are usually deposited with a bank, are not at the disposal of the directors. Directors who accept obligations in the name of the company will be personally liable. If several persons act in the name of the company, they will be jointly and severally liable.

If the company is not registered within ninety days of being set up, the articles of association will forfeit all legal effect, and the members will be entitled to have their contributions returned.

IV. Rules Common to Both S.r.l.s and S.p.A.s

371. In accordance with Article 2463 CC, the provisions relating to S.p.A.s contained in Articles 2329, 2330, 2331, 2332, and 2341, on the conditions for the formation of a company, registration and its effects, grounds for nullity, and founders' rights, will apply to S.r.l.s (*see* Chapter 1, §2).

§3. Contributions

372. The rules on contributions are provided in Article 2464 CC and following, the aim of which is to guarantee the company and its creditors a minimum amount in terms of value.

I. Nature

373. Unlike an S.p.A., in the case of an S.r.l. the members are allowed to contribute not only by cash or in kind, but also in the form of work and services, provided that such a contribution can be economically valued and unless the articles of association provide otherwise.

The rules on contributions paid in the form of assigning a claim or in kind are set forth in Articles 2254 and 2255 CC. The basic concept is that the general rules on contracts on such matters will apply.

In accordance with Article 2254 CC, in the case of contributions of assets, the guarantee provided by the members and the transfer of risk are governed by the rules governing a contract of sale, in that the members must guarantee the ownership and enjoyment of the contribution. Furthermore, if only usage of the asset is contributed, the rules on leases will govern guarantees of enjoyment (Articles 1465, 1478, 1529 CC).

Otherwise, as far as contributions consisting of credits pursuant to Article 2255 CC are concerned, the members will be liable in the event of non-performance by the debtor in accordance with the general rules on assigning credits (Articles 1578, 1585 CC and followings).

In accordance with Article 2465 CC, anyone who contributes by transferring a claim or in kind must produce an appraisal prepared by a registered auditor or by an auditing company. The auditor will be liable for damage to the company, members, and third parties.[27]

The rules on the appraisal are the same as those for the S.p.A. (Articles 2343 and 2343*bis* CC).

If the value of assets or credits is less than one-fifth of the stated value, the company will have to proportionally reduce its capital. The members may either pay the difference in cash or exercise the right to withdraw. In the latter case, the members must be repaid.

In S.r.l.simp. and in S.r.l. with less than EUR 10,000.00 share capital, founding members can only contribute in cash.

II. Payment

374. The value of contributions cannot be less than the amount of the entire declared capital, and the members must deposit at least 25% of their cash contribution with a bank. This initial payment may be substitutes by a bank or insurance guarantee.

Contributions in kind must be paid in full immediately. In case of contribution in the form of work and services, member has to issue a bank or insurance guarantee in favour of the company and, if the articles of association so provide, he or she may at any time replace it with a guarantee deposit of an amount equal to that of the capital contribution.

In the case of a single member company, the single member must deposit his or her entire contribution immediately. If the plurality of the members lapse during the company's life, any contributions still due must be paid within ninety days.

III. Non-performance

375. If a member fails to make his or her contribution within the required deadline, the directors will invite the member to comply within thirty days. On the expiry of this period, the directors may either sue the member to obtain the contribution or sell the insolvent member's quota to the other members in proportion to their quota of capital. If the members do not buy the insolvent member's quota and unless otherwise provided, his or her quota may be sold by auction. If the auction fails, the directors may remove the member, withholding his or her contribution for the company. In such an event, they must reduce the company's declared capital accordingly.

376. In any cases of default, the debtor is not entitled to vote at the members' meeting.

27. The auditor's report is also required if the company purchases receivables or assets from founders, members, or directors of an amount equal to at least 10% of the declared capital within two years of the company's incorporation. Unless otherwise provided, such purchases must be established by the members' meeting (Article 2479 CC).

§4. MEMBERS' FINANCING

377. In small and medium-sized enterprises, usually the members finance the company in ways that do not imply changing the declared capital. Therefore, it is important – especially in the event of bankruptcy – to distinguish between facility financing and capital financing (including loans with either no repayment deadline or bearing no interest, which are basically a capital contribution).

An example of a capital contribution is that of financing granted by members at a time when, because of the type of business carried on by company, there is an excessive imbalance between the company's debt and its asset capital (undercapitalization) or in cases in which a capital contribution would be reasonable. In such cases, it is hard to establish the method by which this kind of contribution is recognized.

The method adopted by the CC is the 'standard based on reasonableness', according to which the financial standing of the company should be taken into account and compared with the conduct reasonably expected by the market.

In the case of capital financing, the repayment of member financing is subject to the prior reimbursement of other creditors and, if this occurs the year before the company filed for bankruptcy, it will be repaid to the trustee (Article 2467 CC). In the case of facility financing, on the other hand, the member will be considered just like other ordinary creditors.[28]

The balance sheet will report on any loans made by members to the company.

§5. SHARES

I. General Principles

378. In accordance with Article 2468 CC, the stakes held in an S.r.l. may not be represented by stock (which means that share certificates are not permitted), nor may they be the subject of investment soliciting.

Unless otherwise provided in the articles of association, the members' rights are proportional to the quota they own. Provision may, however, be made for certain members to be entitled to special rights regarding the management of the company or the distribution of profit. In such a case, any special rights can be modified only with the agreement of all members – unless otherwise provided by the articles of association – and the members affected by the modification are entitled to withdraw pursuant to Article 2473 CC.

In the case of an S.r.l., a member owns just one quota of a variable value based on the share of capital that he or she buys or sells. The member may, therefore, only exercise his or her right to withdraw in respect to the entire quota, unlike the case of

28. The aforementioned principles also apply to S.p.A.s, in which the members may decide to subscribe to a capital increase not yet resolved by the members' meeting or pay contributions into a capital account (or without security). In these latter cases, some of the contributions paid into the capital account could be considered as loans lent by the members to the company and therefore, they should be repaid just like other contributions.

the S.p.A., in which: (i) members hold shares attributing rights independent of the owner; and (ii) they may withdraw in respect to just a part of their shares.

In the event of joint ownership, the owners' rights must be exercised by a mutual agent appointed by the joint owners. The joint owners are jointly and severally liable as far as their obligations vis-à-vis the company are concerned.

II. Assignment

379. The assignment of shares may be subject to: (a) acceptance by management, members, or third parties; and (b) special conditions, if any, or limitations barring inheritance.

In cases in which assignment is not permitted, a member may exercise his or her right to withdraw, apart from cases in which the articles of association envisage that this should not be permitted for two years after the date on which the company was set up or after the quota was subscribed.

Article 2470 CC envisages that the assignment be drawn up in the form of private deed by a public notary or by a *dottore commercialista* (certified accountant), who must register it at the Registro delle imprese. Within thirty days of registration, the assignment must be recorded in the share ledger at the request of either the seller or the buyer.

In the case of death, the assignment must be registered and recorded by the heir or legatee.

The assignment will be enforceable vis-à-vis the company, provided that it has been registered.

Registering the assignment at the register solves the problem of a conflict between more than one purchaser. In such a case, the first bona fide buyer to register the assignment at the register obtains sound title to his or her property, regardless of the time of the assignment.

In any case the assignee is liable within a three-year period of the registration for the contributions due by the assignor.

380. The quota may be subject to expropriation. In such a case, the distraint on the quota will be enforced by: (i) formally notifying the debtor and the company; and (ii) registering it at the Registro delle imprese. After this, the directors will arrange to record it in the share ledger. The judicial order decreeing the sale of the quota must be notified to the company by the creditor.

If the quota cannot be assigned and the creditor, the debtor, and the company fail to reach agreement on the sale, it will be necessary to proceed by auction. The sale by auction will, however, be ineffective if, within ten days of the auction, the company proposes another purchaser who makes the same bid.

The above provisions also govern the event of insolvency of a member.

381. As long as the shares are subject to a pledge, usufruct or distraint, Article 2471bis CC refers to the rules on S.p.A.s envisaged in Article 2352 CC.

In the event of shares being subject to a pledge or usufruct, unless otherwise provided, the pledgee or usufructuary is acknowledged the right to vote, but, if the share has been made subject to distraint, the holder will have such right.

§6. Member's Withdrawal

I. The Purpose of Withdrawal

382. Withdrawal is the right by which a member can obtain payment of his or her quota without having to negotiate with other members or third parties. As with an S.p.A., the rules regulating the right to withdraw seek to balance the company's interest in keeping the assets to achieve the corporate purpose with the member's right to sell his or her shares if essential aspects of the business or the company change. In the case of an S.r.l., the right to withdraw is more important than it is with an S.p.A., because the members do not usually have an opportunity to sell their shares to third parties.

II. Legal and Contractual Grounds for Withdrawal

383. The legal grounds for withdrawal are as follows:

- changes to the corporate purpose clause involving a significant modification of the business;
- operations that substantially alter the corporate purpose, without altering the articles of association (i.e., selling a branch of business, taking over another company, or formation of a joint venture);
- transformation, merger, or demerger of the company;
- transferring the company's registered office abroad;
- revoking of the state of liquidation;
- eliminating one or more grounds for withdrawal set forth in the articles of association;
- relevant changes to the rights of members, involving the distribution of dividends or management and control;
- a resolution introducing, amending, or eliminating an arbitration clause envisaged in the articles of association;
- excluding the right of option in the event of a capital increase (Article 2481bis CC);
- developments involving the entity exercising powers of guidance and coordination of management, as envisaged in Article 2497quater CC (*see* Part III, Chapter 1);
- the articles of association exclude transferring shares or make their transfer subject to the total discretion of the directors;
- it is impossible for an heir to acquire the status of member.

Furthermore, if the S.r.l. is set up without an expiry date, a member may withdraw without having to explain why, after giving 180 days' prior notice. The period of notice may be extended to as much as one year in the articles of association. Case law extends the power of withdrawal if the expiry date of the company exceeds the life expectancy of the member.

The articles of association may envisage other cases of withdrawal.

384. It is important to highlight certain differences between S.p.A.s and S.r.l.s: (a) the second ground does not apply to S.p.A.s unless there is a specific clause in the by-laws; and (b) in the case of S.p.A.s, a member may withdraw with respect to a part of his or her shares.

III. Withdrawal Procedure

385. As far as the withdrawal declaration is concerned, the CC does not envisage specific rules for an S.r.l. Therefore, unless the articles of association make specific provision, reference may be made to Article 2437bis CC relating to the S.p.A.

386. The value of the shares will be proportional to the fraction of declared capital owned and must be established on the basis of the 'market value' of the corporate assets at the time of withdrawal. If the parties fail to reach an agreement on the market value, they may ask the court to appoint an expert.

The repayment may be made within 180 days by the other members purchasing the shares or, with the consent of the other members, by a third party. If the shares are not purchased, the company will arrange to make the repayment without them. Otherwise, the repayment will come from available reserves or, if this is not possible, by reducing the share capital. If the company is not in condition to repay the quota, it has to be liquidated.

In any case, the right to withdraw will be excluded if: (i) the reason for this is eliminated; or (ii) the company is placed under liquidation.

§7. A Member's Removal

387. As the CC envisages, if a member fails to arrange to pay the contribution within the due date, the directors will order him or her to do so within thirty days. If he or she fails to comply, the directors may either take him or her to court or sell his or her shares to the other members. If there are no purchasers, the directors will remove the member from the company and withhold the amounts paid.

388. The articles of association may envisage other cases of removing a member based on 'reasonable grounds'. Such 'reasonable grounds' may include the following: (a) if the member fails to meet obligations envisaged by the law or the articles of association; (b) if the member decides to carry out transactions that diminish the reliance of the other members; (c) if the member is in default as director of the company.

389. The articles of association must establish which governing body of the company will decide with respect to removing the member, that is, whether it should be the board of directors, a members' meeting, or the members in the form of an agreement reached in writing or through a written procedure.

A member subject to removal may appeal to the courts.

The repayment of the member thus removed will follow the rules applying to withdrawal, apart from the reduction of capital. If the member removed is not repaid either by the other members or by a third party, or if the S.r.l. does not have available reserves, the company will be placed under liquidation.

§8. Issuing Instruments of Debt

390. Until 2003, Article 2486 CC prohibited an S.r.l. from issuing bonds or other financial instruments. Consequently, the risk capital was created by contributions paid by a small group of partners.

Under the current Article 2483 CC, the articles of association may envisage issuing instruments of debt and, if they do, they will establish the responsibilities of members and directors, as well as the limits, formalities, and quorum required for such decisions. The issuing of instruments of debt must be registered at the Registro delle imprese by the company's directors.

The CC makes no provision with regard to the kinds of instruments of debt, but it is clear that they must be instruments acknowledging the right to repayment of the amount lent to the company. 'Hybrid securities' conferring both proprietary and administrative rights are not permitted, but most authors acknowledge the issuing of instruments of debt convertible into shares.

Furthermore, these instruments cannot be offered to the general public of consumers or listed in a public financial market; only professional investors subject to prudential control under special regulations, such as banks or companies authorized as security dealers (Società di intermediazione mobiliare - SIMs),may subscribe securities issued by an S.r.l. If they transfer the securities to third parties who are not professional investors or members of the same company, they will be held to account for the company's solvency (Article 2483 CC).

If the articles of association so envisage, the conditions and procedures of the loans may be modified with the consent of the majority of holders of the instruments of debt.

§9. Company Bodies

I. Members' Decisions

A. Matters Covered by Members' Decisions

391. Pursuant to Article 2479 CC, the members decide on the matters set forth in the articles of association or else on matters brought to their attention by one or more directors or by members owning at least one-third of the capital.

In all events, they will decide on the following matters:

- Approving the balance sheet and distributing the dividends.
- Appointing directors, unless otherwise provided.

- Appointing either the sindaci and chairperson of the collegio sindacale or the external auditor (Article 2477 CC).
- Amending the articles of association.
- Resolutions involving substantial changes to the corporate purpose or involving significant modifications to members' rights.

B. Approval Formalities and Quorums

392. Unlike S.p.A., the articles of association of an S.r.l. avoid the need for a members' meeting to make decisions of minor importance. In such cases, the articles of association may envisage that resolutions be passed in the form of written consultation or through express written consent, in such a way as to certify the matter to be decided and the will of each and every member.

The decisions must, however, be made by a members' meeting in cases that involve the last two matters listed in the previous paragraph or if either the directors or members representing at least one-third of the capital so request.

The decisions must be approved with the votes of members representing the majority of capital, unless the articles of association envisage a different quorum.

393. Pursuant to Article 2419bis CC, the articles of association must provide for a members' meeting to be convened following procedures ensuring due information on the matters to be discussed (faxes and e-mails are considered valid systems of transmission). Unless there are specific provisions in this regard, the call must be delivered by registered letter with a receipt sent to members at least eight days before the date set for the meeting.

A decision may be validly adopted, even with no legal calling, in cases in which the entire capital is represented at the meeting, all the directors and auditors are either in attendance or duly informed, and no one objects to the matter being discussed.

394. The meeting will be validly formed if members representing at least half the capital take part in it. Unless otherwise provided, a member may take part in the meeting by proxy.

Voting rights are proportional to the quota owned by the member.

A resolution is approved with the votes of at least the majority of the capital represented by the members attending the meeting. Two kinds of decisions must be approved by members representing at least 50% of the capital of the company, unless otherwise envisaged in the articles of association. These are (1) decisions involving substantial changes to the articles of association; and (2) decisions involving significant modifications to the corporate purpose or to members' rights.

395. The chairperson will be appointed either in the articles of association or by those who attend the meetings. He or she will guarantee the standard procedure for setting up the meeting, check the identity and right to participate of all those present, regulate the holding of the meeting, and check the results of voting, which must be set forth in the minutes of the meeting.

C. *Invalidity of Members' Decisions*

396. The invalidity of members' decisions is regulated by Article 2419ter CC and by a number of provisions contained in the CC concerning the S.p.A.

Pursuant to Article 2479*ter* CC, resolutions may be challenged if they are: (a) adopted in breach of the law or the company's articles of association; or (b) adopted with the decisive vote of members who, whether they are acting in their own right or on behalf of third parties, have an interest in conflict with that of the company, in cases in which the decisions might harm the company.

In the above cases, the resolution may be challenged – within ninety days of the time it is recorded in the ledger of members' decisions – by dissenting members, by the directors, or by the collegio sindacale, if appointed.

It should be stressed that, unlike an S.p.A., in the case of an S.r.l., a member who challenged a resolution does not necessarily have to represent a minimum percentage of the declared capital.

397. Furthermore, resolutions involving impossible or illegal matters and resolutions passed without adequate prior information may be challenged by anyone concerned within three years of when they are recorded in the ledger of members' decisions, whereas resolutions modifying the corporate purpose or involving impossible or illegal matters may be challenged at any time.

As with an S.p.A., the resolution cannot be declared void if the invalidity of some of the votes does not affect the quorum required to pass the decision. Furthermore, resolutions approving the annual balance sheet cannot be challenged after the resolution approving the following year's balance sheet has been approved (Articles 2377, 2434bis and 2479*ter* CC).

Also applicable to S.r.l.s are the S.p.A. rules on: (i) the procedure for challenging resolutions (Article 2378 CC); (ii) challenging resolutions to increase or reduce the capital or issue bonds (Article 2379*ter* CC); (iii) a number of cases in which the resolution cannot be declared void due to subsequent actions by the members or by the company (Article 2379bis CC); and (iv) the effects of the court decision on invalidity vis-à-vis the members and third parties (Article 2377 CC) (for all these matters, *see* Chapter 1, §5, IX).

During proceedings, the judge may grant a period of six months to allow the company to amend the challenged resolution.

II. Directors

A. *Appointment*

398. The company's management will hinge mainly on the rules set forth in the articles of association, in view of the fact that the CC does not impose a specific model of administration. The articles of association will thus establish formalities with respect to appointing the directors, allocating duties to members, members' and directors' meetings, the model of management, and rules on administration, including specific powers vested in certain members. In practice, depending on the clauses of the articles of association, the management of an S.r.l. may vary from a model typical of a corporation, with a board of directors taking collegial decisions, to a model of administration entrusted to one or more members, as in partnerships, which may also envisage the participation of non-director members in certain decisions.

Pursuant to Article 2475 CC, unless otherwise envisaged, responsibility for managing the company is vested in one or more members appointed under a members' decision. The clause envisaging the appointment of non-member directors is very common. Within thirty days of the members' resolution, the directors must register their appointment at the Registro delle imprese specifying their personal data and indicating which directors represent the company and whether they manage the company individually or jointly.

The voidness or voidability of the appointment of directors representing the company cannot be enforced against third parties after the above-mentioned registration formalities, except in cases in which the third parties were aware of it (Article 2383 CC).

B. Joint and Individual Management

399. If two or more directors are appointed, they will form a board of directors, but the articles of association may envisage either a joint or an individual management. In all events, decisions with respect to drawing up the annual balance sheet, mergers or demergers, and resolutions by the directors envisaging a capital increase can be adopted only by either the sole director or the board of directors.

It should be stressed that, even if the directors form a board, the articles of association may allow directors' resolutions to be adopted in the form of written consultation or through express written consent (this may be by fax or e-mail, provided that they are formally signed).

If the articles of association envisage a joint management, Article 2258 CC (on joint management in partnerships) will apply. Under this article, the directors may perform a deed only if there is unanimous consent of all directors or, if the articles of association so provide, a majority of them. The directors cannot perform any deed individually apart from urgent initiatives required to avert harm to the company.

If, on the other hand, an individual management is envisaged, Article 2257 CC will apply, pursuant to which each member may exercise his or her power of administration individually. Furthermore, if the members are permitted to act individually, each one of them may object to a future operation by another member. The objection will be decided by a majority of members, which will depend on each member's sharing of the profit.

C. Conflict of Interests

400. As far as directors' conflicts of interest are concerned, Article 2475*ter* CC provides that the company may file a claim to void agreements reached by directors who have – whether they are acting on behalf of third parties or in their own right – interests in conflict with the company, in cases in which the third party knew or might have known of the conflict. Furthermore, the directors, members of the collegio sindacale, or external auditors, if appointed, may ask the court to void resolutions passed with the decisive vote of a director affected by a conflict of interest, within ninety days of the date when the resolution was adopted, in cases in which the resolution in question might harm the company. The judgement of invalidation will not affect the rights of bona fide third parties arising from business transactions affected by the resolution.

Unlike an S.p.A., therefore, in the case of an S.r.l. the directors are neither required to declare any interest that they may have in a company operation nor to abstain from voting in such a case. The law provides no definition of conflict of interest, however, and this may give rise to difficulties in interpreting and enforcing the above rules.

D. Liability

401. Generally speaking, directors who fail to comply with the duties envisaged by the law and by the articles of association will be jointly and severally liable vis-à-vis the company for any damage that has occurred (Article 2476 CC). As with an S.p.A., their liability is defined as contractual but is mostly governed by the special provisions of company law. Therefore, to escape liability, the director must prove that he or she did not take part in the operation giving rise to the damage or, if he or she was aware of it, that he or she formally disapproved the decisions taken by the other directors. In the case of joint management, such an exemption is extremely difficult to obtain.

Unlike an S.p.A,, there is no provision in the CC concerning the standards of diligence or other parameters to be applied in evaluating management of an S.r.l. Apart from a number of specific rules, such as the rules on conflicts of interest, the general principles on the diligence of professionals will apply. The criteria and the general limits on directors' liability (i.e., the business judgment rule) envisaged for S.p.A.s may be taken into account by the courts, but there is no specific cross- reference in this respect.

In all events, the approval of the balance sheet does not discharge directors from their liability.

402. In the case of an S.r.l., the members are vested with broad powers in controlling management.

First of all, members not acting as directors must be kept informed of the company's business. Second, they are entitled to inspect – aided by their consultants if necessary – company ledgers and documents concerning management operations. Third, any member may take proceedings with respect to the directors' liability and apply for them to be removed in cases in which management principles and provisions are breached. The company will win damages, but the court may order it to reimburse the claimant's legal expenses. Unless otherwise provided, the claim may be either settled or withdrawn, in cases in which members representing two-thirds of the declared capital agree and provided that there is no objection by members representing one-tenth of the declared capital. Although not explicitly envisaged, clearly, a claim may also be filed by the company following a members' resolution or a decision passed by the (new) directors.

403. The members and third parties may file proceedings if they have suffered direct damage as a result of the directors' activities. Such claims are governed by the law of tort and are unaffected if the claim concerning the damage to the company is settled or withdrawn.

404. A typical feature of an S.r.l. is a rule concerning the liability of members. As S.r.l.s are often small and have close links between members and directors, the Article 2476, paragraph VII, CC envisages that members who have wilfully resolved or authorized corporate acts that have damaged the company, its members, or third parties will share joint and several liability with the directors for such acts, even if they themselves are not appointed as directors.

III. Accounts Supervision

405. Pursuant to Article 2477 CC, the articles of association may envisage the appointment of a supervisory organ or an external auditor. If the by-laws do not determine differently, the supervisory organ is composed of a single member. The appointment of an supervisory organ or of an external auditor is, however, mandatory in cases in which:

(a) the company must draw up a consolidated balance sheet;
(b) the company controls another company subject to the external audit supervision;
(c) the company has exceeded for two consecutive years at least two of the following thresholds envisaged in Article 2435*bis* CC: (1) the balance sheet of the company shows assets equal to or greater than EUR 4,400,000; (2) proceeds from services or sales are equal to or greater than EUR 8,800,000; and (3) there are fifty or more company employees. If the above limits have not been exceeded for two consecutive fiscal years, the company is not obliged to maintain the supervisory organ.

In cases, in which the supervisory organ is mandatory, the provisions relating to the collegio sindacale of an S.p.A. will apply, but, as far as its duties are concerned, it is not clear whether they include only accounts supervision or whether they also include monitoring compliance with the law and the articles of association on management, which would appear to be more logical.

It should, however, be stressed that the power of the collegio sindacale envisaged in Article 2409 CC to file a statement on suspected serious irregularities in management at the court of the district where the company has its registered office is not envisaged for an S.r.l., in which the members have the aforementioned extra power to control management. This means that there are fewer safeguards for third parties than there are with an S.p.A.

406. In cases in which the supervisory organ is not mandatory, the articles of association may envisage its duties and powers, but as far as other elements (i.e., personal requisites, remuneration, and general principles on liability) are concerned, the rules envisaged for an S.p.A. must be applied by analogy. In all events, the members of the supervisory organ must be registered on the Registro delle imprese, report on the annual balance sheet and on its activity, providing suggestions and comments.

IV. Annual Balance Sheet and Distribution of Profit

407. Pursuant to Article 2478bis CC, most of the rules (Articles 2423bis, 2423ter, 2424, 2424bis, 2425, 2425bis, 2426, 2427, 2428, 2429, 2430, and 2431 CC) on the annual accounts of the S.p.A. also apply to the S.r.l. The contents of the annual accounts and the accounting criteria are, therefore, the same as those envisaged for the S.p.A. (*see* Chapter 1, §7).

The annual accounts must be drawn up and submitted to the approval of the members within 120 days of the close of the financial year, or alternatively within 180 days, if permitted by the articles of association, in the case of group-leading companies or in cases in which the structure or business of the company so requires.

The annual accounts are approved either by the members or by a members' meeting, and the directors must deposit a copy of the annual accounts along with the list of members at the Registro delle imprese within thirty days of the date of approval.

Under Article 2463, paragraph 5, CC S.r.l. with capital share below EUR 10,000.00 have to allocate a fifth of its annual net earnings as reserve capital, this procedure is mandatory until the sum of the reserve plus the share capital reach EUR 10,000.00. This reserve can only be used to pay losses or to increase the share capital. The same applies to S.r.l.simp.

After the company has reached EUR 10,000.00 share capital, the ordinary rules on reserves should be applied, following which a twentieth of the annual net earnings have to be put onto reserve.

408. The members by a specific agreement or a members' meeting may approve allocating dividends only if the annual accounts have been legally approved and show profits. In the event of a reduction in the declared capital because of losses, no profit may be distributed until the repayment or reduction of capital.

As with an S.p.A., however, if distribution of dividends is approved and the members have collected in good faith, they will not be obliged to return them even if the resolution approving the balance sheets is cancelled.

§10. Amending the Articles of Association

I. Approval Procedure

409. Amendments to the articles of association must be approved by a members' meeting with the votes of members representing at least 50% of the capital. In cases in which the amendments refer to specific rights of management or profit distribution, unanimity is required, unless the articles of association envisage otherwise (Article 2468 CC).

The minutes of the meeting must be drawn up by a notary. The provisions with respect to the notary or the court verifying the legality of amendments and the subsequent registration of the amended articles of association of an S.p.A. will apply (*see* Chapter 1, §8).

Members who disagree with the decision to amend the articles of association may withdraw in the cases, and following the procedures, described above (*see* this chapter, §6).

II. Capital Increase

410. As with an S.p.A., a capital increase may affect the percentages of capital held by the members. Consequently, the legislative provisions are designed to ensure that the members maintain a role in the company similar to the role they occupied before the capital was modified. However, to avert internal conflicts, the articles of association may exclude or limit this right by allowing third parties to become members and by giving dissenting members the right to withdraw.

411. Increasing the share capital implies that contributions on shares already issued have been paid in full. As far as approval is concerned, the decision must be adopted by a members' meeting, but the articles of association may give the directors the power to do so, specifying the modalities and limits of the increase.

The minutes of the members'meeting or the directors'resolution must be drawn up by a notary and registered at the Registro delle imprese so as to make them public.

412. The capital increase may be carried into effect without contributions from members, using available reserves existing in the company's accounts (a nominal or free increase). In such a case, following a resolution passed by a members' meeting, the increase will be implemented through an accounting operation (i.e., by reducing available reserves by the value of the capital increase), and the quotas of the members will not change.

413. In cases in which the increase requires new contributions, however, once the decision has been passed either by a members' meeting or by the directors, the period for subscribing and making payments will start to run. Payments must be made to the company in compliance with the rules envisaged for incorporation. The decision to increase the capital may envisage a share premium, which must be paid immediately with the subscription. If the capital is not subscribed to the pre-established extent, the increase will not come into effect and the contributions must be returned. The articles of association may, however, envisage that a partial increase be valid.

414. The members are entitled to subscribe new capital issued in proportion to the quotas they own. If the articles of association envisage increasing the capital by offering the subscription to third parties and the members adopt such a decision, dissenting members may withdraw.

415. As with an S.p.A., the capital increase procedure is finalized by the depositing of a report by the directors at the Registro delle imprese certifying that the capital has been subscribed to the envisaged extent, or, if the resolution so permits, to a lesser extent. Once this statement has been deposited, the new capital may be indicated in the company's documents and correspondence.

416. According to the legal theory, when the share capital of an S.r.l.simp. reaches EUR 10,000.00, the corporations switch to the ordinary S.r.l. form. This process is not considered to be a legal transformation, so that the relevant discipline does not apply.

III. Capital Reduction

417. There are two cases in which a reduction in capital may arise: (1) when a members' meeting considers that the capital is excessive in relation to the company's requirements; and (2) when losses have occurred.

To avoid abuses by the majority, the procedures adopted by the company must abide by the principles set forth in Article 2482quater CC, pursuant to which the shares and rights of the members must remain unchanged.

In the former case, the creditors may wish to oppose the reduction because it gives rise to a corresponding reduction in the company's assets. Because of this, the resolution must be registered at the Registro delle imprese and will only take effect ninety days after registration, if no objections are raised. If the reduction is opposed, the court may permit its implementation provided that it does not jeopardize the creditors or they are suitably guaranteed.

The reduction may come about as a result of either relinquishing the payment of contributions still due or distributing to members sums of money and property out of company assets. The reduction must not reduce the capital to below the legal minimum.

418. A capital reduction because of losses is optional if the losses do not exceed one-third of the capital. In such a situation, the directors do not have to convene a members' meeting. If, however, a members' meeting is convened, the capital may either be reduced to adjust it to the residual assets or left unchanged.

419. By analogy with the rules regulating the S.p.a., if, as a result of the losses, the corporate assets have been reduced to less than two-thirds of the capital, Article 2480 CC requires the company bodies to take action to put an end to a situation in which the apparent capital is not reflected in adequate assets. As soon as the directors acknowledge the losses, they must convene a members' meeting and prepare a report on the company's financial position. The report, together with the observations of the collegio sindacale or the external auditor, must be made available to the members at least eight days before the members' meeting. The articles of association may provide for a different period.

The members' meeting may resolve either to immediately reduce the capital or to carry the losses forward to the following year's accounts. If losses in excess of one-third are confirmed the following year, at the very latest, the members' meeting must reduce the company's capital when it passes the resolution approving the balance sheets. If the resolution is not passed by the members' meeting, the directors, the sindaci, or the external auditor may apply to the court, which will direct that the capital be reduced in proportion to the losses incurred by the company. Furthermore, unlike an S.p.A., any person or entity having an interest in the capital reduction may apply to the court. It is unlikely that third parties will have a concrete interest in a capital reduction or sufficient information to apply, but in accordance with this provision, any S.r.l. member may apply.

The resolution to reduce the capital or the court order must be registered at the Registro delle imprese.

420. If the losses reduce the capital to below the legal minimum of EUR 10,000.00 an extraordinary members' meeting must be immediately convened to first reduce the capital and then either increase it to at least the legal minimum or transform the company into a different type of company not requiring a minimum capital. Without any such resolution, the company will have to be liquidated, and liquidators will have to be appointed either by a members' meeting or by the court.

421. It is discussed the case of an ordinary S.r.l. the capital of which falls below EUR 10,000.00. With the introduction of S.r.l.simp. and the S.r.l. with less than EUR 10,000.00 share capital, it could be possible for an ordinary S.r.l. to continue its business. Nonetheless, this perspective is already not supported by relevant jurisprudence.

§11. The Single Member S.r.l.

422. The Twelfth European Council Company Law Directive EC 89/667 on single member private limited liability companies was enacted in Italian legislation through Legislative Decree 88/93, which introduces the first model of a single member Italian corporation with limited liability of the member. This innovation marked the start of a process transforming a number of basic principles of Italian company law (*see* Chapter 1, §8).

The theoretical importance of the single member S.r.l. is diminished as a result of the 2003 Company Law Reform, once the process of allowing the member of a single-shareholder S.p.A. to have his or her liability limited to the contribution has been completed, provided that certain conditions are met. In practice, though, the number of single member S.r.l.s is far greater than that of single-shareholder S.p.A.s.

423. In cases in which the S.r.l. model is adopted by a single member, a number of precautions must be taken to guarantee the integrity of the assets and safeguard third parties. The derogations to the general rules regulating the S.r.l. are exactly the same as that envisaged for the single-shareholder S.p.A.

424. During the incorporation phase, the single member will account unlimitedly for any obligations he or she has assumed on behalf of the company prior to registration, and he or she must pay the entire contribution in cash, and not just 25%, as in the case of multiparty S.r.l.s (Article 2464, paragraph IV, CC). Similarly, if, after incorporation, ownership of the shares is concentrated in a single member, he or she must arrange to pay the contribution in full within ninety days.

425. In the case of a single member, there are also additional disclosure requirements. The articles of association deposited at the Registro delle imprese must provide details of the first name(s) and surname (or company name in the case of legal entities), date and place of birth, domicile, and nationality of the single member. In documents and correspondence, the company's single member status must be specified (Article 2470 CC). Notices to the register must be made by the directors both when the S.r.l. becomes a single member company and also when multiparty status is restored. The name of the company does not, however, have to highlight its one-party status.

426. Violations of the requirement to pay contributions in full and/or make disclosures will give rise to the unlimited liability of the single member – in the event of the company's insolvency (Article 2462, paragraph II, CC) – with respect to any obligations undertaken, until such time as the aforementioned formalities have been met.

As with an S.p.A., a precaution has been introduced to discourage operations that might lead to an impoverishment of the company's assets to the benefit of the member. To be valid vis-à-vis the company's creditors, contracts between the company and the single member, or, in any event, deeds implying a benefit for the single member, must in fact be: (i) recorded in the ledger of meetings and resolutions of the board of directors; or (ii) drawn up in writing in a deed with a certain date preceding the attachment of the asset (Article 2478, paragraph III CC). Otherwise, the creditors will be able to sue both the company and the member as if the operations in favour of the latter had never taken place.

§12. Dissolution and Liquidation

427. See Part III, Chapter 3.

Chapter 3. The Società in Accomandita per Azioni (S.A.p.A.) ('Limited Partnership by Shares')

§1. Definition and Sources

428. The S.A.p.A. is a company with its capital split into shares and characterized by the presence of a particular type of partners: accomandatari (general partners), who are exclusively entrusted with the company's administration and who are liable both jointly and unlimitedly for the company's obligations.

As contemplated in Article 2454 CC, the rules envisaged for an S.p.A. will apply to an S.A.p.A. in every other respect, insofar as they are compatible.

An S.A.p.A., therefore, combines the features of an S.p.A. with those of the S.a.s. (limited partnership), in which we find partners who are unlimitedly liable for the company's obligations and also partners who are liable only to the extent of their quota.

However, while the S.a.s. is different from its reference type, that is, the S.n.c. (general partnership), in that the accomandanti (special partners) are only limitedly liable, the S.A.p.A. differs from its reference type in that the accomandatari (general partners) and/or directors are unlimitedly liable for the company's obligations.

429. The S.A.p.A. type of company is not common in Italy. This is because of excessive costs burdening the accomandatari partners, which are not offset by the stability of management power guaranteed by the fact that administrative power and accomandatari partners status coincide.

In practice, the S.A.p.A. type of company lends itself to group-leading companies, in which entrepreneurial risk is less significant but stability in controlling and managing subsidiaries plays a more important role.

§2. Formation and Registration

430. As far as the formation of, and contributions to, an S.A.p.A. are concerned, reference should be made in full to the rules governing the S.p.A. (*see* Part I, Chapter 1, §1 and following).

An S.A.p.A. is characterized by the fact that the names of the accomandatari partners are highlighted and ascertainable. They must be indicated in the by-laws, and the company name must contain the name of at least one accomandatario partner (this name will remain even if the person in question forfeits this position).

§3. ACCOMANDATARI (GENERAL PARTNERS) AND ACCOMANDANTI (SPECIAL PARTNERS)

431. As with limited partnerships, in S.A.p.A.s, too, we find two categories of partners (who in this case are also members): the accomandatari (general partners) and the accomandanti (special partners).

These two categories differ primarily in terms of liability for the company's obligations: for accomandatari partners liability is both joint and unlimited, whereas for accomandanti partners it is limited to their contributions.

Furthermore, in an S.A.p.A., each accomandatario partner is a director by right. This requires a special set of rules regulating the acquisition and discontinuance of the position of accomandatario partner, administrative powers, and ensuing responsibilities.

432. As far as appointments are concerned, the founding accomandatari partners must be indicated in the article of association. The company may have only one general partner, but in all events the appointment of new accomandatari partners will involve changing the by-laws and require the approval of an extraordinary meeting of members.

The position of S.A.p.A. director coincides by law with that of accomandatario partner. An accomandatario partner may sell all his or her shares to a third party, but such third party will not automatically become an accomandatario partner, because, as we have just said, this would involve changing the by-laws.

The CC makes no provision with regard to the accomandatario partner's right to relinquish his or her position and, therefore, his or her power of administration by becoming an accomandante partner, but, if this is permitted, a resolution passed by an extraordinary members'meeting modifying the by-laws will in any case be necessary.

433. The accomandatario partner will account to third parties for company obligations that have arisen during the period in which he or she occupied this position, whereas a new accomandatario partner will only account for obligations that have arisen after he or she has accepted the position.

In accordance with the combined provisions of Articles 2304 and 2471, first paragraph, of the CC, the liability of the accomandatario partner will always be joint and unlimited. This liability is, however, subsidiary, in that a company creditor must first proceed to enforce his or her credit through the corporate assets and only after this act against the individual accomandatari partners.

434. As far as the accomandanti partners are concerned, on the other hand, they are liable to the extent of their contributions, while in every other respect they enjoy the same status as that of an S.p.A. member (*see* Part I, Chapter 1, §1 and following). There are, however, a number of differences compared to S.p.A. members as far as filing corporate liability proceedings (*see* §4. II) is concerned.

435. The distinction between accomandatari partners and accomandanti partners does not imply any differences in the properties of the company's shares, in that the system of shares is the same. The position of accomandatario partner, therefore, has nothing to do with the ownership of special shares, but only with specific provisions contained in the by-laws.

§4. Company Bodies

I. The Option Between the Ordinary System and the Two-Tier System

436. Under the system adopted in the 1942 CC, the company bodies of a limited partnership with share capital were a members' meeting, the accomandatari partners/directors, and the auditors.

Following the 2003 Company Law Reform, this structure is maintained for S.A.p.A.s that adopt the ordinary organizational model, but the problem of the compatibility of two-tier and one-tier models with the organization of the S.A.p.A. has had to be addressed, because S.A.p.A. rules do not address any such eventualities.

However, on the basis of various references contained in the CC, legal doctrine has held that the two-tier model referred to in Article 2409octies CC may be adopted as an alternative to the traditional model.

This does not apply to an S.A.p.A. with a one-tier type of structure, however, because the figure of director/accomandatario partner is incompatible with the necessity to appoint members of the board of directors having requisites of independence, pursuant to Article 2409septiesdecies and following articles of the CC.

II. The Members' Meeting

437. Generally speaking, a members' meeting is regulated in the same way as in the S.p.A. (*see* Part I, Chapter 1, §5).

Special rules apply, however, to certain resolutions adopted by a members' meeting.

In their capacity as director/members, the accomandatari partners, in fact, have neither the right to vote in resolutions appointing or removing sindaci or members of the supervisory board, nor indeed in resolutions involving the filing of liability proceedings against them.

Changes to the by-laws must, however, be resolved by an extraordinary members' meeting, but they also have to be approved by all the accomandatari partners, who thus dispose of a veritable right of veto over any changes to the original layout of the company.

438. Another particular feature compared to an S.p.A. concerns corporate liability proceedings against the directors or the members of the management board.

Such proceedings may be filed: (i) following a resolution by a members' meeting (in which only the accomandanti partners may participate); (ii) following a resolution by the supervisory board (in two-tier S.A.p.A.s) and, finally; (iii) directly by accomandanti partners holding particular quotas of capital (i.e., one-fifth, or any greater extent envisaged in the by-laws, provided that it is not more than one-third; and one-fortieth, or any lesser extent envisaged in the by-laws, in the case of companies that resort to the risk capital market in accordance with Article 2325bis CC).

III. The Peculiarities of the Ordinary System

439. As far as administration is concerned, we have already highlighted the fact that the directors and accomandatari partners must coincide, and we have already discussed how they are removed and subject to corporate liability proceedings. It should be added that: (i) the accomandatari partners/directors occupy their positions indefinitely; (ii) they are subject to all the obligations and liabilities of S.p.A. directors; and (iii) in cases in which there is more than one of them, they operate collectively.

If their appointment is withdrawn without just grounds, they are entitled to receive compensation for damages in accordance with Article 2456 CC.

440. As far as the supervisory body, that is, the collegio sindacale, is concerned, please refer to the information provided concerning S.p.A.s (*see* Chapter 1, §6). The only differences compared to the S.p.A. are: (i) that resolutions on appointing and removing sindaci (Article 2459 CC) are reserved for the accomandanti partners; and (ii) the sindaci have the power to appoint a provisional director to deal with the company's routine business if all the directors lapse from office at the same time (Article 2458, paragraph 2, CC).

IV. The Peculiarities of the Two-Tier System

441. As far as the management board of an S.A.p.A. is concerned, please refer to the information provided earlier concerning accomandatari partners/directors. In accordance with Article 2409novies, paragraph 2, of the CC, there must be at least two accomandatari partners/directors on the management board.

442. As far as the supervisory board is concerned, the members of this body, like the sindaci in the ordinary system, are appointed and/or removed by the accomandanti partners.

The supervisory board may not appoint, replace, or remove the members of the management board. Furthermore, removal ex lege is also held to be inapplicable, which is envisaged in cases in which a resolution to file corporate liability proceedings against the managers is approved on a majority of two-thirds of the supervisory board.

443. In view of Article 159 of the TUF, the fact that the accomandatari partners are not empowered to appoint and remove the members of the supervisory board also extends, in the case of listed companies, to the appointment and removal of auditing companies.

§5. Dissolution and Liquidation

444. Finally, as far as the grounds for dissolving an S.A.p.A. are concerned, please refer to the rules regulating S.p.A.s (Part III, Chapter 3, §1 and following).

A specific ground for dissolving an S.A.p.A. arises in cases in which all the directors or all the members of the management board lapse from office, and in cases in which, within six months of this happening, no arrangements have been made to replace them, with substitutes having accepted the appointments.

As we have already seen above (*see* §4, III), on the occurrence of this hypothesis of dissolution, the collegio sindacale or the supervisory board is under an obligation to appoint a provisional director entrusted with the company's day-to-day administration.

If, on the other hand, all the accomandanti partners lapse from office, this does not constitute a ground for dissolving the S.A.p.A.

Chapter 4. The Società Europea (SE) ('European Company')

§1. Definition and Sources

445. European Council Regulation (EC) 2157/2001 created the European Company (Societas Europaea, hereafter SE), and, in so doing, aimed to establish a uniform legal framework within which enterprises of Member States can programme or reorganize their activities at the European level. This regulation is accompanied by Directive 2001/86, which lays down the principles ensuring harmonized rules regulating employee involvement in management.

The SE is a new model of a company, with supranational characteristics, which takes its place alongside those envisaged in national legal systems. The SE model has been devised for enterprises with activities, establishments, or multinational capital that need to extend their framework market.

The SE is a company in which the capital is divided into shares and the members of which are liable only to the extent of the capital they have subscribed. It has legal personality, and its starting capital cannot be less than EUR 120,000 (*see* SE Reg. Articles 1 and 4).

446. In the earliest projects, it was envisaged that the SE would have been regulated in full by European sources, but this proved impossible because of persisting differences between national systems of legislation on limited liability companies and the need to abide by the subsidiarity principle.

In spite of this, the SE is regulated first and foremost by EC Regulation 2157/2001, and where the regulation so envisages, by the company's statutes (Article 9 of the regulation). In matters where the regulation makes no provision, the rules applicable, on a subsidiary basis, will be: (i) the national rules implementing the regulation; (ii) the rules that would apply to a public limited liability company in the State where the SE is registered: and, finally; (iii) the provisions of the statutes, to the extent permitted for national public limited liability companies in that State. Furthermore, insofar as the regulation provides, the SE will be treated in each Member State as if it were a public limited liability formed in accordance with the law of the Member State.

In practice, there are many references to national rules covering both the activities preceding the formation of an SE and also the organization and functioning of the SE.

447. The fact that European sources are not self-sufficient means that the formation of an SE registered in a Member State will only be possible after national rules implementing EC Regulation 2157/2001 and Directive 2001/86 have been set in place.

Italy has proceeded to enact the Directive in Legislative Decree 188 of 19 August 2005, but, as things stand, there are no rules providing for implementation of the regulation. This delay results from a lack of interest on the part of the Italian government in the SE instrument, which is presumably attributable to the conviction that the 2003 Company Law Reform has made it possible to satisfy any organizational requirements of national enterprises or enterprises to be registered in Italy. The Company Law

Reform, in fact, contains no rules referring specifically to the SE regulation and its implementation, but the organizational systems of the S.p.A. have been shaped bearing in mind national reference models, in particular, those of Germany, France, and the UK, as well as of the SE. This will, therefore, lead to a trend in which new national models of organization steer towards greater standardization with the SE model, thereby making implementation rules less necessary and gradually facilitating the formation of SEs registered in Italy.

Moreover, the fact that, in Italy, there is a third model of organization of the S.p.A., that is the ordinary model, which differs from both the two-tier model and the one-tier model envisaged in the SE regulation, poses specific problems in terms of coordinating the regulation with the national system of law. Future rules implementing the regulation in Italy will have to clarify whether or not the ordinary model can also apply in the SE, or whether it will be possible to hypothesize that the statutes of an Italian-registered SE may also envisage the appointment of a collegio sindacale.

448. As long as the regulation remains unimplemented – although some Italian enterprises have already participated in forming SEs registered in another Member State – no SE registered in Italy has yet been formed. Indeed, this cannot happen until legislation implementing the regulation is introduced. Some SE, nevertheless, have moved their seat to Italy.

The presentation provided below of the SE system briefly summarizes the basic contents of both EC Regulation 2157/2001 and Directive 2001/86, which will have to be implemented in Italy, without, however, specifying an organizational model that can actually be used for a company that plans to set up its registered office in Italy.

§2. Formation and Registration

449. The regulation facilitates the formation of the SE, envisaging four procedures, one of which, the formation of a holding SE, is not envisaged in Italy for other joint-stock companies.

I. Formation

A. The SE Formed by Merger

450. The prerequisite for formation by merger (merger by forming a new company or merger by acquisition) is that two or more public limited liability companies or SEs registered in an EU country are governed by the law of different Member States.

The SE regulation envisages the entire procedural formation itinerary in terms that conform to the later provisions of Directive 2005/56/EC, on cross-border mergers. First and foremost, draft terms of a merger must be prepared by the governing or administrative bodies of the companies that intend to merge. After this, the draft terms must be published in the journal of the Community States where most of the company's business will be done. Finally, the draft terms of merger must be approved by general meetings of the companies participating in the merger.

Once its legality has been scrutinized by a court, a notary, or another authority considered competent by the States to which the companies participating in the merger belong and also by the State where the SE's registered office is situated, the SE must be registered on the register indicated by the law of the Member State where the SE is registered.

B. The SE Formed by Conversion

451. The prerequisite for this system of formation is the existence of a public limited liability company, which, for at least two years has had a subsidiary (and not just a branch) in a Member State other than that where it is effectively registered.

The procedure consists of the governing or administrative body preparing draft terms of conversion, which, after being publicized in accordance with the law, then must be approved, together with the statutes, by the favourable vote of the company's general meeting. Prior to the meeting, an expert appointed by a judicial or administrative authority of the State whose law will govern the SE must attest to the existence of the capital and the reserves. The State may, however, make the conversion subject to a unanimous vote or to a vote by a qualified majority of the body by which the employees are represented.

C. The Formation of a Holding SE

452. The prerequisite for this system of formation is the existence of two or more public or private limited liability companies having their registered office and head office in two different Member States or having had, for at least two years, an affiliated company or a branch in a different Member State. In such a case, the members of the promoting companies will grant the new SE a percentage of shares or quotas, assigning to the holding SE more than 50% of permanent voting rights. As far as everything else is concerned, the holding SE formation procedure is comparable to that of the formation by conversion procedure. The appraisal by the experts, however, also must include and evaluation of the adequacy of the share-exchange ratio. Once the draft terms have been approved by the members' meetings of the companies participating in the formation, and when necessary by the employees' delegations, the members will then have three months' time to decide whether or not to contribute their own shares or a part of them. If the percentages envisaged in the draft terms are reached, the formation of the SE will be publicized in accordance with the formalities envisaged in the Member State where it is registered, and the shares in the SE will be assigned to the members of the companies participating in it.

D. The Formation of an Affiliated SE

453. In this case, two or more public companies or firms, pursuant to Article 48 of the European Treaty or other legal bodies governed by public or private law registered in different Member States, form an SE in accordance with the legislative provisions of the Member State in which the SE will establish its head office.

II. Registration

454. In accordance with Article 12 of the regulation, the SE must be registered on a special register in the Member State where it has its head office. The registration can take place only after an agreement has been reached on employee involvement procedures (*see* below, §5).

§3. Company Bodies

I. The Option Between One-Tier and Two-Tier Systems

455. Given that in Member States of the EU public limited liability companies may, as the case may be, adopt the one-tier system, the two-tier system, or both, the regulation opts for neither one nor the other, but allows the SE to adopt different organizational sysems, depending on the provisions of the statutes. There is, however, a general requirement, which is that the duties of persons entrusted with management responsibilities have to be defined and distinguished from the duties of the persons entrusted with supervisory responsibilities.

456. The introduction of a European model that leaves the statutes free to choose between two organizational systems characterizing different national traditions thus gives rise to the possibility of forming the SE on the basis of two organizational models throughout the territory of the Community. This is highly significant for countries in which the legal systems envisage that national limited liability companies can be structured on only one of the organizational models (e.g., Germany and, to a lesser extent, the United Kingdom). Furthermore, the regulation also plays an important role in countries such as France and Italy, where the limited liability company can be formed on the basis of both organizational systems because the national and European organizational models are not quite the same.

457. According to the regulation, in the one-tier model, day-to-day management can be entrusted, within the governing body, to one or more directors, in cases when, as in Italy, this is permitted for national limited liability companies. Unlike the S.p.A., though, the assignment of specific supervisory functions to non-executive directors is not envisaged.

458. The regulation envisages that the annual accounts, the consolidated accounts, and the auditing of accounts should be regulated in the same way as in S.p.A.s of the Member State where the SE is registered. No provision has been made, however, with respect to setting up an internal supervisory body, such as the collegio sindacale, of the S.p.A. The rules implementing the regulation in Italy will, therefore, have to specify whether in SEs based on the one-tier system, such a body must or can be set up.

II. The General Meeting of Members

459. The general meeting of members is only indirectly affected by the choice of the system of administration. The rules can therefore be said to be common to the two hypotheses, but in the two-tier system duties and powers are significantly reduced.

460. The general meeting deliberates upon any matters established in the SE Regulation (among such matters we should stress appointing the directors, but not necessarily approving the balance sheet) and in the legislation of the Member State in which it is registered.

The regulation provides that the general meeting may be convened at any time by the board of directors, the administrative body, the supervisory body, or by any other body envisaged in the legislation of the relevant Member State, and also by members holding at least 10% of the shares of subscribed capital or any lesser percentage of shares specified in the statutes or by national law. If the competent bodies fail to convene the general meeting, the judicial authority – in Italy, this is the civil court where the SE is registered – may convene it or authorize the members to do so.

461. The convocation must provide an indication of the agenda. Members disposing of 10% of the capital or of any lesser percentage indicated in the by-laws or by national law may ask for the agenda to be supplemented by further matters.

462. Resolutions usually require a majority of the votes validly expressed, but such votes do not include those inherent in shares with respect to which the member has not participated in the vote, has abstained, or has returned a blank or spoiled ballot paper.

To amend the company's statutes, a qualified majority of two-thirds of the votes expressed is, however, required, even though a Member State may envisage in its legislation a simple majority of votes expressed, provided that it represents at least half of the subscribed capital.

When necessary, the votes of the meeting may be subject to separate procedures if different categories of members are in attendance.

III. The Two-Tier System

A. The Management Board

463. The two-tier model of SE envisages a strict separation of roles between the management board, which is entrusted purely with management, and the supervisory board. The transactions that have to be authorized by the supervisory body are established in the statutes, but national law may specify certain types of transactions, which may be subject to authorization by the supervisory board. On this point, Italy can be expected to adopt a solution coherent with S.p.A.s, not compulsorily envisaging transactions that have to be authorized by the supervisory board, but allowing – for SEs, too – the statutes to envisage that the supervisory board should deliberate upon strategic operations and industrial/financial plans, while, however, not exempting the management board that prepares them from liability.

The management board must, however, keep the supervisory board updated on the progress of the SE's business at least once every three months.

464. As far as appointments are concerned, it is envisaged that the members of the management board should be appointed and removed by the supervisory board, but the regulation allows national law to envisage that the members of the management board may also be appointed by a members' meeting. Such an option is not envisaged for an S.p.A. and will, therefore, probably also not be envisaged for SEs registered in Italy.

The number of members of the management board is envisaged in the statutes, but the minimum and maximum number may be set by national law.

The position of member of the management board is not compatible with that of member of the supervisory board. Therefore, if a member of the supervisory board is also appointed to the management board, even if only provisionally, his or her functions will be suspended.

465. The exercise of the management function may be allocated, within the management board, by entrusting day-to-day management to one or more managing directors, in accordance with the current rules in force for limited liability companies in the State where the SE is registered. In such a case, the combined provisions of Article 2409novies, paragraph 1, and Article 2381, paragraphs 3, 4, and 5, of the CC, will apply to an SE registered in Italy.

B. The Supervisory Board

466. The members of the supervisory board are appointed by the general meeting of members, without prejudice to employee involvement. The elected members will designate the chairperson. If half of the members have been designated by the employees, only a member appointed by the general meeting may be elected chairperson.

The number of members is freely established in the by-laws, unless national law sets it or fixes a minimum or maximum number.

467. The supervisory board must not restrict itself to waiting to receive information from the management board but may also actively intervene and request information that may be useful for it to exercise its supervisory function. Such a request must usually be submitted after a resolution has been passed by the board but, in States which so permit, it may also be submitted by individual members.

The power to directly or indirectly carry out the checks required to fulfil its duties is much more effective. This power may take the form of either: (i) inspections; or (ii) requesting directors or third parties to provide information and documents, as is, moreover, envisaged in the combined provisions of Article 2409quaterdecies and Article 2403*bis* CC for the supervisory board of the S.p.A.

The regulation allows the checks to be carried out by persons delegated by the supervisory board, but fails to specify whether or not they may also be non-members.

468. The instrument with which the supervisory body impacts most on the activity of the management board is that of prior authorization, to the extent that this is envisaged in the regulation, in national law, or in the statutes.

Whereas in an S.p.A., the authorization of the supervisory board may only be envisaged in the statutes for 'strategic operations' and 'industrial or financial plans prepared by the management board', in an SE, the supervisory board has a much broader margin for manoeuvre. Article 48, paragraph 1, in fact leaves the statutes free to specify the categories of transactions subject to authorization, allowing the States only: (a) to entrust the supervisory body with selecting the categories of transactions; and (b) to establish the minimum content of this clause. Therefore, as with S.p.A.s, there is nothing to prevent the national law from imposing the supervisory board's authorization for any category of transaction, unless it decides to leave this to the statutes.

If Italy implements this provision, leaving the statutes completely free to establish the authorization role of the supervisory board, this would give rise to an organizational model different from that of an S.p.A., as it would be characterized by a potentially unlimited extension of the prior control of merit exercised by the supervisory body.

IV. The One-Tier System

A. The Board of Directors

469. In the one-tier system, administration is entrusted to a board of directors formed by at least three members. The States are left free to set, or not set, a minimum or maximum number of members of the governing body. As far as eligibility criteria are concerned, the regulation makes a general reference to national legislations in matters concerning S.p.A.s.

470. The board of directors must meet every three months and the statutes have to establish which transactions are subject to the explicit decision of the board. The matters covered by management are not explicitly specified in the regulation, but only implicitly in that it makes a distinction between day-to-day management (Article 43, paragraph 2) requiring a delegated authority and the higher management function reserved for the board.

471. As far as dividing responsibilities between the governing body and a members' meeting is concerned, the SE is characterized by an approach closely resembling that of the current system in force in Italy. Therefore, Article 2364, No. 5, CC, will apply to an SE registered in Italy. This article permits resolutions by a members' meeting on management matters in cases in which the statutes envisage that authorization of a members' meeting is required for certain transactions but it excludes any possibility of the authorization exempting the directors from liability.

472. The governing body's resolutions are usually made by a majority of votes of members present or represented. If there is a tie, the chairperson will have to cast the tie-breaking vote. For a vote to be considered valid, a quorum of half the members present or represented is, however, required.

473. Since there are no provisions in the Regulation concerning the supervisory function, and since there are no rules requiring the national law to specifically regulate this function, apart from accounts auditing, the national rules on S.p.A.s will, therefore, have to be applied. Therefore, unless the rules implementing the regulation prevent this, it is thought that the statutes of the SE may opt for a one-tier system with an internal management supervision committee, as in the case of an S.p.A.

474. Furthermore, unless the implementation rules envisage otherwise, on applying the S.p.A. rules to the extent indicated in Article 9 of the Regulation, if the statutes do not adopt an internal management supervision system within the governing body, a collegio sindacale will have to be introduced with the functions, powers, and responsibilities referred to in Article 2397 and following articles of the CC.

V. Provisions Common to the Two Systems

475. The Regulation does not address the issue of representation, nor does it refer to either national law or to the statutes on this point. Since there are no explicit provisions, it is thought that representation will be vested either in the body that manages the SE or in one or more of its members. Representation will usually be vested in the management board in the two-tier SE and in the board of directors in the one-tier SE, and any national law providing differently would be in conflict with the Regulation.

476. Article 47 of the Regulation envisages that persons other than natural persons may also be appointed as members of governing bodies, provided that this is permitted by the Member State or by the statutes. The appointment of legal persons is not explicitly permitted for S.p.A.s by the CC, but the Court admits such possibility, and is allowed in European Economic Interest Group (EEIG) registered in Italy. Therefore, it would appear to be reasonable to expect that, for SEs, too, the national law will introduce a set of rules comparable to those envisaged for the EEIG.

477. Decisions passed by administrative and supervisory bodies must be passed with a quorum of at least half the members and on the favourable votes of the majority of those attending. If there is a tie, the chairperson will cast the tie-breaking vote.

478. Over and beyond the aspects that we have already covered, there are no provisions concerning the remuneration of members of governing bodies. Therefore, any decisions on the extent or manner of remuneration and criteria to be applied in establishing the remuneration are regulated in full by national rules on limited liability companies and may be left to the statutes by such national rules.

On the matter of liability for damage suffered by an SE as a result of failure to comply with obligations laid down by the law or in the statutes or with other obligations inherent in members' functions, Article 51 of the Regulation explicitly contemplates that the provisions on limited liability companies of the Member State where the SE is registered will apply. The rule is limited to liability vis-à-vis the company, but in accordance with Article 9 of the Regulation, similar conclusions are thought also to apply to liability vis-à-vis the members and third parties.

§4. Transferring the Registered Office

479. The registered office of the Societas Europaea must be situated within the EU, in the same Member State in which the central administration is based (SE Regulation Article 7). The registered office of the SE will, therefore, always coincide with the head office and is relevant for the purposes of applying national legislation.

480. Therefore, in the event of the registered office being transferred, the company does not have to be liquidated, and there is no need to set up a new legal person.

The transfer procedure opens with either the management board or the board of directors preparing a transfer proposal, to which a report must be attached, explaining the legal and economic aspects of the transfer and the consequences for members, creditors, and employees.

For two months after publication, the competent State authorities may oppose the transfer on the grounds of public interest.

Two months after publication of the proposal and the report, the transfer will be submitted to the approval of the general meeting, in accordance with the statutes. State legislations may envisage forms of safeguarding minority members who have opposed the transfer.

With the certification of the competent authority of the Member State in which the company had its original registered office, it is then possible to register the SE on the register of the Member State where it has its new registered office.

In accordance with Article 8, paragraph 7 of the SE Regulation, before the competent authority issues the aforementioned certificate, 'the SE shall satisfy it that, with respect to any liabilities arising prior to the publication of the transfer proposal, the interests of creditors and holders of other rights involving the SE have been adequately protected in accordance with the provisions of the Member State where the SE had its registered office prior to the transfer'.

On publication of the new registration, the newly chosen registered office will become effective vis-à-vis third parties.

§5. Employee Involvement

481. Registration of the SE can take place only: (i) once an agreement has been reached on how to involve employees or, alternatively; (ii) once the negotiation deadline has passed with no agreement being reached; or else (iii) in cases in which the employees' delegation decides not to open negotiations because it intends to avail itself of the rules on information and consultation in force in one of the Member States where the SE has its employees.

If the conditions are not met, the SE can neither acquire legal personality nor resolve to transfer its registered office.

482. Employee involvement in managing the enterprise's activity may, however, be either 'strong' or 'weak'. A 'strong' involvement implies that the employees' representatives will participate in the supervisory or administrative body of the SE., a 'weak' involvement, on the other hand, is simply designed to guarantee a consultation and/or information procedures between the representative bodies of employees and the SE's governing bodies.

483. By tradition, in Italy, relations between employees and enterprises are managed by the trade unions at either the company or national level, and the employees' representatives are not present in management or supervisory bodies. Unless there are specific provisions in the statutes, therefore, there will be no employees on the boards of directors, management boards, and supervisory boards, even in S.p.A.s with large numbers of employees.

Italy has nevertheless implemented, in Legislative Decree 74 of 2 April 2002, Directive 94/45/EC of 22 September 1994, on formation of a European company committee or an information and consultation procedure for employees of EU-dimension enterprises and groups of enterprises, and, in Legislative Decree 25 of 6 February 2007 – for enterprises with at least fifty employees – Directive 2002/14/EC, which provides a general framework for employees' information and consultation.

484. Legislative Decree 188 of 19 August 2005, incorporating into Italian law Council Directive EC 2001/86, on employee involvement in the SE, was approved at the end of a long debate that led to the finalization of a joint document (Joint Announcement of 2 March 2005) by the main employers' organizations and trade unions confederations.

Legislative Decree 188/95 makes many references to collective bargaining between trade unions and enterprises, especially in the framework of forming the Special Bargaining Delegations (SBD). As far as the form of employee involvement is concerned, the decree makes no choice, leaving its definition to separate negotiations between the directors of the SE and the SBD representing the employees of the various companies to which it refers. The national set of rules pursuant to Article 7 of the Regulation – which will constitute the applicable national law in cases in which the negotiation between the parties fails or in which the parties themselves decide to avail themselves of such rules – is established in the decree, which only envisages information and consultation rights, excluding any form of participation. This means that participation will only be possible in the hypotheses envisaged in paragraph 2 of Article 7 of Directive 2001/86.

§6. Dissolution and Liquidation

485. Finally, as far as SE dissolution and liquidation procedures are concerned, the Regulation goes no further than to refer to the applicable national law, that is, to the provisions that would be applicable if the SE were a public limited liability company formed according to the law of the Member State in which its registered office is located (Article 63 of the SE Regulation).

486. Italian-registered SEs are subject to the rules on dissolution and liquidation applicable to S.p.A.s (*see* Part III, Chapter 3).

Chapter 5. The Società Cooperativa (Cooperative) and the Mutua Assicuratrice (Cooperative and Mutual Insurance Company)

§1. Sources and Main Features

487. The società cooperativa (hereinafter 'cooperative') differs from other types of companies because its ultimate goal is to pursue the so-called mutual benefit purpose, in contrast to the goal of generating profits and distributing them to members. Nevertheless, like other companies, also cooperatives collectively run an economic activity.

The Italian Constitution favours companies that pursue mutual benefit purposes.[29] In spite of this, the set of rules contained in the CC has failed to provide a clear definition of what the mutual benefit purpose is supposed to be. This is probably for fear of restricting the development of the cooperative movement by establishing a clear-cut definition. Furthermore, it is extremely difficult to produce a single definition encompassing all the currently existing forms of cooperation.

488. Cooperatives are regulated by a very complex set of rules, because different laws have overlapped in the course of time.

The general rules originally contained in the 1942 CC were later amended by two laws: the Legislative Decree No. 1577/1947 (so-called Basevi Law) and the Law No. 59/1992.

Later on, the Company Law Reform of 2003 restyled the general set of rules regulating the società cooperativa and the mutua assicuratrice, and introduced the special model of the '*cooperativa a mutualità prevalente*'. Moreover, cooperatives have been allowed to issue financial instruments and their corporate governance rules have been improved in such a way as to streamline their management and favour them in achieving their mutual benefit purpose.

489. Article 2511 CC describes the cooperative only as a 'company with a varying capital and a mutual benefit purpose'. However, the basic concept of mutual benefit consists 'of directly providing goods, services or job opportunities to members of the organization at better economic conditions than those available in the market' (Report on the CC). The mutual benefits may vary according to the different forms of cooperation. There are consumer cooperatives, in which the recipients of the goods or services provided by the company are indeed the members of the company and production and labour cooperatives, where members are the company's workforce. In a nutshell, the persons who benefit from the company's goods or services or from job opportunities created by the cooperative are the very same members of the cooperative.

---

29. §45 of the Constitution of Italy: 'The Republic acknowledges the social function of cooperation carried out for mutual benefit purposes and without aims of private speculation. The legal system shall promote cooperation with any appropriate means and shall acknowledge the fulfilment of its specific purposes by setting in place an appropriate monitoring system.'

In this way the members can bypass the intermediate market stages created by the existence of other contracting parties and can obtain better contractual terms than those available in the market (e.g., savings on the cost of goods, or benefiting of a higher remuneration of the labour, or acquiring goods/services provided by the cooperative at favourable economic conditions).

490. One of the most important feature regulating cooperatives is the distinction between cooperatives with a predominantly mutual benefit purpose (*cooperative a mutualità prevalente*) and other cooperatives.

The distinguishing feature of cooperatives with a predominantly mutual purpose is that they must carry out their major activity either in favour of their members (e.g., consumer cooperatives) or using the labour or goods/services provided by the members (production or labour cooperatives) (Article 2512 CC). In their report accompanying the balance sheet (nota integrativa), the directors and the sindaci must verify that the specific criteria listed in Article 2513 CC, which defines the cooperativa a mutualità prevalente, have been observed. The reason for this is that the mutual benefit is held to prevail over profit interests in cases in which business between the company and its members exceeds 50% of the cooperative's business during the financial year. As a result, the articles of the cooperative have to establish specific restrictions, that is, prohibiting the distribution of profits to members beyond a certain threshold, barring payments on financial instruments subscribed by cooperative's members beyond a specific amount, or prohibiting the distribution of reserves. Furthermore, in the event of dissolution, the cooperativa a mutualità prevalente must transfer all its assets (apart from its capital and dividends, if any) to mutual funds set up to promote the development of the cooperative movement (Article 2514 CC).

The most important effect of meeting these requisites is that the società cooperativa a mutualità prevalente benefits from a special tax relief (favourable taxation on profits, VAT, local taxes, and so on). The other types of cooperatives may, however, benefit only from minor tax and labour benefits even if they also pursue a mutual purpose. The aim of this different treatment is to offset the economic advantage enjoyed by a cooperative that does not have a predominantly mutual purpose, in view of the fact that it operates in a manner akin to that of a profit-making company.

491. The cooperatives without a predominantly mutual purpose may be used as a stepping stone to switching from the standard model of cooperation to a profit-making company model. Article 2545decies CC has in fact now removed the former ban on cooperatives being transformed into profit-making companies, which hinged on the idea that it would not be fair for one generation to benefit from the assets set aside by previous generations and from the State subsidies previously enjoyed by the company.

492. Cooperatives are regulated by the Articles from 2511 to 2548 CC and by the provisions regulating the S.p.A., to the extent they are compatible with the general principles by which cooperatives are governed. Nevertheless, for smaller cooperatives (i.e., those with less than twenty cooperating members and with corporate assets less than EUR 1 million), the articles of the cooperative may provide that the simpler rules of the S.r.l. will apply (Article 2519, paragraph II, CC). Reference to the set of rules applying to S.r.l.s is mandatory in cases in which there are less than nine members (Article 2522, paragraph II, CC). Legislative Decree No. 27 of 27 January 2010 has introduced special rules concerning società cooperative listed at stock exchange, aimed at the harmonization of the regulation of listed cooperatives with provisions of listed S.p.A. The special provisions concern financial reports, audit reports, and members meeting (from Article 135 to Article 135bis of the TUF).

493. A general principle governing cooperatives, as other corporations, is that only the cooperative will account for corporate liability with its own assets (Article 2518 CC). The distinction formerly contained in the 1942 CC between a cooperative with limited liability and a cooperative with unlimited liability was repealed by the reform of 2003. The limited liability is geared towards increasing the protection of individual members and thus strengthening the cooperative in the market. Article 2516 CC codifies an additional general principle, which applies to all types of cooperatives, that is, the principle that members should be treated equally as far as their mutual relations are concerned. This does not mean that all members are treated the same way: the economic rights of each member will be proportionate to the quality and quantity of its contributions; but in terms of voting power, all members are equal. The principle of equal treatment for members must, therefore, be reflected in a rule of conduct for the governing bodies. Another main feature of cooperatives is the so-called *principio della porta aperta* ('open-door principle') that permits anyone to submit his request in order to be admitted as a member of the cooperative, following the procedure explained below. As a consequence of the open character of cooperative, the share capital is variable (Article 2524 CC), since every new member admitted subscribes new share capital without the obligation to amend the article of association.

Several special laws also apply to cooperatives operating in particular sectors or regarding specific areas of the legal system. These laws, which may also be regional laws, lay down particular requisites and grant special benefits for cooperatives pursuing specific social purposes.

§2. Formation and Registration

494. The legal provisions concerning the formation of a cooperative, as indeed its general structure, seek to ensure the fulfilment of purposes of achieving a mutual benefit, while also preventing this type of company from being exploited solely for profit-making purposes.

Nevertheless, the company's articles play a significant role in the cooperative's organization. Article 2521, paragraph II, CC in fact requires that the cooperative's articles of association should establish rules regulating the exercising of the mutual activities, which apply both between members and between members and third parties.

495. The contents of the articles of a cooperative do not differ a great deal from those of an S.p.A. and an S.r.l. As well as identifying the members, the articles of association must establish the following:

- The company's name, registered office, and branches. The company name must specifically include the words società cooperativa (Article 2515 CC). Cooperatives with a predominantly mutual purpose must make a specific reference in documents and correspondence to the nature of società cooperativa a mutualità prevalente and to their registration number on the special list of cooperatives at the *Ministero dello Sviluppo Economico*.

- The corporate activity.
- The amount of share capital to be subscribed by each member. As with an S.p.A. the share capital has to be fully subscribed, and the rules regulating the cooperative are based on those for S.p.A.s. Even if the law does not specify it, following the dominant opinion the 25% of the value of the shares or quotas allocating sums of money has to be paid by a bank at the setting of the cooperative.
- The value allocated to the credits and goods brought into the company.
- The conditions requested to be admitted as member and the deadlines by which the member has to fulfil his contribution.
- The terms and conditions on which a member may withdraw, or be excluded.
- The criteria to be followed in allocating and distributing profits (in various forms mainly different form dividends and correlated with the members' activity).
- Rules on convening members' meetings, choosing the system of management, appointing directors and auditors, and establishing set up costs.

496. In addition to the articles of association of the cooperative, there may also be company by-laws establishing the rules regulating the functioning of the cooperative. Although physically separate, the by-laws are held to be a single document with the company's articles. Furthermore, the company may also adopt rules regulating relations between the cooperative and its members, in particular about their mutual activity. If these rules have not already been included in the articles of the cooperative, they may be drafted by the directors and later approved by a members' meeting, with the majorities required for extraordinary members' meetings (Article 2521, paragraph V, CC).

The personal requisites of members must ensure that the members' activities are coherent with the mutual purpose and the specific sector in which the cooperative operates (Article 2527 CC).

497. The requisites must be predetermined in a non-discriminatory manner and in such a way as to ensure compliance with the so-called open-door principle for the admittance and withdrawal of members.

498. Members who do not have the personal requisites set forth in the articles of the company but will acquire them after special training are also admitted into the cooperative. These members are called "soci in formazione", that is, members who are in the company on a trial basis.

They must be allowed into the company after not more than five years, and they cannot exceed a specific percentage of the total number of cooperating members.

499. For a certain class of members, so-called "soci sovventori" (supporting members), introduced by Law No. 59/1992, no particular personal requisites are required. Although the cooperative seeks to achieve specific, mutual interests, the law allows members with no particular interest in the mutual purpose to be admitted into the cooperative so that they can subscribe fresh capital to finance the corporate activities.

500. The setting up procedure of a cooperative is similar to that of an S.p.A. or an S.r.l. The articles of the cooperative must be drawn up by a notary public in a deed and must be registered at the Registro delle imprese and in a special register kept by Ministero dello Sviluppo Economico: the two registrations are now obtained with a single request. Upon registration, the cooperative becomes a duly incorporated company (Articles 2511, 2512, and 2518 CC). To guarantee transparency, cooperative a mutualità prevalente must be registered in a special section of the register of cooperatives, at which they also have to deposit their balance sheets, and in their documents they also must specify the registration number certifying their essentially mutual status.

If they do not meet the requisites laid down for cooperative a mutualità prevalente for two consecutive years, they will automatically forfeit their privileges (Article 2545octies CC).

501. The minimum number of members required to set up a cooperative is nine (Article 2522 CC), although this may be only three in cases in which there are at least three natural persons (or else società semplici, in the agricultural cooperatives). In this latter case, the rules of the S.r.l. must be adopted. Lower numbers of members may also be allowed by special laws. Compliance with the minimum number of members is essential, and by consequence the cooperative will be dissolved if, during its life, the number falls below the minimum number and the required number is not re-established.

502. It should be pointed out that, unlike S.p.A.s and S.r.l.s, cooperatives are characterized by a variable capital. No minimum capital is required to set up a cooperative. This follows from the fact that in a cooperative, the personal aspect of the members prevails over the economic value of the shares. In other words, the cooperative is a company in which there is a predominant intuitus personae. The share capital may vary freely as members come and go, without having to amend the company's articles of association (Article 2524 CC, the so-called open-door principle).

§3. Financing by Members and by Third Parties

503. The members of the cooperative may subscribe shares or quotas, as prescribed by the articles of the company: the capital must be divided into shares or quotas depending on whether the S.p.A. or the S.r.l. model is used. Most of the provisions relating to the shares of an S.p.A. apply to a cooperative with a capital divided into shares (Articles 2346, 2347, 2348, 2349, 2354, and 2355 CC). In spite of this, there is no need to specify on the share the fixed amount of capital or the value of contribution still due. Nevertheless, to further extend the participation of the members and promote the mutual purpose, the face value of shares or quotas must not be less than EUR 25.00 or more than EUR 500.00.

For the same reason, a maximum limit of EUR 100,000.00 is established on the total holding of each member. This limit neither applies to contributions consisting of credits or natural goods or to members who are not natural persons, nor does it apply to members who have subscribed financial instruments granting administrative rights (Article 2525 CC). Furthermore, if the cooperative has more than 500 members, the above-mentioned limit may be increased by 2% of the value of the share capital.

504. Law No. 59/1992 introduced the aforementioned categories of soci sovventori (supporting members) and azioni di partecipazione cooperativa (shares based on cooperative participation).

Supporting members are in fact members who do not necessarily have the requisites to qualify as cooperating members and who, through their membership, provide the cooperative with financial resources. Their shares or quotas may be freely transferred, unless specific limits are imposed on the cooperative's articles. They may also have preferential treatment compared to cooperating members in distributing incomes or repaying shares. Special provisions have been set in place to prevent supporting members from taking part in the cooperative purely to make a profit and to prevent them from bypassing management control. The revenue index of their holdings may not exceed 2% of the index applicable to the other members. Furthermore, as the articles of the cooperative may give them more than one vote, the number of votes allocated to a supporting member may not be more than five, and together they may not have more than one-third of the votes allocated to the other members.

505. As far as financial instruments are concerned, the problems originally encountered by cooperatives in procuring capital on the market have been gradually overcome. Presidential Decree (DPR) No. 106/1973 first introduced the possibility for a cooperative to issue loans to its members, which had to be redeemed at competitive market interest rates and on special tax terms. Law No. 59/1992 later sought to expand the financial framework of cooperatives by allowing financial instruments to be issued, under which *soci finanziatori* (holders of financial instruments) would not yet come into the mutual mechanism. Since law No. 448/1998, then confirmed by the 2003 Company Law reform cooperatives are allowed to issue bonds and financial instruments as S.p.A.s (Article 2526 CC). The articles of cooperative will establish the administrative and financial rights that have to be linked to them, and they will also establish the terms on which they can be transferred. Particular attention must be paid to ensuring that the holders of the financial instruments do not prevail over the other members of the cooperative. Therefore, even though priority may be given to the holders of such instruments in terms of income and capital repayments, indivisible capital reserves may never be used to this end (Article 2545ter CC). Moreover, the holders of financial instruments may not be entitled to more than one-third of the votes allocated to the other members.

In cases of cooperatives regulated by provisions governing S.r.l.s, only debt instruments without administrative rights may be issued. Furthermore, in this event, they can be allocated only to qualified investors.

506. Finally, financial support may also be provided by the possibility of increasing the share capital through payments from members, in which case the capital increase must be decided by the annual meeting. In this case, however, a right of option to subscribe the new shares or quotas must be granted to the other members. In cooperatives, share capital increases through payment must be compatible with the basic mutual purpose and with the company's nature in terms of intuitus personae. Consequently, all the provisions on such matters as limits on holding shares, personal requisites of members, no competition by members, one vote per capita criterion, and so forth will have to be borne in mind. The members' option may be limited or excluded by a members' meeting, at the management's motivated proposal, on condition that more than half the share capital casts a vote at the meeting (Article 2542, paragraph III, CC). The aim of this is to ensure that careless decisions are not made, which might deprive the members of the right of option.

§4. Admission and Withdrawal of Members

507. As far as changes in the membership are concerned, the so-called open-door principle is the guiding criterion. This means that anyone who has an interest that coincides with the interests of the other members may make an application to be admitted to the management. It also means that a member who no longer has the specific requisites required of the other members must leave the company.

508. There are potentially conflicting interests behind provisions regulating the admittance or withdrawal of a member to or from a cooperative. On the one hand, the cooperative is concerned that its share capital is not depleted by inappropriate capital outgoings or refunds, especially cooperatives that need substantial financial support, whereas, on the other, the members want to be free to leave the cooperative if it no longer meets the interests for which they entered the company. As far as admission is concerned, this means: (a) the member's interest in being admitted and the gain from the mutual benefit; and (b) the company's interest in admitting only those who have the specific requisites.

509. Following the general open-door principle, the admission of a new member, who has the specific requisites, does not give rise to an amendment to the cooperative's articles. Italian case law has clarified that the interest in being admitted cannot be held to be a vested right, as the directors have a certain power of discretion in deciding this. However, in the event of refusal, the directors must convey the reasons to the applicant within sixty days of being so requested.

510. When a member is admitted, the directors must arrange for him or her to be entered on the register of members (libro dei soci). Upon registration, economic and administrative rights are acquired, but the member cannot vote before ninety days have elapsed since registration (Article 2538, paragraph I, CC).

If the application is accepted, the directors must also give the reasons for this to the other members in the report on the balance sheet. This ensures that the decisional process on applications is adequately disclosed, thereby curbing the directors' power of discretion. If the application is refused, the applicant may ask the members' meeting to overturn the directors' decision.

The new members have to pay an extra charge on the face value of the shares or quotas. This extra charge is established by the directors, but it may also be established by members' meetings at the proposal of the directors, in cases in which the company's articles so require.

511. The provisions regulating transfers of shares must take into account the personal aspects inherent in the cooperatives. Transfers of shares or quotas will only be effective as far as the cooperative is concerned if the directors have first agreed (Article 2530 CC). However, if the directors fail to give their consent within sixty days from the request, the approval will be implicit and the member will be entitled to transfer his shares. Furthermore, if the directors disagree, the members may apply to the courts. The implicit assumption and the courts' control reinforced the open-door principle by limiting the discretionary power of the directors.

512. The provisions on transferring shares do not apply to subscribers of financial instruments. The prevalent opinion is that they also do not apply to transfers between cooperating members, in view of the fact that the principle of ensuring specific requisites does not apply in such cases. Special provisions on transfers of shares are established for the credit cooperation sector, applying to both the banche popolari and the banche di credito cooperativo (Article 30, paragraph V, Consolidated Law on Banking (TUB)).

513. The provisions concerning the voluntary withdrawal of members from the cooperative are also influenced by the personal aspects of the members. Provisions on the voluntary withdrawal of members are, moreover, closely linked to whether or not there is any other way in which the members can leave the cooperative. If the articles of the cooperative in fact ban members from transferring their shares, a member must always be given the chance to leave the company. In such a case, however, he or she must give ninety days' advance notice. Furthermore, he or she is permitted to leave provided that he or she has been in the cooperative for at least two years (Article 2530, paragraph VI, CC). The reason for this is based on the mutual interest in keeping members with specific requisites for a firm minimum duration.

Furthermore, the courts often reiterate the fact that when a cooperative is set up for an unlimited duration, a member can always leave by giving six months' advance notice (the articles may also establish twelve months) (Article 2437 CC relating to S.p.A.s, which is considered to apply).

514. In addition to the aforementioned situations, as a rule, withdrawal is permitted as and when the law and the articles of the cooperative so provide. As far as transferring shares is concerned, the directors must ascertain that the necessary conditions have been met and approve the withdrawal within sixty days of the advance notice. Once this period has elapsed, the withdrawal is deemed as having been approved. In the event of refusal, the member may apply to the court (Article 2532 CC).

Partial withdrawal is not permitted (Article 2532, paragraph I, CC).

515. The withdrawal of a member gives rise to two effects. There is an effect on the corporate relationship, as the member forfeits his or her status as soon as his or her application is approved. There is a second effect on the mutual relationship, because the former member cannot benefit from the fulfilment of the mutual purpose after the close of the current financial year (or after the next financial year in cases in which he or she has given notice less than three months before the close of the current financial year, pursuant to Article 2532, paragraph III, CC).

516. Finally, if the articles of the cooperative so provide, the directors or even the participants of the annual meeting may declare that a member has been excluded. It is possible to apply to the court against such a decision.

A member may be excluded from a cooperative in cases in which he or she has failed to pay, or paid only in part, the shares or quotas that he or she has subscribed (Article 2351 CC). The same applies to payments of the extra charge on shares or quotas and the allocation of natural goods. However, in such cases, as an alternative, the company may file an action for performance as opposed to exclusion.

Members of the cooperative may also be excluded in the specific cases set forth in the company's articles. In any event, they may always be excluded for manifestly failing to fulfil the mutual purpose. More specifically, exclusion will apply in cases in which a member forfeits the admission requisites. It will also apply in cases in which a member has been judicially declared non compos mentis, has gone bankrupt, or has been barred from public office for committing a crime. In the event of exclusion, the mutual relationship comes to an end with effect from the time the directors resolve the exclusion. This is not quite the same as the solution adopted for withdrawal (*see* above).

517. In all cases of voluntary withdrawal, exclusion, or transfer of shares, the member will continue to account to the cooperative to the extent of the value of the share or extra charge for one year after his or her withdrawal (Article 2356, paragraph I, CC). This provision is an exception to the general provisions of Article 2949, paragraph I, CC, according to which the limitation on corporate commitments is five years, as well as an exception to the general rule that also extends liability to the transferees.

It should be stressed that some of the aforementioned provisions on admission, transfer, withdrawal, and exclusion do not apply (unless otherwise stated) to members who are not cooperating members, as they need not have any particular personal requisites.

§5. Company Bodies

518. The company bodies of cooperatives are the same as those of S.p.A.s, and the same criteria are applied in allocating responsibilities. These include members' meetings, the board of directors, and the supervisory body, which do not always have to be appointed.

A number of important features have, however, been introduced for cooperatives to take into account their specific nature.

I. The Members' Meetings

519. First of all, as far as the deliberating body is concerned, the capita voting system applies, whereby each cooperating member has a vote, regardless of the value of his or her quota or the number of shares that he or she owns. The one vote per capita principle is an essential manifestation of the controlling role of the people as members of the cooperative (Article 2538 CC).

520. The articles of association may, however, contemplate exceptions to this principle within the limits specifically permitted by the law. The financing member may in fact be granted either just one vote or multiple votes, depending on his or her contribution, but this is without prejudice to the limit set forth in Article 2526 CC, under which the financing members may not express (either on their own behalf or by proxy) more than one-third of the votes of all the members in attendance. If this limit is exceeded, the votes of the financing members will have to be proportionally reduced. Furthermore, if the financing member is also a cooperating member (as in the case of financial instruments offered for subscription to cooperating members, as provided for by Article 2538, paragraph II, CC), the articles of association, may establish limits on the right to vote.

Another significant exception to the one vote per capita principle arises in the case of cooperating members that are legal entities. The articles of association may grant them more than one vote but never more than five, in relation to the amount of their holding or to the number of members by which the legal entity is formed (Article 2538, paragraph IV, CC). This limit has been introduced to ensure that to a legal entity cannot be allocated the majority of votes at a members' meeting, as could occur in the past.

Finally, the current set of rules allows more than one vote to be allocated in cooperatives in which the members achieve the mutual purpose by merging their enterprises or certain phases of them. In the main, these are production and labour cooperatives, in which the vote may be allocated according to participation in the mutual exchange. However, no single member may express more than one-tenth of the votes vested, and collectively, any such members may not have more than one-third of the voting rights of the members present or represented at the annual meeting (Article 2538, paragraph V, CC).

521. In cooperatives, votes may be expressed by correspondence or through other systems of telecommunications (Article 2538, paragraph VI, CC), provided that the articles of association so permit. In this case, the notice of convocation must contain a full description of the proposed resolution. If the meeting deliberates upon a proposal different from that indicated in the notice of convocation, the votes expressed by correspondence will not contribute towards forming the quorum required to set up the meeting.

The articles of association will establish the procedures for convening a members' meeting (if they are in derogation of legal requirements), the majorities required for it to be set up, and for adopted resolutions to be valid, bearing in mind the number of votes due to members on a per capita basis and not on the basis of their holdings in the capital.

522. The will of a members' meeting may be formed through the mechanism of separate meetings. This mechanism is a manifestation of how the democratic principle is applied in the framework of the cooperative, as it seeks to reinforce actual possibilities of participation (Article 2540 CC). Separate meetings may be envisaged either for specific subject matters or with the attendance of particular categories of members. Such meetings are mandatory, however, in cases in which the cooperative has a broad base of members or an extensive territorial presence (more than three thousand members operating in several provinces, or more than five hundred members engaged in various mutual activities).

The provision for a proportional representation of minorities of members is particularly interesting. This has to be guaranteed at the annual meeting.

The separate meetings will deliberate upon the same matters later to be addressed at the annual meeting. They will appoint delegates (who must be members) to participate in the annual meeting, where definitive resolutions will be passed on the matters placed on the agenda. Prevailing doctrine maintains that, in this manner, the delegates have a binding mandate, in that all they have to do is reiterate at the annual meeting the votes expressed at the separate meetings. The members who have taken part in the separate meetings may, however, attend the annual meeting, but without having the right to vote.

As they are only a stage in forming the will of a members' meeting, the resolutions of file in separate meetings cannot be separately challenged, whereas resolutions passed at the annual meeting can even be challenged by absent or dissenting members, provided that it is proven that the quorum required to pass resolutions would not have been reached without the votes expressed by delegates elected at incorrectly held separate meetings (Article 2538, paragraph VI, CC).

523. If financial instruments bereft of voting rights are issued, the cooperative must convene special meetings for each category of these instruments to deliberate upon matters inherent in the specific interest represented. Such meetings will be convened either by the directors or by the joint representative whenever necessary, or, alternatively, when at least one-third of the owners of the financial instruments so request.

The provision for special meetings in cooperatives has a broader scope of application than that of Article 2376 CC, on special meetings of the S.p.A.s, in that it is envisaged that they may also vote over and above cases in which a right acknowledged to a specific category of shares is jeopardized. As well as resolving to designate the joint representative and set up an expenses fund, the special meetings will in fact also decide how the rights attributed to the category are exercised and on other matters of common interest, as well as on any disputes with the company and the relevant settlements or waivers.

As far as listed cooperatives are concerned, Article 135 of the TUF provides that the percentage of the capital required for the exercise of members' rights must be estimated having regard to the total number of members. In this way, it has been confirmed the 'one vote per capita'principle.

II. The Board of Directors

524. As far as the board of directors is concerned, the law also envisages for cooperatives the possibility of adopting different models of administration from those of the traditional models, such as the one-tier and the two-tier models. It has, however, been pointed out that such a multiplicity of models is out of proportion with the type of enterprise and its requirements. Indeed, it is thought that the two-tier model is hardly practicable for cooperatives, because the supervisory board can be formed only by cooperating members, and at least one of its members must be enrolled at the register of chartered accountants.

Regardless of the system selected, in addition to the matters envisaged in Article 2381 CC (issuing convertible bonds, drawing up the balance sheets, increasing the capital during the first five years of the enterprise, reducing the capital due to losses even below the legal limit, and drawing up a merger or demerger project), the directors may not delegate powers in such matters as the admission, withdrawal, and exclusion of members or decisions affecting mutual relations with members (Article 2544 CC).

525. If the two-tier system is adopted, the owners of financial instruments may not elect more than one-third of the members of the supervisory board and the board of management. If, on the other hand, the one-tier system is adopted, the directors elected by the owners of financial instruments may not be more than one-third of the total. They may not be delegated operating powers, and they may not be members of the executive committee. These restrictions have been introduced to ensure that the rights provided to financing members are not such as to jeopardize the pivotal importance of the cooperating members and alter the special nature of the company's mutual purpose.

526. As far as the traditional system is concerned, the rule according to which all the directors must also be members of the company no longer applies. Today, it is sufficient for the majority of directors to be selected from among the cooperating members or from among persons designated by cooperating members that are legal entities (Article 2542 CC). The idea of this is to ensure that management is entrusted in the main to persons directly engaged in carrying out the mutual activities. Nevertheless, non-members may be admitted to the company's board of directors for the purposes of acquiring technical and administrative elements that are necessary for the entity's sound functioning.

In the same vein, the owners of financial instruments may not be given the right to elect more than one-third of the directors, and the cooperative articles may provide that one or more directors be chosen from among persons belonging to different categories of members in such a way as to reflect the interest that each category has in the corporate activities.

It should be observed that the articles of association may reserve the appointment of one or more directors for the State or for public entities, if they have a pre-eminent interest in the company, but in this case they may never represent the majority.

III. The Supervisory Body

527. In the cooperatives structured following the traditional system, the collegio sindacale has to be appointed if the rules of S.pA. are applied or in the same cases for which it is compulsory for S.r.l.s, that is, when the company must draft a consolidated balance sheet, when the company controls another company subject to the external audit supervision, and when for two consecutive financial years, two of the limits referred to in Article 2435*bis* have been exceeded, or alternatively, when the cooperative company has issued nonparticipating financial instruments (Article 2543 CC).

In cases in which the company opts for a two-tier or one-tier system of administration, there is no need to set up a further supervisory body, as this is represented either by the supervisory board or by the internal control committee within the board of directors. The accounts must, however, be audited by an external auditor or an auditing firm.

528. Article 2543 CC makes it mandatory for the right to vote in electing the supervisory body to be allocated in proportion to the value of quotas or shares owned or according to the participation in the mutual exchange, in such a way as to ensure that the body is first and foremost an expression of the cooperating members. Furthermore, the appointment of one-third of the members of the supervisory body may be reserved for the owners of financial instruments in order to ensure an ulterior guarantee to encourage financial investment in companies with a mutual purpose (Article 2543, paragraph III, CC).

529. If the cooperative resorts to the risk capital market or has to draft a consolidated balance sheet, the accounts will be audited by an external auditor or by an auditing firm enrolled with the register of chartered accountants, in compliance with the general reference to the rules regulating S.p.A.s and S.r.l.s. In this case, the collegio sindacale has to verify compliance with: (i) the law; (ii) the articles of association; and (iii) principles of sound administration, with particular stress on the suitability of the organizational, administrative, and accounting framework adopted by the company and its concrete functioning. If the cooperative does not resort to the risk capital market, and does not have to draft a consolidated balance sheet, and the company adopts the traditional governance model, then the articles may envisage that the auditing of accounts be exercised by the collegio sindacale, which must in this case be formed by chartered accountants only.

§6. Members' Rights, Reserves, and Ristorni

530. The rights of members of cooperatives are based on the law, on the articles of association, and on its by-laws.

The members are the persons entitled to partake the benefits arising from carrying out the corporate activities. In cooperatives, the right to profits (or rather, to distributed profits) is, as explained above, subject to particular restrictions geared to safeguarding their mutual purpose. Indeed, the distribution of dividends becomes an accessory, to the mutual purpose of the cooperative and that means that the articles of association must establish the maximum percentage at which dividends can be distributed between cooperating members (Article 2545quinquies CC). In cooperatives with a predominantly mutual purpose, there is, moreover, a general ban on remuneration beyond a certain level for both the shares and for the financial instruments offered to cooperating members (Article 2514 CC).

531. Profits may be distributed only if the ratio between the company's aggregate indebtedness and the net worth is higher than one to four. The same limit also applies to purchasing treasury stock and to distributing divisible reserves to members (Article 2545quinquies). This is a substantive limit, the purpose of which is to guarantee the consistency of the cooperative's assets and to avert a transition from the mutual purpose, an essential element of the cooperative, to the profit-making purpose.

Obviously, the limit on purchasing treasury stock, distributing profits, or distributing divisible reserves to members does not apply to the owners of financial instruments, because this would discourage subscriptions.

532. Divisible reserves may be assigned to members either by granting financial instruments or through a free increase of the holding in the share capital of not more than 20% of the original value (Article 2545quinquies, paragraph III, CC). This limit has been intentionally kept low to avert the risk of excessively inflating the ordinary share capital that has to be paid out.

Finally, if the corporate relationship is discontinued for only one member, the divisible reserves will be allocated to him or her by issuing freely transferable financial instruments, unless the articles provide otherwise. This solution becomes compulsory in cases in which the ratio between its aggregate indebtedness and the company's net asset is less than one to four (Article 2545quinquies, paragraph IV, CC).

533. The indivisible reserves, on the other hand, are appropriations that, under the law or the articles may not be distributed to the members, not even in the event of the company's dissolution (Article 2545ter CC). Such reserves may be used to cover losses (Article 2545quater CC), but only exceptionally, because the utilization of optional reserves and of sums already earmarked to increase the capital must precede that of unavailable reserves (Article 2545ter, paragraph II, CC).

The quota of net annual profits to be destined for the legal reserve fund is 30%.

Furthermore, a quota of the net annual profits, regardless of whether or not the cooperative is a cooperative with a predominantly mutual purpose, must be transferred to mutual funds set up by recognized national associations in order to promote and develop cooperation, at the rate contemplated by the law (Article 2545quater, paragraph II, CC).

The remaining profits, which, therefore, are neither destined for the legal reserve nor transferred by law to the mutual funds, will be used as directed by a members' meeting, which may, therefore, decide to set up voluntary reserves (Article 2545quater, paragraph III).

534. Finally, Article 2545sexies CC regulates *ristorni* that are, like profits, special distributions, sums of money shared between the members, but follow different criteria. Cooperatives may in fact grant members the mutual benefit in two ways, either: (i) directly, in cases of consumer cooperatives, by applying cost prices to them, and, in cases of labour cooperatives, by paying salaries equal to the enterprise's entire net revenue; or (ii) indirectly, by applying to members the current market price or paying them a salary equal to that of profit-making companies, but periodically paying them extra money, which are defined as *ristorni* (e.g., distributing additional price compared to the market price already paid to purchase the members' products or an additional salary 'for members' work). *Ristorni* must not, therefore, be confused with profits, because they are not a remuneration of the capital, but of labour or of goods or services provided by cooperating members.

535. Therefore, Article 2545sexies CC provides that the articles of association have to establish criteria in distributing *ristorni* to members in proportion to the quantity and quality of mutual exchanges and establishes a clear separation between refunds and profits, making it compulsory to enter in accounts figures pertaining to the activities carried out with members under different accounting entries.

The decision to distribute *ristorni* will be made at a members' meeting, which may also resolve that they be distributed in the form of a proportional increase in corporate quotas by issuing new shares or even issuing financial instruments. The members of the meeting will make this decision by a majority, at the proposal of the directors. As with distributing profits, the distribution of refunds is not a subjective right of the participants, as there has to be a prior evaluation of the company's economic situation.

536. Finally, the rights of members of cooperatives include:(a) to the right of inspection mentioned in Article 2422 CC, which consists of the possibility of examining the stock ledger and the minute book of sessions and resolutions of members' meetings; and (b) the possibility for members representing at least one-tenth of the total number (or at least one-twentieth if the cooperative has more than three thousand members) to examine, through a representative, the minute book of sessions and resolutions of the board of directors and the executive committee, if any. This is an important power of control vested in the members over the company's management, but it is not vested in a member who is in default because of failure to pay contributions or other non-compliances, including failing to meet obligations undertaken with the company.

§7. The Cooperative Group

537. The cooperative group was an innovation brought in under the reform of company law provided for by Decree No. 6/2003. In cooperatives, the one vote per capita rule ensures that the coordinated management of several cooperative enterprises is not based on a relationship of control and consequently of one cooperative being subordinated to the others. This means that it is not legally possible for cooperatives to set up a so-called vertical group. The cooperative group regulated by Article 2545septies CC is, therefore, a horizontal, or jointly run, type of group, inasmuch as the control relationship is contractual and not corporate.

The jointly run cooperative group is thus defined as a contract whereby several cooperatives, which may even belong to different categories, regulate the management and coordination of their respective enterprises. The contractual agreement, which falls within the formula of a consortium of entrepreneurs, is designed to set up a shared, unitary business strategy, which is frequent, for instance, in the banking and insurance sectors.

538. The hypothesis considered by the CC is characterized by the basic homogeneity of those participating in the group insofar as the group is usually restricted to cooperatives only. The law establishes the bare contents of the relevant contract, and in so doing, seeks to preserve the mutual nature of the group of cooperatives as a form of association and avert abuses on the part of the controlling cooperative.

Each cooperative belonging to the group is under an obligation to deposit the participation agreement in writing at the register of cooperatives, in such a way as to facilitate checks on this form of mutual aggregation (Article 2545septies, paragraph III, CC).

539. The contract must also specify the duration of the group and the cooperative(s) that have been voluntarily entrusted with powers of guidance and coordination, indicating what these powers consist of. The agreement must also provide information on the eventual participation of other public and private entities and on the criteria applied in adhering to, or withdrawing from, the contract, as well as compensation criteria and the balance in terms of distributing the advantages stemming from the joint activity. In this respect, the concept of 'group mutuality' may be inferred, which has to do with harmonizing the group's interest with that of each enterprise that joins it.

Furthermore, it may be inferred by analogy that Articles 2359/2362 CC, on capitalistic corporate groups, and specifically, Articles 2497/2497septies CC, on the management and coordination of companies, apply, provided that they are compatible with the particular provisions on mutuality and the voluntary nature of the cooperative group. The rules on advertising the group, which are designed to ensure transparent management also within the group, thus apply to the jointly run cooperative group, among other rules. The subsidiary must therefore specify in its documents and correspondence the fact that it is under the management and coordination of others, and this same information must also be provided when it is registered at the special division of the Registro delle imprese.

Each company belonging to the group may withdraw from the contract without any charges being applied if, as a result of joining the group, the conditions of the exchange prove to be detrimental to its members (Article 2545septies, paragraph II, CC).

540. A different instance, which is not considered in the CC but in Article 25, paragraph II of Legislative Decree No. 127 of 9 April 1991, is that of a cooperative company that controls one or more capital companies. In spite of a number of concerns being raised by legal doctrine, it is thought that participation in profit- making companies is not in conflict with pursuing the mutual purpose typical of cooperatives. This is because it is the so-called subjective profit-making purpose that is incompatible with the mutual purpose, that is, the interest in sharing the profits between or among members, and not the so-called objective profit purpose, which consists of making operating surpluses and which the cooperative can achieve in various ways, possibly even reinforcing the pursuance of the mutual purpose. In this case, the law makes it compulsory to draft the consolidated balance sheet of the cooperative group, even if it is controlled by a cooperative. However, the fact that there is no specific set of rules means that the directors of the cooperative are able to run the holding without any power of authorization or ratification being vested in individual cooperating members, and without any particular powers of administrative supervision being envisaged.

§8. Amendments of the Articles of Association

541. As far as amendments to the articles of association and mergers/demergers of cooperatives are concerned, Article 2545*novies* CC makes a general reference to the rules regulating joint-stock companies.

In the specific field of cooperatives, amendments to the articles of association may cover such matters as distributing profits or *ristorni*, introducing financing members by setting up funds for technological development, preparing multi-annual planning procedures to modernize the company with a view to issuing cooperative participation shares, or organizing share capital increases in the forms envisaged in Article 2438 and following articles of the CC. The amendments may not, however, alter the system of liability of members, in view of the fact that cooperatives are based only on limited liability.

542. A merger may arise when a profit-making company is incorporated with a cooperative company, insofar as this is compatible with capital assets allocation obligations and the mutual purposes that characterize cooperatives. Mergers between cooperatives with different corporate purposes are also possible, provided that there is the consent, of the majority required in cases of amendments to the by-laws. Doubts remain, however, in the case of a merger between cooperatives with a predominantly mutual purpose and other cooperatives, which gives rise to a cooperative of the first type. In this case, the rules applicable to the predominantly mutual cooperative should in any case be held to apply.

543. Furthermore, if the decision is made by special qualified majorities (at least half the members, save exceptions in cases in which there are less than fifty or more than ten thousand members) in the course of a special members' meeting, the cooperative may resolve its transformation into an informal partnership, a general partnership, a limited partnership, a joint-stock company, or a consortium (Article 2545novies CC).

The rules regulating the transformation of cooperatives were introduced to remove obstacles and to adapting company models to developments in the corporate structure and the markets. It thus superseded the ban previously imposed by Article 14 of Law 127/1971 on cooperatives being transformed into profit-making companies, for fear that this would make it possible for benefits obtained from the State to be transferred to legal entities operating outside the cooperative sector.

544. Cooperatives are allowed to be transformed into profit-making companies on clear conditions prescribed by the law. Such a transformation is possible only for cooperatives other than predominantly mutual cooperatives and on condition that the assets of the transformed company are transferred to the mutual funds pursuant to Article 2545undecies CC.

If we examine this more closely, though, the ban on transformation for predominantly mutual cooperatives is more apparent than real, because Article 2545octies CC provides that the cooperative will also forfeit its status as a predominantly mutual cooperative (in addition to cases of failing to comply with the conditions of predominance for two consecutive financial years, pursuant to Article 2513 CC, *see* above in paragraph 1), if the statutory provisions referred to in Article 2514 CC are changed by amending the articles of association. In this case, as the company is no longer a predominantly mutual cooperative, it will acquire the possibility of adopting a transformation resolution pursuant to Article 2545decies CC.

It should be observed that the transition from a predominantly mutual cooperative to a not predominantly mutual cooperative and vice-versa does not constitute a transformation. Indeed, these two different models are subcategories of mutual enterprises belonging to the same category. However, if the requisite of predominant mutuality is forfeited, the directors are under an obligation to inform the Ministry for Economic Development and to draw up a balance sheet to determine the effective value of the assets to be ascribed to unavailable reserves.

545. On the question of the requirement to transfer the assets to mutual funds in the event of transformation, this is implied by law as a result of adopting the transformation resolution. The transfer refers to the effective value of the assets – after deducting the paid in and revalued capital and dividends not yet distributed – increased, if need be, up to the minimum amount of the new company's capital existing as of the date of the transformation (Article 2545undecies CC).

The directors must attach to the proposed transformation resolution a sworn report by an expert designated by the court of the district where the cooperative has its registered office, certifying the effective value of the enterprise's assets (Article 2545undecies CC). In this respect, Article 2500sexies CC, which refers to the transformation of a joint stock company into a partnership, is thought to apply. The appraisal must, therefore, be deposited at the registered office for thirty days prior to the members' meeting, and the members are entitled to inspect it and obtain a copy of it free of charge.

546. Article 2545decies CC, final paragraph, clarifies the effects of the transformation on the members, providing that after the transformation has taken place, any financial instruments with voting rights will be converted into ordinary shares, while maintaining any privileges. The assignment of quotas or holdings proportional to the quota originally subscribed and the maintenance of privileges, which are usually capital privileges inherent in the distribution of profits or repayment of capital, allow the owners of such instruments to thus maintain their position unchanged within the cooperative.

§9. Administrative Control

547. The Italian Constitution envisages that cooperatives are subject to a system of external controls aimed at ensuring their specific nature and their objectives. The legislature's historical leaning towards making all cooperatives (and not only cooperatives with a predominantly mutual purpose) subject to a system of external supervision is, in fact, based on general values that the system aims to pursue.

548. Unlike joint-stock companies, which are subject mainly to judicial control, cooperatives are, therefore, subject to a twofold administrative control.

A first form of administrative control seeks to monitor the cooperative phenomenon as a whole. This is the Register of Cooperatives kept at the Ministry for Economic Development, at which cooperatives have to register under penalty of not qualifying for tax relief and other benefits.

Second, cooperatives are subject to the control of the supervisory authority, which is designed to ensure that they undergo regular administrative and auditing checks and that the conditions required for tax relief and financial aid to be granted are duly met.

This supervision (apart from certain categories of cooperatives) is entrusted to the Ministry for Economic Development, which exercises this power of control in the form of regular and special inspections of individual cooperatives (Legislative Decree No. 220/2002). Regular inspections are carried out once every two years, while special inspections are carried out whenever they are deemed necessary. The main purpose of the inspections is to verify due observance of legislative, regulatory, and mutual purpose requirements, the existence of the requisites imposed by general and special laws to qualify for tax relief, the company's regular bookkeeping and administration, the correct technical approach and performance of the company's specific activities, the extent of its assets, and the situation of its assets and liabilities.

In fulfilling its supervisory function, the Ministry usually avails itself of national associations that represent, assist, and protect the legally acknowledged cooperative movement, pursuing both ideal and political objectives. This gives rise to the phenomenon of self-control of the cooperative movement, that is, a control over the cooperative movement organized through associations of member cooperatives.

549. If irregularities are ascertained in the way in which a cooperative functions, after issuing a warning, the supervisory authority may remove the directors and sindaci and entrust the company's management to a government commissioner, establishing his or her duration in office and powers (Article 2545sexiesdecies CC).

The supervisory authority may moreover order that the cooperative be dissolved if, in its opinion: (a) it is not pursuing the mutual purpose; (b) it is unable to achieve the purposes for which it was set up; or (c) for two consecutive years, it has not deposited balance sheets or carried out operations (Article 2545septiesdecies CC).

550. The management of cooperatives is placed under the judicial control as envisaged in Article 2409 CC for S.p.A.s. Before 2003, this control was excluded for cooperatives, which had traditionally been placed only under government supervision. It was thought that, as the government's control is based on broad public aims, any intervention on the part of the courts would have been inappropriate and superfluous.

Nevertheless, at the moment ministerial supervision operates alongside judicial control pursuant to Article 2409 CC, which may be sought either by cooperating members holding one-tenth of the share capital or by one-tenth of the total number of members (this falls to one-twentieth in cooperatives with more than three thousand members). The thinking behind this is to ensure adequate protection for persons/entities that participate in the capital simply as financing members.

The Code establishes rules coordinating the two forms of external control. A court faced with a claim against the directors and sindaci of a cooperative cannot render any decision – and, therefore, has to declare the proceeding a non-suit – if an administrative control procedure has already been started, with the appointment of an inspector or a commissioner (Article 2545quinquiesdecies CC). The claim filed with the court must in any case be notified to the supervisory authority, which must always be consulted during the course of proceedings.

The supervisory authority will, however, suspend the administrative proceeding if the court has already designated a judicial inspector or administrator with respect to the same events. Consequently, administrative controls exclude judicial controls, and vice-versa.

§10. Mutue Assicuratrici (Mutual Insurance Companies)

551. Cooperatives and mutue assicuratrici (hereafter 'mutual insurance companies') both fall within the general framework of mutual companies. In spite of this, the history and raison d'etre of cooperatives are quite independent from those of mutual insurance companies, which are linked to the history of maritime and insurance law. Cooperatives, on the other hand, are a typical product of the twentieth century trade union movement.

The very essence of mutual insurance companies is that membership is only possible by taking out an insurance policy with the company, whereas membership is forfeited when the insurance policy is cancelled (Article 2546, paragraph III, CC). This means that, in mutual insurance companies, the insurance contract is part and parcel of the corporate contract and they together form a single contract. The consequence of this is that the contribution provided by members, which may be established in the articles of association in the form of fixed or variable contributions (Article 2546, paragraph I, CC), is both a contribution to the company and an insurance premium. The member is thus insured as such, without having to stipulate a separate insurance contract. Therefore, although mutual insurances are subject to the rules created for cooperatives as by nature they are compatible with them, they are an exception to the rule of achieving the mutual purpose through separate exchanges between the company and the members.

Leaving aside the financing members, the mutual insurance company thus gives rise to a special legal relationship that embodies a special associative relationship and an insurance relationship in a single contract.

552. Mutual insurance companies are not only subject to the rules regulating cooperatives in view of their compatibility, but also to the set of rules on running insurance enterprises (Legislative Decree No. 209/2005, the Private Insurance Consolidation Act). Supervision over insurance cooperatives is entrusted to the Ministry for Economic Development and to the Institute for Surveillance over Insurances (IVASS).

553. The corporate assets of a mutual insurance company, which consist of the contributions of the insured members and are calculated in accordance with technical criteria applying to insurance premiums, may be supplemented, if the articles so envisage, by guarantee funds set up to pay indemnities, created with contributions from insured members or third parties. Any such third parties will become members, even if they do not take out an insurance policy with the company (Article 2548, paragraph I, CC).

554. Two categories of members may thus coexist in mutual insurance companies: insured members and financing members. The latter have profit-making, as opposed to mutual, interests, which means that a mutual insurance company with financing members has the combined characteristics of a mutual purpose/profit- making contract.

However, to ensure that the financing members do not prevail in the company's management, the law provides that the articles of association may allocate to each financing member (including private individuals) more than one vote but not more than five, depending on their contribution. The votes allocated to financing members must, however, not be less than the votes granted to insured members. Furthermore, although financing members may be appointed directors, the majority of the directors must be formed by insured members (Article 2548 CC).

§11. Dissolution and Liquidation

555. The same causes of dissolution apply to cooperatives as those envisaged for joint-stock companies in Article 2484 CC, except, of course, for the cause inherent in reducing the share capital to below the legal minimum, as by its very nature a cooperative is a company with a varying capital. Therefore, only the total loss of the share capital will be a cause for dissolving a cooperative (Article 2545duodecies CC).

Two specific causes for dissolving a cooperative are: (i) when the number of members falls to below the minimum number of nine (or three), unless it is re-established within one year; and (ii) the compulsory administrative liquidation by order of the supervisory authority in pathological cases of cooperatives that elude mutual practices, giving rise to forms of unfair competition in the market.

556. Under Law Decree of 23 December 2013 No. 145, converted in Law of 21 February 2014 No. 9, during an insolvency procedure, in case of business lease or purchase, labour cooperatives, set up by workers of the insolvent enterprise, have the right of first refusal.

557. The only particular feature of the procedure by which the cooperative is liquidated, after it has been dissolved, is that the supervisory authorities are given powers to replace the liquidators if there are irregularities or excessive delays in the liquidation (Article 2545octiesdecies CC). Furthermore, as far as appropriating the assets left over from the liquidation is concerned, in the case of predominantly mutual cooperatives, the entire net corporate assets (i.e., after deducting only the paid in and revalued capital and any dividends that have already accrued) must be transferred to mutual funds for promoting and developing cooperation (Article 11.1 of Law No. 59/1992).

Reference is also made in toto to the rules regulating joint-stock companies as far as the liquidation procedure is concerned. The only special provision there is that a reciprocal exclusion exists between compulsory administrative liquidation by order of the supervisory authority in case of insolvency and the company's bankruptcy, inasmuch as the adjudication of bankruptcy excludes the compulsory liquidation and vice-versa. The cooperative can become bankrupt only when it carries out commercial activities (Article 2545terdecies CC).

Part II. Partnerships

Chapter 1. The Società Semplice ('Non-business Association')

§1. Definition and Sources

558. The società semplice is the most elementary kind of company derived from the 'società civile' pattern, provided for in the 1865 CC and inspired by the 'societas' of the Roman times. After the introduction of the mandatory registration and because of the restricted number of activities that they can perform, this type of partnership is used in few cases.

The società semplice presents a simplified structure and, even though it must have an economic activity as its subject, it cannot be used to conduct in associated form a commercial activity, as provided for in Article 2249 CC. In practice it is used mainly for managing real estate and controlling interest, as well as to conduct an agricultural, non-industrialized activity.

Articles from Article 2251 to the Article 2290 CC, regulating the società *semplice*, are applied, in absence of derogation, also to S.n.c. and to società in accomandita, in spite of the fact that these are intended for performing commercial activities.

§2. Formation and Registration

559. In order to set up a società semplice, specific forms are not imposed, and particular fulfilments are not requested for that purpose. Thus, the agreement can be stipulated even orally or *per* facta concludendo.

Nevertheless, the articles of a società semplice must be in writing any time the nature of the contributions requests that form (i.e., a typical case is that of an estate contribution). Prevailing authors hold that this form concerns only the contribution clause, and not the entire agreement.

560. The società semplice in any event must be registered in the Registro delle imprese and, for that purpose, a request signed by all the members is sufficient. Registration has a different effect, depending on whether the società semplice carries out agricultural activity or not. In the first case, registration involves legal knowledge from third persons who cannot invoke ignorance of the act; in all the other cases, registration makes known the act, but the association must prove the effective knowledge or knowability from suitable means (i.e., personalized or specific communications).

§3. Structure

561. The law does not impose specific partnership bodies.

In a società semplice, a board of directors or a members meeting is not necessary because members' deliberations are not expressions of a unitary partnership and will, but express only the sum of the members' single wills.

Thus, to make a decision, a partnership does not have to follow particular procedures; a meeting of the members is not required, the members' will can be expressed in any way (also through facta concludentia), and it is required only to collect the members' will, in case of a unanimous decision, or the majority of the members' decision.

Recently, the courts declared that the fact that the CC does not request for the società semplice a members meeting or other partnership organs does not mean that their constitution is forbidden.

§4. Management and Power of Representation

I. Management

A. Disjoint Management Principle

562. In a società semplice, the management and the performance of acts aimed to attain the partnerships' objects are due to each partner separately (Article 2257 CC); then, each one can perform acts binding the partnership without a previous permission of the other partners.

Disjoint management is the legal system, but it is possible to depart from it.

B. Derogations of the Disjoint Management

563. Partners can adopt a different management regime, choosing a joint management (ruled by the unanimity principle or by that of the majority) or conferring the management to one or some of the partners.

In the case of a joint management, the management is granted to a board of partner managers. Single-partner managers cannot perform on their own any kind of act, apart from a case in which it is urgent so as to avoid damage to the partnership.

When the management is granted to one or just some of the partners, the non-managing members can ask for information, but they cannot interfere with the management activities.

C. *The Non-partner Manager*

564. It is doubtful whether a third person can be appointed as manager. According to the prevailing opinion, this is not possible, because the partners derive an unlimited liability for partnership debts from their direct involvement in the management.

According to some authors, in any event, it could be possible that the members with managing powers appoint to a third person the task of performing all the activities related to the partnership's objects.

D. *Managing Partners*

565. Managers' rights and duties are governed by the contract of mandate rules.

According to the prevailing opinion the manager cannot be perfectly identified with the mandate, and the mandate rules can be applied only within the limits in which they do not depart from the partnership's relationship discipline.

Confirming this opinion, while Article 1708 CC limits the mandatory powers within the performance of the ordinary acts of management, managers, unless the contract or a subsequent agreement do not exclude it, can perform all the ordinary and extraordinary acts of management related to the partnership's objects.

566. A manager must act personally, he or she can be substituted only if expressly authorized, and, must act with bonus paterfamilias reasonable care.

Unless expressly and otherwise agreed managers are entitled to receive fair compensation.

567. As concerns managers' liability, managers are liable jointly to the partnership for the discharge of the duties imposed upon them by law and the agreement partnership. However, such liability does not extend to those who prove that they are free of fault.

Joint liability exists also when the management is disjoint, being any manager appointed with the task of controlling the others' activities, and, eventually, of opposing a veto.

Liability refers to facts and behaviour that damage the partnership, and, therefore, only the partnership, through its representatives, can bring an action for damages.

E. *Managers' Appointment*

568. Lacking in this regard a specific rule in the CC, it is held that managers can be appointed in the articles of the partnership or at a subsequent time by means of an appointment deliberation.

F. *Managers' Office Termination*

569. The law does not expressly rule cases of termination of a manager's office, except for the revocation. In other cases, therefore, apply the contract of mandate rules.

Termination causes, apart from revocation, are term expiry, waiver, death, prohibition for an incompetent person, or a person under care.

In the case of joint management, unless otherwise agreed, a termination cause concerning only one manager extends also to all the others.

Waiver is considered effective only when the manager is substituted.

570. The manager revocation is regulated in different manners if the manager is appointed in partnership agreement or with a separate act.

In the first hypothesis, the manager can be revoked only for cause and, in any case, with the unanimous consent of the members.

In the case of a separate act, the manager can be revoked, even though there is not a cause, with a unanimous deliberation or with the majority of the votes, if it is so provided for.

Revocation for cause can be in any case requested by each partner to the court. There is a cause for revocation in a case in which an activity performed by the manager violates the loyalty, fairness, and reasonable-care duties so that the violation negatively affects the relationship of trust and confidence.

Among facts that can provoke a revocation are the following:

- non-performance of the management activities;
- delegation to other persons of management power;
- performance of acts of management separately if the joint form was provided for; and
- violation of a prohibition of competition.

II. Power of Representation

571. The power of representation has to be distinguished from the power of management.

In fact, the management consists of the assumption of decisions aimed to realize the partnership's purpose, while the representation power consists of those decisions' effects on third persons and through acts performed on behalf of the partnership.

Therefore, exercising the power of representation, consequences of the act performed are produced within the partnership's legal sphere.

If it is true that the power of representation can be defined as a natural attribution of the manager appointment, it is not an essential aspect concerning the partnership management. It is, in fact, possible that the partnership agreement limits the representative power, granting it to one or just some of the managers.

Unless otherwise agreed, in any event, the CC provides for the principle according to which the partnership representation is granted to all the members separately.

572. The partnership acquires rights and assumes obligations through the partners who have the power to represent it and appears in judicial proceedings in person of such partners. Unless otherwise provided for in the partnership agreement, the power of representation belongs to each managing partner and extends to all acts that are within the object of the company.

Thus, if it is not otherwise provided for, each managing partner represents the partnership for any act relating to the partnership's objects, but partnership agreement can limit the power to represent the partnership on behalf of one or just some of the members.

573. Power of representation is normally linked to the managing power, and, thus, the limits of the second one extend to the first one. In any event, it is possible that the power of representation is limited more strictly in the partnership agreement; for example, providing for a joint representation (with the signature of two or more representatives) for acts of relevant value, even though the management is disjoint. These limits must be made public by appropriated means, such as Registro delle imprese, otherwise they will not have effect against third persons that have no knowledge of it.

574. Regarding the representation before courts, the power of representation extends also to judicial acts.

Therefore, unless otherwise provided for in the partnership agreement, each manager appointed with the power to represent the partnership can act before courts, and he or she can be sued for the partnership.

Thus, if the partnership agreement provides for a joint representation, without providing for representation before courts, it is held that the partnership has to act before courts and it has to be sued in person of all the managers.

§5. Invalidity

575. The partnership agreement's invalidity must be considered by examining general rules referring to contract law because a specific rule in the CC does not exist.

To this extent, the following articles must be considered:

- Article 1418 CC, according to which 'a contract is null and void if contrary to mandatory rules, unless differently provided for by law. A contract is void when one of the requirements indicated in Article 1325 CC is missed, when causa (i.e., the socio-economic function) is unlawful, when motives in the case considered in Article 1345 are unlawful, and when one of the object requirements indicated in Article 1346 is missed'.
- Article 1325 CC, according to which 'contract requirements are: (a) agreement, (b) causa, (c) object, and (d) form, whenever requested for contract validity'.
- Article 1345 CC, according to which 'a contract is unlawful whenever the parties intended to stipulate it only for an unlawful motive common to both of them'.
- Article 1346 CC, according to which 'a contract object must be possible, lawful, determined, or possible to be determined'.
- Article 1425 CC, according to which 'a contract is voidable if one of the parties was incompetent to contract. It is also voidable when conditions imposed by Article 428 are present, that is, the contract stipulated by a person unable to distinguish right and wrong'.
- Article 428 CC, according to which, after providing for acts performed by a person unable to distinguish right and wrong, even though he or she is not declared incompetent at the time the acts were performed provides that 'contract voidability can only be declared if the other party's fraud results from the detriment that is derived or that could be derived to the person unable to distinguish right and wrong or from the contract quality or elsewhere'.

§6. Contributions

576. According to Article 2235 CC, a partner is required to make the contribution specified in the partnership agreement. If contributions are not specified, it is presumed that the partners are required to contribute in equal parts among themselves, that which is necessary in order to attain the scope of the partnership.

Thus, conferring contributions is a duty of the partner on behalf of the partnership and not towards the other partners, and the partnership can ask for damages deriving from breach of this duty.

Duty to perform contributions is not subject to limitation of actions until the partnership is in force. Time limits, in fact, start only after the partnership's expiry.

I. Object

577. Contributions in a società semplice can consist of cash, goods, or services, but they must be determined or it must be possible to determine them, or they can have as objects an enterprise since its beginning.

According to the prevailing opinion, contributions can all be services, with an initial lack of capital.

The CC does not indicate the object of the contributions, so it is held that they must be presumed in cash, unless the nature of the activity does not lead to a different conclusion or unless it is not expressly agreed in a different way by the partners themselves.

II. Modality and Warranty

578. Lacking a specific provision, rules related to the single kind of contribution contract should be applied (i.e., sale, in case of contribution related to goods conferred in property; and loan, in case of contributions related to goods conferred in use).

If these rules are contrary to the ones imposed by company law, the last one will apply.

579. Article 2254 CC provides that the warranty that the partner has to provide for goods conferred in property and all the risks related to it are regulated by the rules for the contract of sale. Risks for goods conferred in use rest on the conferring partner, and the warranty is regulated by the loan contract rules.

Article 2255 CC adds that the partner who confers a credit is liable in case of breach of his or her debtor within the limits indicated by Article 1267 CC in case of conventional assumption of a warranty.

Thus, three hypotheses have to be distinguished:

(1) Goods conferred in property: the contract of sale rules are applied, both the ones related to the implied condition as to title and the good defects.

(2) Goods conferred in use: the rules on the contract of loan are applicable, so that the risk of a fortuitous destruction of the goods conferred rests on the conferring partner.
(3) Credits contributions: in case of debtor insolvency, the partner is liable within the limits indicated in Article 1267 CC (providing that in case of assignment of credit, the assignor is liable within the limit of what he or she has received). The partner liability towards the partnership will only be limited to the value attributed by the partnership agreement to his or her contribution (plus, of course, expenses and interest).

III. Partner for Work and Skill

580. A partner for work and skill is obliged to provide for his or her own work activities, manual or intellectual, on behalf of the partnership.

If the partnership agreement does not provide for the entity of the partner for work and skill participation in profits and losses, the general presumption of equality does not apply, but on equitable basis the participation is determined by a judge.

581. A question arises in the case of the partnership being liquidated. Judges and authors hold that, unless otherwise agreed, the partner/worker is not entitled to be reimbursed for the value of his or her contribution, but only to participate in the distribution once the value contribution is given back to the other partners who conferred cash, goods, and credits. A minority jurisprudence holds that, in addition, the partner for work and skill is entitled to receive the value of what he or she conferred.

Article 2282 CC, providing for the principle that 'the partnership debts having been settled, surplus funds are destined to reimburse the contributions', does not distinguish contributions according to their object.

§7. Status of Partners

I. Partners' Rights

A. Right to Profits

582. A partner is entitled to receive periodically a share of the partnership profits.

Unless otherwise agreed, profits are shared once the statement of affairs is approved.

The shares of the partners in the profits and losses are presumed to be in proportion to their contributions. If the amount of the contributions is not specified in the contract, they are presumed to be equal. The share belonging to a partner who has contributed his own services is established by the court on an equitable basis, if it is not specified in the contract. If only the share of each partner in the profits is specified in the contract, it is presumed that participation in the losses is to be determined in the same proportion (Article 2295, No. 7 CC).

Departing from this criterion is possible within the limits, in any event, of the so-called leonina societas prohibition. In fact, Article 2265 CC provides that a stipulation by which one or more partners are excluded from any participation in the profits or losses is void.

As has already been said, agreements are void as well if, even if they do not expressly exclude profits and losses participation, actually prevent it, because, for example, the partner's right to profits is subject to a certain level of earnings achievement that is in actuality impossible to attain.

Nevertheless, shares preferred in the reimbursement in case of liquidation are admitted.

B. Right to Manage and Control the Partnership Management

583. A member is entitled to manage and perform all the acts necessary to attain the partnership purpose, unless otherwise agreed.

A partner not directly involved in the management is, in any event, entitled to control the partnership management.

More precisely, the partners who do not participate in the partnership management have the right to receive information from the management and to an accounting when the business for which the company was established has been completed. The partners have the right to an accounting of the management at the end of each year, unless a different time is established in the contract.

The right to information is realized either through an information request or through a documents consultation, and concerns not only the management's overall state of affairs, but also detailed information relating to single operations.

The right of information is recognized also for the partners' managers in case of disjoint management.

Partners not involved in the management are also entitled to receive a statement of affairs (normally, it is annual).

According to the prevailing opinion, in absence of an explicit rule, the statement can be approved by partners with a majority of the votes.

C. Right to the Share Reimbursement in Case of Partnership Liquidation

584. The right to the share reimbursement in case of parthership liquidation is recognized, once the partnership debts are paid, to the partners who made a capital contribution. Thus, according to the prevailing opinion, the right to reimbursement is not recognized for a partner for work and skill.

II. Partners' Duties and Prohibitions

585. Contribution is an essential and fundamental obligation for the partner's status, and therefore, in case of breach of that duty, the CC provides for the exclusion of the partner.

Lacking a different contractual provision, a partner can manage and represent the partnership, but he or she is not obliged to. Partners who perform management activities assume all the related duties and liability for the consequent obligations.

A member, only with the other members' consent, has the possibility of using goods that are part of the partnership's assets for purposes unrelated to those of the partnership.

III. Partners' Liability

A. *Imperfect Patrimonial Autonomy*

586. The società semplice has an imperfect patrimonial autonomy because, even though it is a proper autonomous subject with its own capacity of holding rights ('capacity to have rights') and exercising them ('capacity to exercise rights').

Members are liable for partnership obligations jointly and severally and without limits. More precisely, according to Article 2267 CC, partnership's creditors can exercise their rights on the partnership's assets. For the partnership, obligations are also liable personally and without limits all the members acting on behalf of the partnership and, unless otherwise agreed, the other members.

In the internal relationships between and among members, in any event, each member can assert the exclusive liability of the person abusing management power.

Members who have paid in have a right to recourse pro quota.

B. *Managers 'Partners' and Other Partners' Liability*

587. According to Article 2267 CC, there is a difference between these partners who acted on behalf of the partnership (managers) and the other partners. In fact, the assets of the former can be exhausted by the partnership creditor, and the joint and several liability rule is binding. The liability of the members who acted concerns all the partnership's obligations, and not only the ones deriving from the acts that they performed.

Non-managing members' liability instead can be excluded or reduced by an express clause in the partnership agreement.

Liability imposed by Article 2267 CC is considered a case of liability for someone else's debt, because concerning third persons, the principal debtor is the partnership, while the partners are liable for the partnership debts, with the exception of the beneficium escussionis (*see* section D).

C. *The Agreement Excluding Non-managing Members' Liability*

588. Article 2267 provides for the possibility that the partnership agreement excludes the liability or the only joint and several liability for those members who do not act on behalf of the partnership: the agreement shall be brought to the knowledge of third persons by the appropriate means; if not, the limitation of liability or the exclusion of the in solido obligation cannot be claimed against those who had no knowledge of it. In any event, the mere publication on the Registro delle imprese is not sufficient to make the agreement objectionable to third persons.

The agreement limiting some partners' liability is only possible for a società semplice, and not for the S.n.c. or the società in accomandita. In practice, this clause is very rare.

D. Beneficium Excussionis

589. Article 2268 CC provides that the partner requested to pay the partnership debts can ask for the right of discussion on the partnership's assets, indicating the goods on which the creditor can satisfy his or her right. The article so entitles the partner to the beneficium excussionis, on the condition that he or she indicates those goods that the creditors can easily liquidate.

E. The New Partner

590. According to Article 2269 CC, the new partner of an already established partnership is liable with the other members for partnership obligations incurred prior to his acquisition of the status of partner.

This principle is also valid in case of a new partner joining the others and, in case of a new partner substituting an associated precedent (in this case, the new member's liability is added to that of the outgoing member).

Considering Article 2268 CC provisions, the new member also can be excluded from liability if he or she is not involved in managing the partnership.

IV. Personal Creditors of the Partners

A. Imperfect Patrimonial Autonomy Consequences

591. Article 2270 CC provides that as long the partnership is in existence, a personal creditor of a partner can enforce his rights on the profits belonging to his debtor and take conservative measures with respect to the share to which the latter is entitled on liquidation. If the property of debtor is insufficient to satisfy his claim, the personal creditor can also demand liquidation of his debtor's share in the partnership at any time. The share shall be liquidated within three months from the petition, unless it has been decided to dissolve the partnership.

In a società semplice, the partners' personal creditors cannot bring an action against the partnership's assets, even within the limits of a partner-debtor's share.

It is not even possible to set off the credit with a partner and the partner's credit with the partnership.

A personal partner's creditor is, in fact, entitled to seize the partner's share of the partnership profits, and he or she is entitled to perform preventive measures on the share.

B. Right to the Liquidation of the Share

592. If it is demonstrated that the debtor has no goods that allow credit satisfaction, at any time of the partnership's life, the creditor can ask for the participation share upon liquidation (Article 2270, paragraph II, CC).

Goods cannot be considered insufficient just because of the difficulty or the slowness in the executive action (as in the case of an estate execution).

V. Partial Termination of the Status of Partner

593. The partnership contract can be terminated for all the members or for one or just some of the members.

There are three hypothesis in which there is a partial termination: (1) death of the partner; (2) exclusion; or (3) withdrawal.

A. Death of a Partner

594. Following Article 2284 CC, unless otherwise provided for in the partnership contract, in case of the death of one of the partners, the others shall settle the deceased's share with the heirs, unless they prefer to dissolve the partnership or to continue it with the heirs, and the latter consent.

595. There is a share liquidation whenever surviving partners do not want to be involved in the partnership with the heirs of the deceased partner or whenever the heirs themselves do not want to join the partnership. In this case, heirs are only entitled to an amount of money representing the share value. Share liquidation is made according to the general principles concerning liquidation of the single partner.

On the whole, payment of the partner's share, according to Article 2289, last paragraph, CC, has to take place within six months from the day on which the relationship ended.

Alternative to a share liquidation, surviving partners who do not want to continue the partnership with the heirs of the deceased partner can choose the anticipated dissolution of the partnership.

596. Partners can also choose to continue the partnership with the heirs; in this case, it is necessary that they agree.

In fact, by joining the partnership, the deceased partner's heirs undertake all the obligations concerning the contract of partnership.

The personal element in the partnerships prevailing, it is excluded, therefore, that, in case of a partner's death, the relationship automatically continues with his or her heirs.

Heirs of the partner become partners as a result of an inter vivos act and not iure successionis.

The agreement does not require the written form and can result from facta concludentia.

597. The partnership agreement may provide for a binding share liquidation or for dissolution, or provide for a continuation clause.

In the praxis, there are three kinds of continuation clauses: those that entitle the heirs to the continuation, those that impose their continuation obligation, and those that provide for an automatic continuation (the so-called succession clause).

A facultative continuation clause entitles the deceased partner's heirs to join the partnership. The clause binds the surviving partners, but not the partner's heirs, who can choose to have a share liquidation.

A binding continuation clause imposes the duty to continue the partnership on the heirs, so that if they do not intend to do so, they will be considered liable for damages suffered by the surviving partners.

A succession clause provides for the automatic entrance of the heirs into the partnership. Therefore, heirs accepting the estate of the deceased person automatically become partners. According to the prevailing authors and decisions, the first clause is valid, while the others are void because they are in conflict with the provisions concerning partnerships and succession.

B. Partner Withdrawal

598. Each partner can withdraw from the partnership when it is contracted for an indefinite time or for the entire life of one of the partners. He or she can also withdraw in the cases contemplated in the partnership agreement or for cause.

The CC distinguishes the hypothesis of an indefinite time partnership (or a lifetime partnership) from that in which the partnership is established for a determined period of time. It is considered an indefinite time partnership even if the partnership is established for a period of time greater than a normal human lifetime. In this case, the withdrawal does not require justification but shall be communicated to the other partners at least three months in advance.

In cases different from those considered in the previous paragraph, withdrawal is not free, but only possible in cases indicated in the partnership agreement or for cause. Decisions concerning the interpretation of the cause are strict. Cause exists only if there is a violation, attributable to another partner, of the contractual obligations or of the loyalty and care duties related to the fiduciary relationship typical of partnerships.

599. It is not required that there be a specific form for the withdrawal declaration, and it has effect when it is received by the partnership.

Withdrawal has an immediate effect in cases in which it is based on cause; otherwise, it produces its effects after three months from the communication, apart from the case in which partnership agreement prescribe a longer period of time.

As a consequence of withdrawal, the partnership has to proceed, within six months, to a share liquidation on behalf of the outgoing member.

If it is not otherwise provided for, the competition prohibition does not apply to the withdrawing partner, but the prohibition that the CC imposes does apply to the one who sells the enterprise (Article 2557 CC).

The articles of the partnership cannot completely avoid for the partner the possibility of withdrawal, even though they can discipline in different manners its exercise.

C. Partner Removal

600. The removal of a partner can take place for serious non-performance of obligations arising from the law or the partnership agreement, as well for interdiction, even if temporary, from public office. A partner who has contributed his or her services or the use of his or her goods to file partnership can also be removed for his or her supervening unfitness to perform such services or for the loss of goods resulting from causes not imputable to the managers.

Likewise, a member who, as his or her contribution, has agreed to transfer the ownership of something can be removed if that thing was lost before ownership was acquired by the partnership (Article 2286 CC).

601. According to Article 2288 CC, removal is automatic for a partner who becomes bankrupt and for a partner whose creditors, according to Article 2270 CC, obtained a share liquidation.

In the first case of automatic removal, the relationship ends from the day on which the bankruptcy of the partner has been judicially declared; in the second case, the relationship conclusion as to the removed partner starts only from the time at which the share is effectively liquidated.

602. In all other cases, removal does not occur automatically, the other partners' decision being required.

Deliberation and its related motivation are communicated to the removed partner, who, in the following thirty days, can bring an action against the partnership.

The court can suspend the removal and thereby verify the removal's legality and confirm or void it ex tunc.

D. Liquidation of a Partner's Share

603. As mentioned above, according to Article 2289 CC, in cases in which the partnership relation is terminated for a single partner, that partner or his or her heirs are entitled to receive an amount of money only representing his or her share value.

The member (or his or her heirs) therefore has a right of credit towards the partnership, and he or she can never obtain goods conferred in ownership on behalf of the partnership.

For goods conferred in use instead, restitution will be excluded only in the case in which they have been conferred for the duration of the partnership.

Share liquidation happens on the basis of the patrimonial assets of the partnership on the day on which the termination takes place. In determining the share value, the business's goodwill also must be considered.

This rule may be derogated by the partnership agreement.

§8. Amendments of the Partnership Agreement

604. Partnership agreement modifications can be objective or subjective.

The former concerns clauses related to the partnership's life, while the latter refers to the members' group composition.

605. According to the Article 2252 CC, partnership agreements can be modified only with the all members' consent, unless it is differently agreed.

The società semplice, like other partnerships, is based on the unanimity principle. From this principle derives that the partnership agreement can be modified only by unanimous consent of all the members, resulting from any act or behaviour that clearly shows all the members' will.

Members have the possibility of departing from the unanimity principle, providing for majority principle, of course, with unanimous consent.

Unless it is differently agreed, a majority must be considered per person and not related to shares. The unanimity principle also applies to the place of business modification.

606. The unanimity principle must also be respected when there is a members' modification. Without consent of all the other members, a member's share cannot be assigned to a third person.

The courts in this respect hold that, without a corresponding will of all the other members, a share assignment transfers to the third person the status of member, but this is only limited to the patrimonial rights related to that status.

A partnership agreement clause providing for a free assignment of the share is in any case valid.

§9. Dissolution and Liquidation

607. Regarding dissolution and liquidation, *see* Part III (Common Rules), Chapter 3.

Chapter 2. The Società in Nome Collettivo ('General Partnership')

§1. Definition and Sources

608. Rules concerning the S.n.c. govern the 'commercial activities' exercised in an associated form, if the parties did not adopt a different type provided in the CC, and it is characterized by the joint and several liability of all the partners. Commercial activities are defined in Article 2195 CC, providing a list of economic activities. Following the prevailing interpretation, the concept is extended to all business activities, excluding the agricultural one.

Therefore, in case of the constitution of a partnership intended for commercial activities, unless otherwise agreed, the organization and regulation are those established for S.n.c.s.

An S.n.c. can have as its purpose also non-commercial activities, provided that Article 2249 CC, paragraph II, establishes that the company having as its object the exercise of an activity different from commercial activities is regulated by rules concerning the società semplice, excepting a different choice of the partners.

609. An S.n.c. is governed by those articles of the CC specifically intended for it (Articles 2291 to Article 2312) and by provisions concerning the società semplice.

To those latter, in fact, Article 2293 refers in relation to anything that is not expressly and differently regulated by the section concerning S.n.c.s.

According to this reference, for example, it is possible to apply to the S.n.c. different rules of the section related to the società semplice as those concerning partnership agreement modification, management, liquidation, and causes of exclusion, as provided in Articles 2252, 2260, 2272, and 2287 CC.

Considering the reference in Article 2293 CC to rules governing the società semplice, unless specifically derogated, only rules pertaining to S.n.c.s will be illustrated in this chapter, referring for any other aspect to the preceding chapter.

The partnership agreement can establish, concerning the organization, rules that are different from the legal rules but cannot change, regarding third persons, the liability regime – without limits and joint and several – of the partners and, as we will see in the following chapters, a partner's liability in an S.n.c. is joint and several towards the other partners, but it is subsidiary towards the partnership. A further source is the partners' will as expressed in the partnership agreement.

§2. Formation and Registration

I. Written Form

610. An element that distinguishes the S.n.c. from the società semplice is the one related to the method of formation.

Article 2296 CC requires that, to record an S.n.c. in the Registro delle imprese, the partnership must be established by a deed drafted by a notary or in a written document with certified signatures.

Written form is not required ad probationem nor ad substantiam, but only as a condition to register the partnership in the Registro delle imprese, so that the S.n.c. orally established, without written form, is validly constituted, but cannot be registered in the Registro delle imprese.

II. Elements of the Partnership Agreement

611. The partnership agreement's fundamental elements are indicated in Article 2295 CC, from which it results that the partnership agreement shall contain: (a) the surname and the name, the place and the date of birth, the domicile, and the citizenship of the partners; (b) the business name; (c) the partners who have the power of management and representation of the partnership; (d) the legal address of the partnership and branch offices, if any; (e) the purpose of the partnership; (f) the contribution of each partner, the value attributed to such contributions, and the manner in which they were evaluated; (g) the services that the working partners are obliged to render; (h) the rules according to which profits are to be divided and the share of each partner in the profits and losses; and (i) the duration of the partnership.

III. Business Name

612. According to Article 2292 CC, for an S.n.c., the business name must indicate the name of one or more partners and the reference to the existence of a partnership.

The partnership can keep in its name the name of a deceased or retired partner, if the retired partner or the heirs of the deceased partner consent.

Non-observance of the above-mentioned article determines the partnership name irregularity and the impossibility of publishing and registering the partnership in the Registro delle imprese.

The expression name of one or more partners, used in Article 2292 CC, is to be considered as referring to the first name and surname of the partner, the second one not being sufficient, because of the confusion that it could create to third parties.

A business name can be transferred, and its variation is considered a partnership agreement modification that must be approved by all the partners.

IV. Registration and Irregular S.n.c.s

613. An S.n.c. has to be registered within thirty days from its formation. The registration is requested by the managers, the partners, or the notary public, if the partnership is established by a deed drafted by a notary.

The lack of registration of the partnership agreement, as explained above, makes an S.n.c. irregular but not invalid.

Article 2297 CC refers to irregular S.n.c.s, providing that until such time as the partnership is registered in the Registro delle imprese, the relation between the partnership and third persons are regulated by the provisions relating to the *società semplice*, with unlimited and joint liability of all the partners.

According to Article 2297 CC, paragraph II, if the partnership is not registered, it is presumed that each partner who acts for the partnership has the power of representation, even in judicial proceedings. Stipulations that grant representation to some of the partners only, or that limit the powers of representation, cannot be set up against third persons, unless it is provided that the latter had knowledge of them.

The fundamental element of an irregular partnership discipline, therefore, notwithstanding the reference to the società semplice, is the impossibility of limiting the unlimited and joint liability, also for the partners that do not have management and partnership representation.

Limits to the power of representation are instead possible.

§3. S.n.c.s and Società Semplice

614. Registering the partnership in the Registro delle imprese, a partnership gains some characteristics that make it different from the società semplice, in particular:

- according to Article 2298 CC, limits to the power of representation cannot be set up against third parties if they are not recorded in the Registro delle imprese or if it is not proved that they had knowledge of them;
- according to Article 2304 CC, partnership creditors, even though the partnership is in the process of liquidation, cannot claim payment from an individual partner, until after the discussion of the partnership's assets (whereas, for società semplice, partnership creditors can directly go after the partner's assets, even though the partner can object to the previous discussion of the partnership, indicating goods by which the creditors can easily satisfy their interests); and
- according to Article 2305 CC, a personal creditor of a partner, as long as the partnership is in existence, cannot claim liquidation of the share of the partner who is his or her debtor.

§4. Status of the Partners

I. Position Towards a Partnership's Creditors

A. Unlimited and Joint Liability

615. In an S.n.c. all the partners are jointly and without limits liable for the partnership's obligations. Compared to the società semplice, in any event, a contrary agreement does not have effect towards third parties (Article 2299 CC).

On the other hand, a partnership's creditors, even though the partnership is in the process of liquidation, cannot demand payment from the partners, except after the partnership's assets are exhausted; it is, therefore, clear that the partner's liability is subsidiary, with the possibility of discussing the assets only after the unsuccessful exhausting of the partnership's goods.

It is not, in any event, necessary to obtain the partnership's bankruptcy or to complete the executive action as long as the inadequacy of the partnership's assets to satisfy the credit is proved.

The beneficium excussionis applies only for the execution, and, therefore, the creditor can obtain a title empowering him or her to levy such execution on the partner before starting an executive action against the partnership.

The titre exécutoire allows the creditor to register a judicial mortgage towards the partner even before the partnership's discussing of assets.

If the unlimited liability partnership goes bankrupt, according with Article 147 of the Insolvency Law, also partners, even if they are legal persons with limited liability, are declared bankrupt. On the other hand, if an unlimited liability partner goes bankrupt, according with Article 149 of the Insolvency Law, the partnership is not declared bankrupt.

B. The Reduced Relevance of the Limiting Liability Agreement

616. An agreement limiting a partner's liability is valid but effective only among the partners, except for the leonina societas prohibition.

This aspect makes an S.n.c. different from the società semplice, in which an agreement limiting a partner's liability, under certain conditions, is enforceable also towards third parties.

Enforceability towards third parties concerns not only the liability limitation, but also, the exclusion of the joint obligation and the variation of the terms for the exercise of the partnership's creditors actions.

An S.n.c. partner who paid a partnership debt as a consequence of his or her unlimited and joint liability can bring an action against the partnership and against the other partners, to whom he or she can claim the liability limitation.

C. New Partner's Unlimited and Joint Liability

617. A new partner is liable without limits and jointly for the partnership obligations that arose before he or she entered the partnership, according to Article 2269 CC, to which Article 2293 CC refers, and according to which, one who joins an already established partnership is liable with the other members for the partnership obligations incurred prior to his or her acquisition of the status of partner. On the contrary the withdrawing partner is liable for obligation arisen before his discharge, as provided for in Article 2290 CC.

II Competition Prohibition

618. According to Article 2301 CC, a partner cannot exercise an activity in competition with that of the partnership for his or her own account or for the account of others without the consent of the partners. Nor can he or she participate in other competing partnerships as a partner with unlimited liability.

This rule can be derogated by the partners either by an express act or by facta concludentia; the other partners' consent can be presumed in case of the exercise of a competing activity (or in case of participation in a competing partnership) existing before the partnership relationship constitution and known by the other partners.

The prohibition of competition ceases when a cause of liquidation happens and the partnership is liquidated.

III. Particular Creditors of the Partner

A. Request of Share Liquidation

619. According to Article 2305 CC, as long as the partnership is in existence, a personal creditor of a partner cannot demand liquidation of the share of the partner who is his or her debtor.

The rule deviates, therefore, from the principle provided in paragraph II of Article 2270 CC for the società semplice.

It is also regarded as being impossible for the creditor to levy execution for the liquidation of the share that will be due to the partner, nevertheless even though it is possible for an attachment of assets on profits.

B. Share Liquidation in Case of Partnership Prorogation

620. In case of implied prorogation of the partnership duration or, in any event, in case of prorogation for an undetermined period of time, according to Article 2307 CC, a partner's creditor, whenever he or she proves the non-suitability of the partner's personal goods (other than the partnership's share) to satisfy his or her credit obligations, can request at any time the liquidation of his or her debtor's share.

On the other hand, in case of prorogation for a determined period of time, express and resulting from the enterprises register by means of a modification of the partnership agreement, the creditor is entitled to judicially object to it within three months of the registration.

§5. Management and Power of Representation

I. Management

621. Management and power of representation in S.n.c.s are governed by rules concerning the società semplice.

The power to manage a partnership, unless otherwise agreed, is due to each partner liable without limits.

Linked to the power to manage an S.n.c. are some duties of the managers, who must:

- request the Registro delle imprese, within thirty days, to register modifications of the partnership agreement and to register all the other facts related to the partnership that must be registered (Article 2300 CC);
- keep the account books prescribed by Article 2214 CC (Article 2302 CC); and
- indicate in acts and business correspondence the place of business and the Registro delle imprese in which the partnership is registered.

Apart from limitations of the partnership agreement or of the power of attorney, a manager can perform all the acts comprised in the partnership purpose, including those that are considered as acts of disposition.

As for the società semplice, according to judicial decisions, only the partners can be managers. According to some authors, instead, it could be possible that all the partners decide on entrusting a third person with the management without losing the qualification of managing partner.

II. Power of Representation

622. Representation, also before courts, of an S.n.c,, unless otherwise agreed, is due to each partner liable without limits.

Therefore, the managing partner who represents the partnership can perform all the acts that are part of the partnership's object.

Unlike the società semplice, those who represent an S.n.c. must be expressly indicated in the partnership agreement.

Furthermore, limitations of their powers, apart from those resulting from the partnership agreement or the power of attorney, according to Article 2298 CC, last part, do not have effects towards third parties if they are not registered in the Registro delle imprese or if it is proved that they had knowledge of them.

Limitations of the power of representation cannot make impossible the management and cannot deprive the general character of representation, reducing it to individual acts.

§6. Amendments of the Partnership Agreement

I. Unanimity Principle

623. To amend a partnership agreement, Article 2252 CC, concerning the società semplice and also valid relating to S.n.c.s according to the general reference in Article 2293 CC, requires consent of all the partners, unless otherwise provided.

II. Accomplishments

624. The partnership agreement amendments must be publicized according to Article 2300 CC, from which results that managers shall apply to the Registro delle imprese within thirty days for the registration of the partnership agreement amendments and of other information concerning the partnership, whose registration is mandatory.

If the partnership agreement amendments are based on a partners' resolution, a certified copy of it shall be filed.

Until they are registered, amendments to the partnership agreement cannot be used against third parties, unless it is proved that they had knowledge of them.

III. Principal Amendments

625. Among possible amendments of the partnership agreement, the most relevant concern the partnership's duration and the partnership capital.

A. Partnership Prorogation

626. A prorogation of the partnership duration can be decided by means of a partners' resolution or can be derived by *de facto* conduct.

In the first case, the prorogation resolution must be registered in the Registro delle imprese, and the expiry date must be determined; in the second case, the partnership's activities *de facto* continue after the previous expiry date and the prorogation does not have a determined duration.

In this case, each partner can always withdraw from the partnership, giving notice of this, and a particular creditor of the partner can require his or her debtor share liquidation.

B. Partnership Capital

627. The CC does not mention the partnership capital among those elements that the partnership agreement shall indicate. In any event, the partnership agreement, as already indicated, shall specify each partner contribution and their value; the global value in this way drawn by partnership agreement is the partnership capital, which is subject to two fundamental rules protecting its destination for the attainment of the partnership's purposes and the partnership's creditors' satisfaction.

1. Limits to the Profits Distribution

628. Only profits effectively gained can be distributed among the partners (Article 2300 CC).

As capital integrity protection is also provided, if the capital is reduced because of losses caused by management, profits coming from subsequent conduct cannot be distributed until the assets have been brought back to the contributions' value or until the capital indicated in the partnership agreement has been reduced.

2. Capital Reduction

629. The capital value can be reduced owing to losses or because the partners consider its value as exceeding the partnership's needs.

In the first case, reduction consists of a formal modification of the partnership agreement and does not imply restitution on behalf of the partners; in the second case, capital reduction also implies restitution on behalf of the partners (or cancellation of the contributions' debt) and, therefore, reduces the asset value on which the partnership creditors can act in execution.

For this reason, resolutions implying an asset's reduction cannot be executed before three months from its recording in the Registro delle imprese. During this period, the partnership creditors can stop the reduction with a petition addressed to the Tribunal of the place of the partnership. The capital reduction can be, in any case, performed if the partnership provides suitable securities of performance.

§7. Dissolution and Liquidation

630. Regarding dissolution and liquidation, *see* Part III (Common Rules), Chapter 3.

Chapter 3. The Società in Accomandita Semplice ('Limited Partnership')

§1. Definition and Sources

631. According to Article 2313, paragraph I, CC, in the società in accomandita semplice, general partners (soci accomandatari) are jointly and without limits liable for partnership obligations, and special partners (soci accomandanti) are only liable to the extent of the share contributed by them. The shares of participation of the partners cannot be represented as share certificates.

Therefore, in an S.a.s, beside those who manage the partnership and are liable for managing it (accomandatari), there are partners (accomandanti) with limited powers and risks, only financing the partnership activity without managing it (the so-called managing prohibition).

632. As for the S.n.c.s, the S.a.s discipline also results, as well as from the rules in the CC dedicated to them, also from the reference to rules established for the società semplice.

Moreover, Article 2315 CC establishes that the provisions relating to an S.n.c. apply also to the S.a.s.s, insofar as they are compatible.

Some supplements and modifications are, in any event, imposed by the presence in the S.a.s. of different kinds of partners.

§2. Formation and Registration

I. Formalities

633. Rules established for S.n.c.s also apply to S.a.s.s.

Article 2316 CC specifies that the partnership agreement shall indicate the partners accomandatari (general partners) and the partners accomandanti (special partners).

Lack of this indication makes the partnership agreement irregular, and the partnership cannot be registered in the Registro delle imprese.

The partnership contract, within thirty days, shall be deposited so as to register and to publish it in the Registro delle imprese.

II. Registration and Irregular S.A.S.

634. As happens for an S.n.c., in case of lack of registration, a partnership will be irregular, and it will be governed by rules established for the società semplice.

Article 2317 CC, paragraph I, establishes that until the partnership is registered in the Registro delle imprese, Article 2297 CC applies to relationships between the partnership and third persons.

Nevertheless, with respect to partnership obligations, the partners accomandanti are only liable to the extent of their shares, unless they have participated in the partnership transactions.

From this principle, it is derived that personal creditors of the partners can ask for the share liquidation of their debtors and that the partnership creditors can ask directly for exhausting the partners, also without previously exhausting the partnership's assets.

The only difference between an irregular S.a.s. and a non-registered S.n.c. consists of the fact that the accomandante continues to have a liability limited to the promised contribution, if he or she does not interfere with the partnership's management.

III. Business Name

635. In a business name, at least the name of one of the accomandatari and the S.a.s. must necessarily be indicated.

Article 2314 CC, paragraph II, establishes that the accomandante, who consents that his or her name is included in the business name, is liable with respect to third persons without limits and jointly with the accomandatari for partnership obligations.

This extension of liability does not imply that the accomandante acquire qualification and powers of the accomandatario, but only operate towards third persons who are partnership creditors.

Again, the aforementioned article, in the first paragraph, referring to Article 2292 CC, allows the keeping in the business name the name of a retired or deceased partner if his or her heirs consent.

§3. Partners Accomandatari ('General Partners') and Partners Accomandanti ('Special Partners')

636. An S.a.s. has two kinds of partners: the accomandatari, with a joint and without limits liability for partnership obligations and with a position corresponding to that of S.n.c. partners, and the accomandanti, only bound to perform the promised contributions.

According to prevailing authors, it is not possible for the accomandante to be a partner for work and skill.

A partner accomandante is in an intermediate position between that of a partner in a business corporation (società di capitali) and that of a non-manager partner in an S.n.c.

It is held that, in doubtful cases, because of a lack of legislation casus omissus, in the discipline relating to the accomandante, the position of the latter is close to that of a non-manager partner in an S.n.c.

For the accomandatari, it is forbidden to perform competing activities compared to the ones performed by for an S.a.s. *Accomandanti* partner does not suffer any limitation on carrying out competing activities.

§4. Management and Power of Representation

I. Position of the Partners Accomandatari

637. According to Article 2318 CC, paragraph II, partnership management pertains only to the accomandatari, but it is not specified if such role is exercised individually or jointly.

In practice, if is not provided otherwise, there is a disjoined management system.

In this case, decisions of a single manager can be opposed by any other partner entitled to manage the partnership, and in relation to the objection, the accomandatari majority will decide.

According to paragraph II of Article 2318 CC, establishing that the partnership management can only be conferred upon partners accomandatari, it is derived that is possible to provide in the partnership agreement that some accomandatari may not be managers.

Therefore, the partnership agreement can confer managing power individually or jointly on behalf of all the managers, on behalf of their majority, or on behalf of some of them.

In those last cases, the partners accomandatari not managers are entitled to control the management as provided for in the Article 2261 CC.

II. Position of the Partners Accomandanti

A. Management Prohibition

638. Article 2320 CC provides that, the accomandanti can neither perform acts of management, nor conclude transactions in the name of the partnership, unless they received a special power of attorney for individual transactions.

A partner accomandante infringing upon this prohibition assumes an unlimited and joint liability to partnership obligations.

In case of such a prohibition infringement, moreover, the partner accomodante can be excluded from the partnership.

Prohibition concerns all the acts of management, both internal and external, as well as simple negotiations.

Some authors consider as forbidden not all the acts that can affect the partnership's management, but only those with a direct disposition of the partnership's assets and those that, for relevance and frequency, reveal the acquisition for the partner accomandante of a power conflicting with relationships between the partners.

B. *Faculties of the Partners Accomandanti*

639. Article 2320 CC, paragraph II, provides that partners accomandanti can, however, render their services under the supervision of the managers, and, if the articles of the partnership permit it, they can give authorization and advice for specified transactions and perform acts of inspection and supervision.

According to the last paragraph of the aforementioned article, moreover, the partners accomandanti are entitled to receive the annual accounts and loss statement, and to verify their accuracy by consulting the books and other partnership documents.

From all the examined dispositions, therefore, the results are that the partners accomandanti have the possibility of the following:

- concluding transactions in the name of the partnership as auxiliary to the managers, as long as they have a special power of attorney for one or more specified acts;
- performing their material or intellectual work, under managers' direction;
- giving authorization or advice;
- receiving annual accounts and the profit and loss account; and
- consulting books of accounts and partnership documents.

§5. Partnership Participation Transfer

I. Accomandanti's Share Transfer

640. Because of the fact that towards them there is no relevance of intuitu personae, Article 2322 CC establishes that the share of participation of a partner accomandante is transferable at death. According to paragraph II of the same Article 2322 CC, unless the partnership agreement provides otherwise, the share of an accomandante partner can be assigned and such assignment is effective against the partnership subject to the consent of the partners representing a majority of the capital.

The partnership agreement can prohibit the transfer or can allow it without limitations, or can also recognize a pre-emptive right on behalf of the other partners.

II. Accomandatari's Share Transfer

641. The transfer on a share of an accomandatario is considered like an amendment to the partnership agreement, and the discipline of Article 2252 CC is applied. Therefore the consent of all the other partners, accomandanti and accomandatari, is required; furthermore, if the transfer is due to the death of the accomandatario, its heirs have to express their agreement.

§6. Dissolution and Liquidation

642. Under Article 2323 CC, the partnership is dissolved when one category of partner (*accomandanti or accomandatari*) extinguishes. In such case, it is possible, within six months, to restore the composition of the partnership by admitting new partners of the extinguished category. If during this period there are no accomandatari, it is up to the accomandanti to appoint a director, who is not qualified as accomandatario, and who is entitled only to ordinary acts of disposition.

643. Regarding dissolution and liquidation, *see* Part III (Common Rules), Chapter 3.

Part III. Common Rules

Chapter 1. Groups of Companies

§1. Purposes of the Law Regulating Groups of Companies

644. Organizations made up of several companies provide a useful tool for coordinating the activity of different, formally autonomous legal entities. This is, therefore, a fairly frequent phenomenon in Italy, where the economic system is characterized by large numbers of small and medium-sized enterprises. The group is based on the control and on the unitary direction among member companies. It entails that the strategic policies governing the activity of each member company are established on the basis of an economic framework encompassing the group as a whole as opposed to the single company. Because of this, there is a risk that the aims pursued by the group and its management policies might conflict with those of the single company or a member of the group. In such a situation, especially in the short term, a company that is forced to comply with the group's management policies may suffer negative consequences on its economic results or assets. Being a member of a group can, however, bring benefits (financial benefits, economies of scale, and benefits in terms of image and market penetration), which the company might not be able to enjoy on its own. This is why the efficient management of undertakings has to be encouraged by, inter alia, exploiting the instrument of groups of companies, while at the same time averting or discouraging operations that might give rise to unjustified harm to one or more group members and, therefore, to their shareholders (above all, minority shareholders, who cannot be involved when it comes to adopting the group's strategic decisions), employees, and creditors.

645. Following the 2003 company law reform, a set of rules regulating groups of companies was added to Article 2497 and following CC. Having defined the characteristics of a group with legal relevance, the rules contain numerous safeguards against the risks of abuse by group-leading companies. These safeguards cover such matters as disclosure obligations, rules on economic liability, obligations on how the decisions of subsidiaries are adopted, and the right of minority shareholders of subsidiaries to withdraw. These provisions apply to any companies or other types of entities that control companies of any kind, as well as to controlled companies. Some requirements are, however, established in the framework of rules regulating S.p.a.s, which is the type of company most frequently found in groups.

§2. MANAGEMENT AND COORDINATION OF COMPANIES

I. Control and Dominant Influence over Companies

646. The rules on groups apply to companies or entities (private or public, but the State is excluded) that are engaged in the activities of 'managing and coordinating companies'. The CC gives no specific indication of how a company or entity may 'manage and coordinate companies'. However, in accordance with Article 2497sexies CC, the management and coordination of companies is assumed to arise in situations: (i) in which there is an obligation to consolidate the financial balance sheets (*see* Part I, Chapter 1, §7, III, F), and (ii) when the company is controlled pursuant to Article 2359 CC. Under this latter provision, a company is held as being controlled if the holding company has the majority of votes or sufficient votes to exercise a dominant influence at a shareholders' meeting or else exercises a dominant influence through contracts. The holding company does not necessarily have to own the shares or securities, but it is sufficient for it to be in a position to either vote or orient voting, even through trustees or subsidiaries. A dominant influence may also be wielded in the form of contracts inherent in the subsidiary's business (e.g., sale concessions, patent or trademark licenses, and franchising), if and when the contract also grants powers to the governing bodies (e.g., the prior approval of directors).

647. The hypotheses set out in Article 2497sexies are, however, mere assumptions of 'management and coordination', which means that evidence to the contrary may be provided. For instance, a large conglomerate holding company, which, pursuant to Article 2359 CC, controls many companies or sub-holding companies operating in different sectors, could seek to demonstrate that it does not actually manage and coordinate all the subsidiaries. In practice, it is very difficult to provide such evidence. Besides, the provision does not rule out the possibility of a company being engaged in management and coordination even in different ways from those described in Articles 2497*sexies* and 2497septies CC.

II. Contracts and Provisions of the Articles of Association

648. By tradition, the Italian legal system has no such thing as the Beherrschungsvertrag typical of the German system. Any contracts or clauses in the by-laws envisaging that a company is subject to the management policies of another company ought to be considered null and void. In spite of this, Article 2497septies CC envisages the hypothesis of a company also being managed and coordinated on the basis of contractual clauses or provisions of by-laws. The purpose of the current system is, in fact, not to prevent the coordinated management of the operating policies of several companies, but rather, to avert and discourage operations imposed by the group without considering the interests of the subsidiary and its stakeholders. Therefore, even in cases in which group management and coordination are based on contractual clauses or provisions of by-laws, the rules contained in Article 2497 and following CC will apply.

§3. Disclosure Requirements Concerning Groups

649. Article 2497bis CC lays down specific disclosure requirements for companies under the management and coordination of another company. The name of the group's leading company or entity must be indicated both in mail and in a special section of the Registro delle imprese. The duty to issue notices updating the information thus publicized rests with the directors, who will account for any harm caused to shareholders or third parties in the event of non-compliance.

650. The accounting documents must also indicate that a situation of management and coordination exists between companies. In addition to the eventual need for consolidated financial balance sheets, the supplementary note attached to the companies' financial balance sheets must contain a summary of the financial balance sheets of the company that manages and coordinates the group. Furthermore, the directors' report must provide explicit information on dealings with both the group-leading company and with other companies under joint management and coordination, and explain what this has meant for the company.

§4. Intragroup Financing

651. One of the most frequent functions of groups of companies is to rationalize financial management and to make loans or render guarantees between group's companies. To be more specific, it is not infrequent for the group-leading company or for other controlled companies to make intragroup loans, with or without interest, partly to limit contributions to subsidiaries. For this reason, the same rules as those envisaged for shareholder financing in S.r.l.s (*see* Part I, Chapter 2, §4) apply to financing either by the group-leading company or between companies coming under its management and coordination. Therefore, if the financing is granted at a time when, as a result of the type of business carried on by the company, there is an excessive imbalance between the company's debt and its asset capital (undercapitalization), or in cases in which a capital contribution would be reasonable, the repayment of shareholder financing is subject to the prior reimbursement of other creditors, and, if this occurs the year before the company filed for bankruptcy, it will be repaid (Article 2467 CC). Nevertheless, under Article 182*quater*, paragraph III, of the Insovency Law, if the financing made by a shareholder is granted according to procedures of *Concordato Preventivo* or *Accordo di Ristrutturazione* (a sort of Company Voluntary Arrangement), then the financing is preferred up to the 80% of the total sum financed, and up to the 100% when the financing company has become shareholder by virtue of the procedures.

§5. Decisions Made by Controlled Companies

652. Safeguarding minority shareholders and third-party creditors of companies belonging to the group implies verifying the grounds for operations carried out by the management bodies. Therefore, in cases in which an operation is influenced by group relations, the management bodies have a duty to justify the reasons for the decision in writing and explain the interests that have been considered (Article 2497*ter* CC). This information must then be provided to both shareholders and third parties in the directors' report on operations.

653. In the holding company, the chief executive officers must inform the board of the most important decisions passed by subsidiaries. Control over the operations set in place by controlled companies is provided either by the collegio sindacale, by the supervisory board (companies adopting the two-tier system) or by all the members of the board (companies adopting one-tier system), by exchanging information with the subsidiary's governing bodies.

§6. Right of Withdrawal

654. A further instrument safeguarding the minority shareholder in a subsidiary is provided by the right of withdrawal (Article 2497*quater* CC). In the framework of group operations withdrawal is possible in three hypotheses.

First of all, the shareholder is entitled to withdraw if there are changes in the group-leading company (e.g., conversion or a change in the corporate purpose) such as to significantly impact on the subsidiary's economic prospects.

Second, the shareholder may withdraw if he or she successfully sues the company responsible for management and coordination for damages because of the breaching of principles of sound management.

Third, withdrawal is possible when the company either enters or leaves a group, as these are situations in which the risk perspective changes. Exceptions to this are provided by listed companies and by situations in which a takeover bid has been launched, because in such cases, the shareholder in any case has an opportunity to disinvest.

In all cases, the withdrawal procedure and the manner in which the price is determined and paid are covered by the general rules on withdrawal by shareholders (Part I, Chapter 1, §8).

§7. Liability of the Holding Company

655. A company that manages and coordinates other companies is not on this account automatically liable for obligations assumed by its subsidiaries. The group holding will, however, be liable in cases in which the management and coordination is in conflict with the principles of sound management of the subsidiaries or harms them purely in the interests of the group leader or third parties. Such liability therefore hinges on the damage caused to shareholders or creditors of the subsidiary in consequence of directives on management issued by the holding company. The damage caused to the shareholders arises as a result of the loss of value or loss of profitability of shareholdings in the company, while the harm caused to creditors arises as a result of the reduction in the company's assets.

656. Whether or not any such damage exists will, however, have to be viewed in the light of any negative and positive effects arising from the operation and from the company's participation in the group. It is, in fact possible that the group leader may issue instructions that give rise to a worsening of the economic results and the assets framework in the short term, which is later offset by direct or even indirect benefits resulting from membership of the group. Evaluating the damage/benefit ratio and the compensatory benefits is a highly complex process. In particular, the compensatory benefits are not easy to quantify and arise at a different time compared to the damage. A time lapse, therefore, needs to be established within which the evaluation should be made, and the annual interval of the financial balance sheets imposes a time limit within which the benefits have to be considered, even if they have already accrued.

657. If damage has been caused but not been offset, any person who has taken part in the operation that has caused the damage will account jointly and severally with the group-leading company. In particular, liability will rest with the directors of the subsidiary who allowed, or failed to prevent, the operation, not consistent with the interests of the company that they were managing. Any person (other shareholders, other group companies, or third parties) who has benefited from the harmful operation will also be liable.

658. The lawsuit can only be filed by the shareholders or by third parties against the holding company if they have not been indemnified by the subsidiary. It has to be noticed that, being a tortious liability, during the trial it is up to the claimant to prove that the suffered damage was caused by a conduct of the holding company. In cases of bankruptcy, insolvency, or administration procedures envisaged by the law, the lawsuit will be filed by the body charged with the procedure.

659. Any justified suspicion of operations carried out to the detriment of subsidiaries may also justify adopting preventive measures. In accordance with Article 2409 CC, such operations may, in fact, be reported to the court by shareholders of the holding company who hold the percentages of capital indicated in this article, as indeed by the control and supervisory bodies, or even by the public prosecutor, in cases of companies that resort to the capital market, pursuant to Article 2325bis CC (*see* Part I, Chapter 1, §6, II C).

§8. Subsidiaries and Branches of Foreign Companies

I. Subsidiaries

660. The rules described above on the management and coordination of companies, disclosures regarding groups, intragroup financing, decisions passed by subsidiaries, the right of withdrawal, and the liability of the holding company also apply to the Italian subsidiaries of foreign companies.

661. As far as types, organization, special operations, and liquidation are concerned, there are no significant differences compared to other companies subject to Italian law. The incorporation procedure has no special characteristics, apart from the need to submit to the notary public official translations of the articles of association, the Chamber of Commerce's certificate regarding the foreign company, and the resolutions passed by the foreign company authorizing the setting up of the new Italian company and appointing the legal representative to sign the articles of association.

II. Branches

662. *See* Introduction §5, IV.

Chapter 2. Conversion, Merger, and Division

§1. Conversion

I. Notion and Forms of Conversion

663. The rules on conversion apply to all types of companies and also to conversions of società di capitali into entities of a different legal nature established by law and, likewise, of such entities into società di capitali. The Italian system provides numerous possibilities for modifying the organizational structures of entities without having to dissolve and reincorporate them. The goal is to make it simpler to adapt organizations carrying out economic activities to requirements emerging in the course of their activities, avoiding the costs and formalities of dissolution and reincorporation.

664. The main aim of the conversion rules is to safeguard: (i) those participating in the original company or entity when it comes to adopting decisions and attributing rights, obligations, and duties in the converted entity; and (ii) creditors and third parties generally, in view of the fact that the different model of organization could jeopardize rights that they have already accrued or rights in any way associated with dealings with the entity. It is evident, though, that to some extent, the requirements and, therefore, the rules are common irrespective of the type of conversion, whereas to some extent, they also will depend on the nature of the original entity or of the entity resulting from the conversion. The next paragraph will, therefore, focus on common rules, whereas the paragraphs that follow will focus on the rules applying to the various types of conversion.

II. Registration, Efficacy, and Invalidity

665. All forms of conversion are subject to a number of common rules concerning prerequisites, advertising, efficacy, and invalidity.

666. Companies are allowed to convert themselves during the time of their activity. Nevertheless, conversion is also possible if the company is in the process of being liquidated, because in this case – provided that no arrangements have been made to distribute the assets – the shareholders can still make the company operational once again. If the company is subject to judicial or administrative procedures, we have to distinguish between two situations: (1) situations in which the aim of the procedure is to control the administration, in which case conversion is possible; and (2) situations in which the aim of the procedure is to distribute the assets to creditors and shareholders, in which case conversion is not possible as it is incompatible with such an aim.

667. The form of the deed of conversion will clearly vary according to the type of company, but in all cases, the fact that it has to be registered at the Registro delle imprese implies that the deed must be in writing. Furthermore, if the company resulting from the conversion is an S.p.a., an S.A.p.A, or an S.r.l., a notary deed is required containing all the elements required for incorporating such companies.

668. According to the legal doctrine, the conversion neither entails the setting up of a new subject, nor the succession from the original company to the company resulting from the conversion. Under a legal point of view, there is a perfect continuity and the legal person is the same both before and after the conversion: only the legal qualification, and the consequent status, changes.

669. To ensure that third parties are duly informed, the conversion requires two forms of publication. Rules on disclosure obligations will apply to the respective types of companies or entities that give rise to, or result from, the conversion. The conversion will only take effect once these advertising obligations have been met in full.

670. In view of the important consequences the conversion implies for all the stakeholders, the eventual invalidity of the deeds of the converted entity will not deprive the conversion of effect, and the conversion cannot be withdrawn after it has been registered at the Registro delle imprese.

However, both the members of the converted entity and third parties can claim compensation for any damage they prove they have suffered because of a conversion procedure contra legem.

III. Homogeneous Conversion

A. Conversion of a Partnership into a Corporation

671. Partnerships can be converted by the favourable votes of the majority of the partners. The majority is not calculated based on a headcount, but according to the quota of profits due to each partner. The partnership agreement may however, envisage a unanimous vote for the conversion. In any case, a partner who has not voted in favour of the conversion may withdraw from the company.

672. If the partnership is converted into a società di capitali (so-called 'evolutional conversion'), it must first be ascertained that the value of the assets is equal to at least the minimum capital envisaged by law for the selected type of company. To this end, the estimate of the company's assets and liabilities must be made by an expert, just as with contributions of assets on setting up a joint-stock company. Furthermore, the directors will be responsible for the valuation and, within 180 days of the conversion's registration at the Registro delle imprese, they must verify the fairness of the value attached to the converted company's assets. Alternatively the simplified procedure provided for by Article 2343*ter* CC for the contribution in kind of S.p.A. can be adopted (*see* Chapter 1, §3, II). If the new company is an S.p.A. or an S.A.p.a. and the value of the assets is less than four-fifths of the estimated value, the directors must reduce the capital. Generally speaking, in view of the fact that the estimate refers to the total value of the converted company's assets, unless the shareholders decide differently, there is no possibility for an individual shareholder to supplement the assets with further contributions or withdraw from the company.

673. The shares or quotas in the new company are allocated in proportion to the quotas of profits due to the shareholders in the converted company. Partners for work and skill are also entitled to a stake in the capital proportional to their quota of participation in the new company's profits. If there is no clear indication in the by-laws, and if the shareholders fail to reach agreement, the quota of participation in the capital will be established by the court on an equitable basis.

674. A conversion from a partnership into a corporation radically changes the liability of the partners and, therefore, the guarantee covering creditors. The partners will, however, continue to be unlimitedly liable for the company's debts prior to the conversion, in accordance with the provisions of the by-laws or the rules applying to the converted company and with Article 2500*quinquies* CC, unless the creditors approve the conversion. The creditors' consent will be tacitly assumed unless they notify their disapproval of the conversion within sixty days of notification of the conversion resolution, which must be made in such a way that there is confirmation of receipt.

B. Conversion of a Corporation into a Partnership

675. The conversion of a joint-stock company into a partnership must be resolved by a shareholders' meeting. The directors must deposit at the Registro dell imprese, and make available to shareholders, a report illustrating the reasons and effects of the conversion at least thirty days before the shareholders' meeting. The meeting will deliberate on the majorities envisaged – either in the by-laws or by law – for amending the by-laws. In all events, the shareholders are entitled to withdraw.

676. If a joint-stock company is converted into a partnership (so-called 'regressive conversion'), the favourable votes are required of the shareholders who assume unlimited liability in the company resulting from the conversion. This is necessary in view of the fact that such shareholders are unlimitedly liable also for obligations assumed by the company prior to the conversion.

677. In all events, the shareholders are entitled to a quota of participation in the new company proportional to their quota of capital in the converted company.

IV. Heterogeneous Conversion

678. The heterogeneous conversion, provided for by Articles 2500octies and 2500novies CC regulates the conversion of società di capitali into a consortium, consortium company (società consortile[30]), joint ownership of enterprise, incorporated association (associazione riconosciuta), or foundation. Likewise, only the conversion of these latter entities into società di capitali is envisaged.

679. In the first case, the rules envisaged for converting limited liability companies into partnerships will apply, apart from the matters explained below.

A resolution passed by a shareholders' meeting must be adopted by a favourable vote of at least two-thirds, and this percentage cannot be reduced by the by-laws.

30. The *consorzio* (consortium) is an agreement under which two or more undertakings set up a joint organization to regulate or carry out certain phases of their activity. The società consortile (consortium company) is either a partnership or a società di capitali, which has as its corporate purpose that of a consortium.

However, the favourable votes are required of the shareholders who assume unlimited liability for the obligations of the new entity and of the converted company.

The effects of the conversion, as far as the new entity is concerned, are regulated by the rules applying to each type. In particular, resolutions passed by a company converted into a foundation are subject to the rules regulating the deed of constitution of a foundation, which, unlike the other hypotheses, does not allocate a quota in the new entity to the shareholders of the converted company.

680. The manner of approval of a conversion into a società di capitali of a consortium, consortium company, joint ownership of enterprise, incorporated association, or foundation will follow different rules, according to the converted entity.

First of all, for associations and foundations set up before the Company Law Reform came into force (1 January 2004), when there was no such possibility of conversion, heterogeneous conversion is not permitted if it means using securities formed by funds of third parties contributed to the entity for purposes other than those of the company resulting from the conversion. If the entity has benefited from tax relief, conversion is permitted provided that the relevant taxes are paid. In no event may bank foundations set up before 2004 be converted into società di capitali.

Second, in cases for which it is permitted, the conversion must be approved, and the shareholdings are allocated, following different rules applying to each converted entity, as specified in Article 2500octies CC.

681. In all cases of heterogeneous conversion, the radical modification of the entity's nature calls for special safeguards for creditors. To this end, Article 2500novies CC envisages that the conversion will take effect only if the creditors have been paid, if they have agreed to the conversion, or if the period of time within which they are allowed to object has elapsed. Creditors may oppose the conversion within sixty days of its publication at the Registro delle imprese. If the court considers that there is a risk, it may make the effects of the conversion subject to the issuing of credit guarantees.

§2. Merger

I. Notion and Forms of Merger

682. When two or more companies merge, they unite to form a single entity. The merger may lead either to the incorporation of a new company or to the incorporation of one or more companies into a preexisting company (merger by incorporation). In economic terms, the merger gives rise to a concentration between undertakings, which usually leads to dimensional growth and, thanks to this, rationalization and economies of scale. Mergers may be between independent companies, between companies belonging to the same group, between a holding company and a subsidiary, or between companies that are linked by capital ownership. In such cases, the merger gives rise to an administrative simplification, as well as a reduction in the costs of the governing bodies, and it also facilitates direct control over activities previously managed by subsidiaries. Moreover, the merger may alter the balances between and among shareholders, the purposes pursued, and the assets with respect to which creditors can act. For this reason, the rules on mergers are designed to safeguard both minority shareholders and third parties.

683. The rules on mergers are contained mainly in Articles 2501–2505quater CC, which have been adjusted to the requirements of the third and sixth EC directive, and more recently the discipline of the CC has been amended by Legislative Decree of 22 June 2012, n. 123, implementing Directive 2009/109/CE. For listed companies, certain requirements regarding disclosures to shareholders and the market are laid down in the TUF. Finally, implementing the European Parliament and Council Directive 2005/56/EC, Legislative Decree No. 108 of 30 May 2008 established a number of requirements for cross-border mergers of limited liability companies within the EC.

684. Merging is permitted at any stage of the life of a company, even during liquidation. In cases of companies in which the capital is split into shares, however, merging is not permitted once the distribution of assets has commenced (Articles 2501, paragraph II, and 2505quater CC).

685. Merging is also possible between different types of companies and entities, within the limits contemplated by conversion rules. In such cases, both the rules on mergers and the rules on conversion will apply.

686. A special case of merger arises when one of the companies has contracted debts to acquire control of the other and, as a result of the merger, the assets of the latter either guarantee, or are the source of repayment, of such debts. Such operations are known as leveraged buy-outs. These are based on the financing capacity offered by the activities of the target company with respect to guaranteeing debts usually contracted with banks so as to acquire the entire capital or a controlling quota of the target company. Often, the company involved in such a merger by incorporation is set up ad hoc. This hypothesis has been explicitly regulated by Article 2501*bis* CC, and special safeguards have been envisaged in view of the serious risk it involves for the financial equilibrium of the company resulting from the merger. Therefore, in addition to the requirements laid down for other mergers, the draft terms of merger must provide information on the plans to finance the debt of the company resulting from the merger. In addition to this, the directors' report must explain the reasons justifying the operation and present an economic and financial plan specifying both the sources of financing and the objectives. This information must be confirmed in the experts' report on the draft terms of merger (*see* the next paragraph) and in a report by the auditing company of either the target company or the purchasing company. Finally, the simplified procedures generally envisaged for fully owned or 95%-controlled subsidiaries do not apply.

II. Draft Terms of the Merger

687. The first step of the merger procedure is for the management or administrative bodies of each of the merging companies to prepare common draft terms of merger. Article 2501ter CC provides an indication of the minimum contents of the draft terms of merger. These are:

– the form, name, and registered office of the merging companies;

- the by-laws of the company resulting from the merger;
- the ratio applicable to the exchange of securities or shares representing the company and the amount of any cash payment (not more than 10%, if companies issuing securities, that is S.p.As., S.A.p.As., or Soc. Coop. per Azioni, take part);
- the terms of allotment of securities or shares of the company resulting from the merger;
- the date from which the holding of such securities or shares representing the company capital will entitle the holders to share in profits;
- the date from which the transactions of the merging companies will be treated for accounting purposes as being those of the company resulting from the cross-border merger (the date may be prior to the date of merger);
- the rights conferred by the company resulting from the merger on shareholders enjoying special rights or on holders of securities other than shares representing the company capital, or the measures proposed concerning them; and
- any special advantages granted to members of the administrative or management bodies of the merging companies.

Together with the draft terms of merger, the management bodies must draw up a financial balance sheet for the companies taking part in the merger based on a date not preceding the date on which the draft terms are deposited by more than 180 days. After the amendments introduced by Legislative Decree No. 123 of 2012, it is now possible to disclose to the public the merger by a notice published on the website of the company. The financial balance sheet must be drawn up in accordance with the rules applying to the balance sheet for the financial year and may indeed be replaced by the latest balance sheet if it has been deposited within the aforementioned deadline. The aim of this requirement is to provide shareholders and third parties with updated data on the companies taking part in the merger. In particular, on the basis of this document, third parties can evaluate the benefits and risks produced by the merger by acquiring information on the assets, credits, and debts of each company involved. Nevertheless, such document is not required if the balance sheet for the financial year has been approved no more than six months before the merger. Furthermore, the shareholders of the merging companies, as well as the holders of financial instruments, may vote unanimously to renounce the balance sheet, as indicated by Article 2501quater CC.

688. Furthermore, the management bodies must prepare a joint report explaining two basic aspects: (i) the economic aims of the merger, the procedure, and its legal effects; and (ii) how the ratio applicable to the exchange of securities or shares has been established and any difficulties that have been encountered. The ratio does not necessarily have to be established in proportion to the assets of the companies taking part in the merger. In this respect, the directors exercise their technical discretion, ultimately establishing a joint evaluation criterion. All the shareholders of the merging companies, as well as the holders of financial instruments, may vote to renounce the report of the directors.

689. The fairness of the method and criteria adopted by the directors in establishing the ratio applicable to the exchange of securities or shares must be examined in the reports prepared by one or more experts appointed by each merging company. If all the shareholders agree, the experts' report is not necessary.

The report must also highlight whether and how different criteria have been adopted in valuing the companies, explaining the resulting values, and any valuation difficulties.

The experts must be registered on the Registry of Accounting Auditors (*see* Part I, Chapter 1, §7, IV), and, to safeguard the shareholders and creditors of each merging company, they must be appointed autonomously by each one. The companies may, however, ask the court of the place where the company resulting from the merger will be registered to appoint one or more experts in the interest of all the merging companies. The court appointment is a guarantee of the experts' independence and is always required in cases in which an S.p.A. or an S.A.p.A. takes part, or results from, the merger. As far as listed companies are concerned, only auditing companies supervised by CONSOB can be appointed.

The experts will be liable for any damage caused by an erroneous valuation of the ratio applicable to the exchange of securities or shares vis-à-vis the companies, shareholders, and third parties, and they will be subject to penal consequences in cases of gross negligence (Article 2501sexies CC and Article 64 of the Code of Civil Procedure).

The shareholders of the merging companies, as well as the holders of financial instruments, may vote unanimously to renounce the report of the expert.

690. To make them public, the draft terms of merger must be deposited at the Registro delle imprese, and published on each company's website, at least thirty days prior to the shareholders' meeting called to approve them (fifteen days for companies not issuing securities). If all the shareholders agree, this deadline may be shortened.

691. In cases of merger by incorporation of fully owned companies, the draft terms of merger will not contain the third, fourth and fifth element set out above, and neither the directors' report nor the experts' report are required.

692. In cases of merger by incorporation of 90%-controlled companies, on the other hand, only the experts' report will not be necessary if the controlling company grants the other shareholders the right to sell their securities or shares at a price established according to the rules on withdrawal.

III. Merger Resolution

693. In cases of limited liability companies, the resolution approving the merger must be passed by a shareholders' meeting, which will deliberate on the majorities envisaged for amending the by-laws. In cases of partnerships, on the other hand, unless the partnership agreements provide differently, the resolution must be passed by the favourable votes of the majority of partners, which is calculated according to the participation in profits criterion. In such companies, though, any partners who are not in favour of the merger will be entitled to withdraw.

In any case, in view of the fact that the draft terms of merger are the result of an agreement between or among the management bodies of several companies, the shareholders can only make amendments that do not affect the rights of shareholders or third parties.

694. If the by-laws so envisage, the merger by incorporation of a fully controlled company may be resolved by the subsidiary's management body, although this is without prejudice to the obligation to deposit the draft terms of merger at the Registro delle imprese and deposit them on the company's website, together with the other documents specified above and the last three balance sheets (Article 2505 CC). In this case, however, shareholders holding at least 5% of the incorporating company's capital may ask for the decision to be passed by a shareholders' meeting.

Similarly, the by-laws of the incorporating company may envisage that the merger by incorporation of a company controlled by at least 90% should be resolved by the management body (Article 2505bis CC). Furthermore, deposit formalities are simplified for the incorporating company, as envisaged in the previous case, and a decision passed by a shareholders' meeting may be required by shareholders holding at least 5% of the incorporating company's capital.

695. The minutes of the shareholders' meeting or of the directors' resolution approving the merger must be drawn up by a notary. The same notary must ensure that the resolution and the new by-laws comply with the law. The resolution, together with the documents and reports already deposited by the merging companies, must be deposited at the Registro delle imprese within thirty days. The rules on amending the articles of association will apply (Article 2346 CC, *see* Part I, Chapter 1, §8).

IV. Creditors' Rights

696. To safeguard creditors' rights, the merger will not take immediate effect. The merger will take effect only once all those who have a credit preceding registration at the Registro delle imprese have been paid or have agreed to the merger, after an amount equivalent to that of the credits has been paid into a bank, or else on the expiry of the deadline within which the creditors may object. Depositing this amount at the bank will, however, not be necessary if the report by the auditing company appointed pursuant to Article 2501sexies CC certifies that the guarantee is not necessary in view of the company's assets and its financial situation.

697. Creditors may object to the merger within sixty days of it being advertised at the Registro delle imprese (thirty days for companies not issuing securities), or on each company's website (Article 2503 CC). If the court considers that there is a risk, it may make the effects of the merger subject to the issuing of credit guarantees.

698. A special safeguard is envisaged for bondholders. According to Article 2503*bis* CC, holders of convertible bonds prior to the merger must be given an offer to convert the bonds into shares. This offer must be advertised in the Official Gazette at least ninety days prior to the shareholders' meeting called to approve the merger, allowing at least thirty days for acceptance. If the bondholders do not agree to the conversion, the company resulting from the merger must maintain unaltered the rights they enjoyed prior to the merger, except in cases in which the meeting of bondholders has agreed to a change.

Holders of nonconvertible bonds may, on the other hand, file an objection on the same terms and conditions as the other creditors, in cases in which the meeting of bondholders has not agreed to the merger.

V. Registration, Efficacy, and Invalidity

699. The merger procedure closes with the deed of merger, which must be stipulated in the form of a notary deed. The deed of merger must be registered at the Registro delle imprese for all companies taking part in the merger. The merger will take effect only after the last registration. The registration of the company resulting from the merger must be the last one, in such a way as to ensure that companies already expired as a result of the merger do not even temporarily appear in the Registro delle imprese.

700. Following the merger, any receivables and payables of the merged companies will be transferred to the company resulting from the merger. Without the creditors' consent, though, the shareholders who are unlimitedly liable in the companies merging with a joint-stock company will continue to be unlimitedly liable for obligations arising prior to the merger.

Furthermore, neither the company resulting from the merger nor the incorporating company may allocate to the shareholders shares or quotas in place of the shares or quotas of the companies taking part in the merger previously held, even by means of trustees, by such companies or by the incorporating company.

701. The merger will take effect from the time of the last registration, unless a later date is established in the merger by incorporation. However, the deed of merger may establish an earlier date from which: (i) the securities or shares attribute the right to profits, or (ii) the operations of the merged companies are ascribed to the company resulting from the merger.

702. For accounting purposes, the merger ought not to alter the valuation of the assets, in view of the fact that the activity continues. It is, therefore, envisaged that the assets and liabilities must be entered in the first post-merger balance sheet at the value indicated by the merged companies at the time of the merger. However, in cases of merger by incorporation, these values may be modified in such a way that, on aggregate, they coincide with the value of the investment appearing in the last balance sheet of the incorporating company prior to the merger.

703. As for cases of conversion and division, the Italian legal system provides comprehensive safeguards for shareholders and third parties in the course of the merger procedure, but offers no possibility for them to obtain a decision restoring the situation to the *status quo ante* once the merger has taken effect. Once the deed of merger has been registered, the court cannot, in fact, be asked to annul the merger or declare it null and void. The only action that can be taken is to claim damages as a result of a merger contra legem.

VI. Cross-Border Mergers

704. Legislative Decree No. 108 of 30 May 2008, which incorporated into law Directive 2005/56 EC, lays down requirements concerning cross-border mergers between Italian società di capitali companies and joint-stock companies that have their registered office, head office, or main centre of activity in another EC Member State.[31]

To establish the applicable law, the decree provides that Italian rules on mergers should apply to merging Italian companies and that, if there is a conflict of laws, the law of the Member State to which the company resulting from the merger belongs will apply.

705. Here are some of the main characteristics of cross-border mergers:

- the right to withdraw of the shareholders of the merging Italian companies;
- wider-ranging contents of the draft terms of merger; the obligation to publish in the Official Gazette at least thirty days before the shareholders' meeting;
- information on the merging companies including, inter alia, the name, registered office, governing law, register, and registration number, and how the rights of creditors and minority shareholders are exercised;
- the possibility of the experts appointed to draw up the report pursuant to Article 2501sexies CC being appointed for all the merging companies – at their joint request – by the judicial or administrative authority competent in pursuance of the law applicable to one of the merging companies or to the company resulting from the merger;
- the issuing by a notary of a certificate attesting the regular fulfilment by the Italian company of deeds and formalities preliminary to the merger's implementation;
- verification of the legitimacy of implementing the cross-border merger – within thirty days of receiving the preliminary certificates and the resolutions approving the joint draft terms of the cross-border merger of the merging companies – by the authority designated by each state (in Italy, this is the notary);
- depositing – within thirty days of the aforementioned verification – the deed of merger, the deed certifying the verification, and the preliminary certificates at the respective Registro delle imprese, with the ensuing efficacy of the merger;
- in cases in which one or more of the merging companies have at least 500 employees and envisage the participation of the employees' representatives in management, the participation of employees in the Italian company resulting from the merger established either on the basis of trade union agreements or, if there are no such agreements, by applying the rules contemplated in such cases in the European Company Regulation.

31. The decree will apply to companies of another type or to companies that do not have the quoted requisites only if this is contemplated by the laws applicable to all the merging companies of other EC Member States.

§3. Division

I. Notion and Forms of Division

706. Through division, a company allocates to two or more companies all or part of its assets, and the shareholders of the first company become shareholders of the companies to which the assets are allocated. If the entire assets are allocated, the divided company will close without being liquidated (total division). If, on the other hand, only some of the assets are allocated, the divided company will continue its activity and the division may be for the benefit of just one company (partial division). The division may allocate the assets either to new companies set up as a result of the division or to preexisting companies.

707. Division is regulated by Articles 2506 to 2506quater CC. Since many aspects of division are, however, covered by the rules on mergers, reference can be made to Part III, Chapter 2, §2.

708. A division differs from a contribution of assets, in that when there is a contribution, the company making the contribution is a shareholder of the company that receives the assets, but when there is a division, the shareholders of the former become shareholders of the latter.

709. Generally speaking, the division allocates to the shareholders shares or quotas in the companies resulting from the division in proportion to the shares or quotas they hold in the divided company. However, it may be established for the division: (i) to attribute to the shareholders different percentages in the beneficiary companies; or even (ii) to exclude certain shareholders from participating in one or more beneficiary companies of the division and allocate shares or quotas of the divided company to them. In the first case, the draft terms of division must give shareholders who do not approve of the division the right to sell their shares to other shareholders, specified in the draft terms, at the price they would be entitled to receive in the event of withdrawal. In the second case, the consent of all the shareholders is required.

710. A cash adjustment of a maximum of 10% of the nominal value of the shares or quotas may be allocated to the shareholders.

711. Division satisfies various economic and organizational requirements. It can be used in cases of partially transferring activities between companies with different owners, but it can also be used for internally reorganizing an undertaking in cases in which it is necessary to separate a part of the activity, differentiating the powers and duties inherent in its management by setting up a company ad hoc. Division can also be an instrument for settling disagreements between shareholders, by separating groups of shareholders in conflict into two or more different companies.

712. Division is permitted for all types of companies, but it is not possible during liquidation once the distribution of assets has commenced.

II. Draft Terms of Division

713. Like the merger procedure, the division procedure consists of four stages: (i) drawing up and approving the draft terms of division; (ii) advertising; (iii) opposition by creditors, if any; and (iv) the deed of division with its registration at the Registro delle imprese.

714. The management bodies of the companies involved in the division have to prepare joint draft terms of division with the same contents envisaged for mergers, together with some important additions.

First and foremost, the draft terms of division must specify which assets and liabilities of the divided company are to be allocated to each of the beneficiary companies. This is extremely important because, if an asset is not allocated, it will remain the property of the divided company in the case of a partial division, whereas, in the case of a total division, it will be allocated to the beneficiary companies in proportion to the quota of assets allocated to them. The quota of assets allocated to the beneficiary companies is based on the ratio applicable to the exchange of securities or shares. As far as liabilities are concerned, if they are not allocated to a company, the divided company and the beneficiary companies will be jointly and severally liable. The liability of the beneficiary companies will, however, be limited to the value of the allocated assets.

Second, the draft terms of division must specify the criteria adopted in allocating to shareholders the shares or quotas of the beneficiary companies and the shareholder rights described above in the event of a non-proportional allocation. If there is an adjustment in cash, this must also be specified.

715. As with the draft terms of merger, the draft terms of division must be deposited at the Registro delle imprese or published on the company's website, at least thirty days prior to the shareholders' meeting called to approve them.

716. The management bodies of the companies taking part must also prepare the financial balance sheets of the companies and the reports on the division, in the same way as for mergers. More specifically, the reports must explain the criteria applied in distributing shares and quotas, as well as the quotas of assets allocated to the beneficiary companies and the quota remaining with the divided company.

An experts' report is required for divisions, too, following the same rules as for mergers. The experts' report will, however, not be necessary in cases in which the division is implemented for the benefit of two or more new companies and the shares or quotas are allocated on a proportional basis, as in this case there is no risk of any harm to the shareholders.

With the consent of all the shareholders and of any other persons entitled to vote in the companies taking part in the division, the management bodies may be authorized not to present the reports and documents referred to above.

717. Approving the draft terms of division and advertising the resolution are regulated in the same way as for mergers. Articles 2505 and 2505bis CC also apply in cases of operations between fully owned or 90%-owned companies.

718. Under Article 2506*ter* CC when the division is executed through a capital increase with contributions in kind or credits, the report provided by Article 2343 CC is required (*see* Part I, §3, II).

III. Creditors' Rights

719. The division modifies the assets and liabilities of the divided company and the beneficiary companies and thus affects the risk of both creditors and bondholders. To safeguard them, the rules on merging contained in Articles 2503 and 2503bis CC on the right of opposition and on the right to convert convertible bonds (Article 2506ter CC) also apply to divisions.

IV. Registration, Efficacy, and Invalidity

720. Just like the merger procedure, the division procedure closes with the deed of division being drawn up by a notary and registered at the Registro delle imprese for all the companies taking part in the division. The division will only take effect after the last registration. In cases of divisions implemented for the benefit of preexisting companies, it may be envisaged that the division will come into effect at a later date. As far as participating in profits and balance sheets are concerned, earlier dates may even apply, as with mergers. The merger rules on balance sheet valuations also apply.

721. As it has been already pointed out, the transferee company will account for the liabilities of the divided company. As far as any unallocated liabilities are concerned, though, the divided company and the beneficiary companies will be jointly and severally liable to the extent of the assets respectively allocated to them. Furthermore, all the beneficiary companies (within the aforementioned limits) and the divided company (to the extent of the assets left with it) will be jointly and severally liable for any debts of the divided company that are not satisfied by the companies to which they are allocated. Therefore, in concrete terms, for the purposes of liability towards third parties, the division will only be completely effective with respect to obligations that have arisen after the division.

722. As with conversions and mergers, a division cannot be declared invalid once it has been registered at the Registro delle imprese. If the division has prejudiced the rights of shareholders or third parties, the only action they can take is to claim compensation for the damage they have suffered.

Chapter 3. Dissolution and Liquidation

§1. Dissolution of Corporations

I. Grounds

723. According to Article 2484 CC, corporate initiative, as defined in the Articles of association, will lapse as a result of: (i) a series of grounds specifically contemplated by law; and (ii) a series of factors internal and external to the company's business.

724. Limited liability companies are dissolved for two main reasons that may affect their internal activity, that is:

(1) in cases in which the company's period of duration has elapsed, if this is envisaged in the articles of association. The duration may, however, be extended prior to expiry under a resolution passed by an extraordinary meeting of shareholders; and
(2) in cases in which the corporate purpose has been achieved or has become impossible to achieve, whether materially or legally (even though, in this latter case, in abstract terms, an amendment of the statutory purpose would be possible).

725. Limited liability companies may also be dissolved because of a series of external factors, that is:

(a) because of the fact that it is impossible for a shareholders' meeting to function, or its ongoing inactivity is brought about by the failure to reach the quorums required to deliberate, or else, more simply, because of problems of inertia;
(b) because of the capital being reduced to below the legal minimum (barring resolutions to increase or balance the share capital);
(c) in cases in which it is no longer possible to meet the cost of paying off a withdrawing shareholder by reducing the share capital, provided that any third party's objection is upheld;
(d) under a resolution of an extraordinary meeting of shareholders (this is the case of so-called early dissolution);
(e) for any other reasons contemplated by the by-laws;
(f) for reasons compulsorily envisaged by law (as, for instance, in the hypotheses of nullity of joint-stock companies mentioned in Article 2332 of the CC).

726. For S.A.p.A.s., two typical grounds for dissolution are contemplated, that is:

(1) in cases in which all the directors lapse from office, unless within 180 days arrangements have been made not just to replace them, but also to make new appointments;
(2) in cases in which the shares of all the general partners lapse and, as a result of this, the administrative body is unable to function for over 180 consecutive days.

II. Consequences

727. The effects of the dissolution come about on the date of registration at the Registro delle imprese of the balance sheet in which the directors ascertain the reason, whereas in cases of dissolution following a resolution passed by an extraordinary meeting of shareholders, the effects of the dissolution will come about on the date when the relevant resolution is registered.

Prior to publicizing the dissolution, the effective existence of the grounds for dissolution must be verified. This obligation is incumbent on the company's directors.

The directors are, in fact, under an obligation to verify the reason for dissolution 'without delay' and register a statement on them at the Registro delle imprese, under penalty of their having to account both personally and jointly for any damage suffered by the company, the shareholders, the company's creditors, and third parties. In practice this is one of the most common case of directors' liability, in case of bankruptcy, because the directors are held liable for the losses suffered by the company after the moment in which the ground for dissolution arose, if the directors did not file a dissolution statement.

728. With effect from the public declaration of dissolution, the directors maintain the power to manage the company, but only to preserve the integrity and value of the corporate assets in accordance with the provisions of Article 2486 CC.

'New' company operations aimed at achieving the corporate purpose are only possible if the inherent level of risk is compatible with the aim of preserving the share capital.

Here, too, the directors will be personally and jointly liable.

729. Once the directors have ascertained one of the grounds for dissolution, this is followed by the next phase of liquidating the company, even if the dissolution has not yet been legally publicized.

The shareholders' meeting will deliberate on how the liquidation should take place, unless this has already been regulated by the by-laws.

If the directors do not call a shareholders' meeting, the sindaci – or, in extreme cases, the court – will do so in their place.

If the shareholders' meeting is not formed or if it fails to resolve liquidating the company, the court will make arrangements to open the liquidation phase and appoint the liquidators.

III. Liquidation Procedure

A. Liquidators

730. A shareholders' meeting in extraordinary session will appoint one or more liquidators, establishing their remuneration, the manner in which they make decisions, their representative power, and the criteria according to which they have to carry out each liquidation operation.

The shareholders' meeting may in any case revoke this appointment, while individual shareholders and sindaci (as well as the public prosecutor) have the power to ask the court to remove the liquidators for cause.

Although Article 2489 CC declares that the liquidators must carry out 'any acts that may be useful with respect to liquidating the company', a shareholders' meeting may explicitly and concretely guide the activities of the liquidators towards: (i) selling the entire company (or some of its units); (ii) selling individual assets and/or rights; or (iii) acting in such a way as to preserve, as far as possible, the value of the enterprise. To this end, following the recommendations of the shareholders' meeting, the liquidators may proceed to provisionally run the activities of the company or one of its units.

Both the supervisory body and the shareholders' meeting will continue to perform their regular functions even during the liquidation phase. For this reason, the company's state of liquidation may be revoked in cases in which resolutions incompatible with the state of liquidation are passed or when they are such as to lead to the elimination of the ground for dissolution: such a situation will arise, for instance, if the share capital is restored to the legal minimum.

The liquidators must arrange for their appointment to be published at the Registro delle imprese and for the directors to provide them with the company books and the balance sheet of accounts, accompanied by a report covering the period subsequent to the latest approved financial balance sheets.

The aim of the activities of the liquidators is to sell, on the best possible conditions, the property forming the company's assets (always bearing in mind the instructions issued by a shareholders' meeting), after which they will proceed to pay the company's debts with the proceeds.

Furthermore, the liquidators may call on the shareholders to pay in full contributions that have only been partially paid to the company, and they may also make immediate arrangements to distribute the company's assets in such a way as to meet all the company's obligations. In this latter case, however, advance payments on the result of the liquidation can only be distributed if, in the financial balance sheets, there are sums available to pay the company's creditors in full.

B. Liquidation of Assets

731. During the liquidation phase, the liquidators must submit to a shareholders' meeting (or to the members, if the company being liquidated is an S.r.l.) the balance sheets for the results of each financial year in the course of which the liquidation continues.

These are veritable financial balance sheets, as envisaged in Article 2423 and following CC, but with the special characteristics required by the liquidation, especially in terms of the criteria applied to evaluate assets. In particular, the first financial balance sheets after the start of the procedure must provide an illustration of the new valuation criteria adopted, bearing in mind the imminent sale of the assets.

The directors must take account of these particular characteristics both in their report about operations and in the supplementary note. However, once the resumption of the company's business is authorized, the manner in which the accounts are portrayed must conform to that envisaged for the ordinary financial balance sheets.

C. The Final Balance Sheet

732. Once the assets have been liquidated and the company's debts paid, the liquidators must draw up the final liquidation balance sheet. In this balance sheet, the assets will show the value produced as a result of selling assets and any further sums of money available, whereas the liabilities will indicate the sums due to each shareholder or for each share.

The balance sheet must be deposited at the Registro delle imprese together with a report by the sindaci and the chief accountant in charge of the audit. Any shareholder may lodge a complaint within ninety days of the aforementioned registration. Any complaints are then examined together in such a way as to establish a single judgment.

IV. Distribution of Assets

733. If no complaint has been lodged within the deadline or in cases in which complaints are rejected, the final liquidation balance sheet becomes unchallengeable, and the liquidators may consider themselves definitively discharged vis-à-vis the shareholders, apart from their obligations inherent in the distribution of the sums due.

Furthermore, legal doctrine considers that the payment receipt issued by the shareholders, without reservation, upon payment of the last distribution instalment, implicitly means that the liquidation balance sheet has been definitively approved, even if the deadline for lodging a complaint has not yet elapsed.

V. Cancellation and Dissolution

734. Once the assets have been distributed, the liquidators deposit the company books at the Registro delle imprese, requesting the cancellation of the company, which can be held to have been definitively closed, in accordance with Articles 2494 and 2495 CC.

The cancellation may take place not only at the end of the liquidation procedure that we have just described, but also in cases in which, for more than three consecutive years, the financial balance sheet of the company under liquidation is not deposited, in such case the cancellation will follow *ex officio*, in accordance with Article 2490, final paragraph, CC.

735. In both cases, registration of the cancellation closes the company with effect *ex nunc*. When the company closes, however, not all of the legal dealings it has entered into are automatically extinguished, or any proceedings stemming from its 'past life' be barred. Indeed, in accordance with Article 2495 CC, without prejudice to the company's closure, even after its cancellation, any company creditors who have not been satisfied may enforce their credits against both the shareholders (to the extent of distribution collected by them, on the basis of the final liquidation balance sheet) and the liquidators (in cases in which the failure to pay was a result of an omission on their part).

Furthermore, within one year of cancellation, any unsatisfied creditors may act to have the company adjudicated bankrupt if the legal requisites arise. The eventual bankruptcy will not resuscitate the company, but simply serve to settle any outstanding matters. Similarly, any property that reaches the company after its discontinuance is held to be the common property of the shareholders.

§2. Dissolution of Partnerships

I. Grounds

736. The grounds for dissolving società semplice, which also apply to S.n.c. and S.a.s. are envisaged in Article 2272 CC. They are as follows:

(a) the expiry of the deadline established in the partnership agreement (but, if the partners continue their activities, the company will be held as having been indefinitely extended);
(b) the achievement of (or impossibility to achieve) the corporate purpose;
(c) the will of all the partners, unless the partnership agreement envisages a majority resolution for this;
(d) the lapsing of the plurality of partners, unless this is re-established within six months;
(e) any other possible grounds specifically envisaged in the partnership agreement;
(f) insolvency (for S.n.c.s. and S.a.s.s. that carry out commercial activities);
(g) a measure passed by governmental authority ordering the compulsory administrative liquidation of the company.

737. Furthermore, an S.a.s. will be dissolved in cases in which only accomandatari partners or only accomandanti partners remain, unless the category of partners that has lapsed from office is re-established within six months (Article 2323 CC).

Unlike for limited liability companies, the reduction or total loss of assets does not constitute a ground for dissolution, because partnerships do not have to have a minimum capital or equivalent assets.

II. Consequences

738. Should a ground for dissolution arise, the company automatically moves into a state of liquidation. This situation must be properly represented to third parties in documents and in correspondence, and also at the Registro delle imprese, if the company is registered.

For partnerships, too, the principle applies according to which, even if a ground for dissolution has arisen, the company is not immediately closed. Instead, a liquidation phase starts, the aim of which is to satisfy company creditors and distribute any residual assets.

In accordance with Article 2274 CC, the directors will remain in office, but their powers of management will be limited to 'urgent business' only. By analogy with the rules applying to limited liability companies, the concept of urgent business is held to include any operations aimed at preserving the value of corporate assets.

In the case of S.a.s., if the accomandatari partners lapse from office, the accomandanti partners must appoint, among themselves, a provisional director to deal with day-to-day business. The provisional director does not become an accomandatario and is, therefore, not unlimitedly liable for the company's obligations.

III. Liquidation Procedure

A. Liquidators

739. The liquidators must be appointed, and may be removed, by the partners' unanimous decision, unless otherwise envisaged in the partners agreement. At the request of one or more partners, the president of the court may appoint the liquidators in cases in which the partners fail to reach agreement, and he or she may remove them on just grounds. The partners may, however, decide unanimously to resume the company's day-to-day management by removing the grounds for dissolution.

The directors must deliver the corporate assets and documents to the liquidators, as well as the latest balance sheet. Together, the directors and liquidators must then draw up an inventory, which will serve as a balance sheet opening the liquidation and represent the company's balance sheet of assets and liabilities.

The liquidators are entrusted with the company's legal representation, in addition to the task of settling any legal dealings associated with the company's business. They may, therefore, do anything required for the liquidation, including selling the corporate assets en bloc and concluding transactions.

Finally, the liquidators may ask individual partners to pay any contributions still due (if the company's funds are insufficient to satisfy the creditors), and indeed further sums of money, within the limits of their respective responsibilities, and in proportion to each partner's participation in the company's losses.

In no event may the liquidators undertake new company operations (if they do, they will be liable both jointly and personally), and they cannot even partially distribute the corporate assets to the partners, unless company creditors have first been satisfied.

As far as anything else is concerned, the rules applying to liquidators make reference to the rules applying to directors.

B. *Liquidation of Assets*

740. On this point, please refer to the explanation provided in paragraph 1 for limited liability companies.

C. *The Final Balance Sheet*

741. As far as closing the liquidation procedure is concerned, the CC makes no provision for società semplice, but for S.n.c.s. and S.a.s.s., the liquidators have to draw up the final liquidation balance sheet and the distribution plan. The balance sheet and the distribution plan are sent by registered letter to the partners and will be held as having been approved unless the partners challenge them in court within two months from the notification. Once the balance sheet is approved, this formally closes the procedure, and the liquidators have no further obligations vis-à-vis the partners, since they are not obliged to proceed to distribute the assets too.

IV. Distribution of Assets

742. Once the company's debts have been extinguished and both the balance sheet and the distribution plan have been settled, the positive balance resulting from the liquidation goes towards reimbursing the nominal value of the contributions. Any surpluses, as envisaged in Article 2282 CC, may be distributed to the partners in proportion to each partner's participation in earnings. Contributions are reimbursed in cash or, if agreed, in kind, in accordance with the rules for dividing shared assets. In cases of contributions of services, the shareholder is simply released from the obligation.

V. Cancellation and Dissolution

743. The regular closing of the liquidation procedure gives rise to the closing of a società semplice and of an irregular S.n.c. In the event of procedural flaws or failure to formally close the liquidation procedure, the company is considered as still existing.

S.n.c.s. and S.a.s.s., on the other hand, are held as having been closed, once the final liquidation balance sheet has been approved and they have been cancelled from the register, activity that must be carried out at the liquidators' request. The company documents and accounting entries must then be delivered to a person designated by the majority of shareholders, who must preserve them for ten years. This is the standard time after which rights are time-barred (Article 2312 CC).

Once cancelled from the register, the aforementioned companies close, but this does not mean that unsatisfied creditors are left unprotected. They may in fact act against; (i) partners who are unlimitedly liable for the company's debts; and (ii) the liquidators, if the failure to pay is attributable to the liquidators' fraudulent or wilful misconduct.

As far as S.a.s.s. are concerned, unsatisfied creditors may act against the special partners (*accomandanti*) only to the extent of the amounts such partners have received as their quota of liquidation.

Finally, if the legal requisites arise, creditors of partnerships that carry out commercial activities may ask for the company to be adjudicated bankrupt within one year of the company being cancelled from the Registro delle imprese.

Chapter 4. Criminal Rules

§1. Interests Protected by Criminal Provisions

744. Both the 1882 Code of Commerce and the 1942 CC included a series of criminal provisions designed to protect the basic values by which company law is inspired.

On the occasion of the Company Law Reform embodied in Law No. 366 of 3 October 2001, Parliament authorized the Government to issue one or more legislative decrees containing criminal provisions, the main contents of which had already been outlined in the law.

Under Legislative Decree No. 61 of 11 April 2002, changes were thus made to the articles of the CC containing criminal provisions in corporate matters. This came even before the company law rules were changed by Legislative Decree No. 6 of 2003. Finally, minor amendments have been introduced by recent legislation, both in the CC and in TUF.

Upon a brief analysis of the current legislative texts (Articles 2621–2642 CC), it emerges that the main legal interests protected by these criminal provisions are as follows:

(a) the transparency of corporate information, that is, institutionally ensuring the reliability and truthfulness of sources of economic information;
(b) the effectiveness (and integrity) of the company's share capital and its non-available reserves, especially in the interest of third-party creditors;
(c) the corporate assets, which have to be protected against eventual abuses on the part of the directors;
(d) the sound functioning of the governing bodies;
(e) general interests inherent in the regular and sound functioning of the market.

It is clear, however, that the current system of criminal offences in corporate matters is inspired by the desire: (i) to generally reduce the hypotheses of offence; and (ii) to make the charging of offences subject in many cases to the existence of the particular interest of the persons concerned, purely from a property perspective.

§2. The Main Offences

I. Protection of the Transparency of Corporate Information

745. Article 2621 CC envisages the offence of 'false company announcements', which consists of two alternative types of conduct: (i) expounding material facts that do not correspond to the truth; and (ii) omitting to provide information required by law.[32] The persons who can be punished for such an offence are the directors, general managers, senior executives entrusted with drawing up accounting documents, sindaci, and liquidators. For the offence to take shape and its perpetrator to be punished, however, a series of further requisites have to be met. These are: (i) there must be the aim of gaining an unjust profit for oneself or for others; (ii) there must be the intention to deceive the recipients of the announcements; (iii) the announcements must be such as to mislead recipients with regard to the company's or the group's economic and financial situation; (iv) there must be a significant alteration of the company's or the group's economic framework; (v) the objectively relevant threshold percentages must be exceeded, that is, 5% of the year's result, including tax, as well as 1% of net asset and, just in cases of alteration of valuation assessments, a 10% difference from the correct assessment.

746. Article 2622, paragraph I, CC envisages a criminal offence similar to the previous one, known as 'false corporate announcements to the detriment of companies, shareholders, or creditors', which differs from Article 2621 CC in that it also includes a detriment to assets, caused directly by the conduct of the perpetrator.

In such a case, the crime is punished with detention from six months to three years, but the offence is only indictable following charges by a party concerned.

747. Article 2622, paragraph III, CC on the other hand, envisages a more serious sentence (detention from three to eight years), and the indictment of directors, *sindaci*, liquidators and top managers may go ahead even without charges by a party concerned, in cases in which false corporate announcements have been made concerning a company that issue shares, bonds and other financial instruments on regulated markets in Italy or elsewhere in Europe. Their controlling companies, or companies '*che fanno appello al pubblico risparmio*', indeed, in such an event, it is thought that the general interest in ensuring truthful information in the financial market has to be protected, even in the absence of a specific claim by a party concerned.

748. The penalty envisaged for this offence is imprisonment from one to five years for directors, *sindaci*, liquidators and top managers of non-listed companies, nevertheless milder penalties (imprisonment from six months to three years) are provided in case of conducts of slight magnitude, considering the little dimension of the company and/or the limited damages caused (Article 2621*bis* CC). Extremely slight facts are not punished when the damage provoked to the company, the shareholders and the creditors is marginal (Article 2621*ter* CC).

749. Article 2625 CC contemplates a pecuniary fine for directors who prevent or make obstacles to the control activity of shareholders or of other company's organs. If shareholders suffered some damages, the directors upon claim of the shareholders may be punished with imprisonment up to one year (two years for listed companies).

32. Under Italian law, *reati* (offences) are distinguished from *delitti* (crimes, which tend to apply to more serious cases) and *contravvenzioni* (infringements), which produce different consequences concerning, *inter alia*, the relevance of wilful or negligent conduct, sentences, time-bars, court rules and the possibility of extinction. Depending on the gravity of the offence, sentences of detention (life sentence and detention for *delitti*; *arresto* (arrest) for infringements) and/or pecuniary fines *multa* (penalty) for *delitti*, *ammenda* (fine) for *contravvenzioni)* may be envisaged. For some *reati* specific *sanzioni* (sanctions) can be additionally imposed by administrative authorities.

II. The Integrity and Effectiveness of the Company's Capital and Its Non-available Reserves

750. Various offences have been defined to protect this legal interest. The main ones are:

- undue restitution of contributions, an offence punishable with detention for up to one year (Article 2626 CC);
- illegally distributing profits and reserves, an offence punishable with detention for up to one year, but if those responsible return the profits and/or reserves prior to the last date envisaged for approving the financial balance sheets, the offence is extinguished (Article 2627 CC);
- unlawful transactions by directors involving the shares and quotas of the company or the holding company, an offence punishable with detention for up to one year. Here, too, if the capital or the reserves are re-established prior to the last date envisaged for approving the financial balance sheets, the offence is extinguished (Article 2628 CC);
- transactions to the detriment of creditors, an offence punishable, following charges by a party concerned, with detention from six months to three years, but if the damage is reimbursed the offence is extinguished (Article 2629 CC);
- fictitious formation of capital, an offence punishable with detention for up to one year (Article 2632 CC);
- undue distribution of corporate assets by the liquidators, an offence punishable, following charges by the party offended, with detention from six months to three years. In any event, this offence is extinguished if the damage is indemnified prior to the sentence (Article 2633 CC).

III. Protection of the Corporate Assets Against Abuses by the Directors

751. There are basically two offences defined that protect the aforementioned legal interest: (i) disloyalty involving assets; and (ii) disloyalty after giving or promising a benefit.

The case of disloyalty involving assets – which is envisaged in Article 2634 CC and is punishable with detention from six months to three years – arises when the directors, general managers, or liquidators of a company, to gain an unjust profit or any other benefit for themselves or for others, commit, or concur in bringing about, acts disposing of the corporate assets, thereby intentionally causing damage to the company's assets.

Disloyalty after giving or promising a benefit – an offence envisaged in Article 2635 CC and punishable, following charges by the person offended, with detention of up to three years (the sentence will be doubled in cases in which the company is listed on the stock exchange) – arises when the directors, general managers, senior executives, sindaci, liquidators, after giving or simply promising a benefit, commit or omit acts in breach of their official duties, thereby causing damage to the company.

IV. The Sound Functioning of the Governing Bodies

752. The criminal offences contemplated by the CC to ensure the sound functioning of the governing bodies are:

- impeding control, an offence that arises when, either by concealing documents or by other forms of artifice, the directors hinder or prevent control by the shareholders, governing bodies, or auditing companies. This offence is usually punishable with an administrative penalty. In cases of damage or on charges, however, the offence is punishable with detention of up to one year, and the sentences are doubled in cases of listed companies (Article 2625 CC);
- omission to notify a conflict of interest on the part of directors of listed companies or companies subject to supervision, an offence punishable with detention from one to three years, but only if damage has been caused either to the company or to third parties as a result of the violation (Article 2629bis CC);
- failure to arrange to file balance sheets, notices, or deposits at the Registro delle imprese, by mail or informatic means, an offence punishable with an administrative penalty (Article 2630 CC);
- failure to convene a shareholders' meeting on the part of the directors and/or the sindaci, an offence punishable with a pecuniary fine (Article 2631 CC);
- unlawful influence on a shareholders' meeting, an offence punishable with detention from six months to three years (Article 2636 CC).

V. General Interests Inherent in the Regular and Sound Functioning of the Market

753. The only cases of offence contemplated by the CC to protect the regular and sound functioning of the market are envisaged in Articles 2637 and 2638 CC, respectively entitled aggiotaggio (manipulation) and 'hindering the exercise of the functions of public supervisory authorities'.

The offence of manipulation arises in cases in which a person either disseminates false news or sets in place simulated transactions or artifices such as to: (a) produce a significant alteration in the price of unlisted financial instruments; or (b) significantly jeopardize the public's confidence in the economic stability of banks or groups of banks (as far as the offence of manipulation in listed companies is concerned, *see* the next paragraph).

This offence is punished with detention from one to five years.

Hindering the exercise of the functions of public supervisory authorities concerns anyone occupying a position in the company who by law has to account to public supervisory authorities. The conduct consists of adopting practices that are of hindrance to exercising supervisory functions. This could, for instance, consist of stating facts not corresponding to the truth or fraudulently concealing facts regarding the company's economic situation.

This offence is punished with a sentence of detention from one to four years, and the punishment is doubled in cases in which companies listed on the stock exchange are involved.

VI. Criminal Provisions Concerning Listed Companies

754. In addition to the offences contemplated in the CC, the TUF also envisages criminal offences and practices punished by administrative authorities in the framework of the governing bodies of listed companies. In some cases, the practices are the same as those envisaged in the CC, but the penalties are harsher because of the need to protect the financial markets.

The main offences include insider trading ('abuse of privileged information', Article 184 TUF), manipulation (Article 185 TUF), directors irregularly purchasing, or failing to compulsorily sell, shares (Articles 172 and 173 TUF), untruthful information and data in prospectuses (Article 173bis TUF), and a series of practices by auditing companies such as untruthful information provided in reports and notices, corruption, illegal remuneration, disclosure of confidential information, and unlawful economic dealings (Articles from 174*bis* to 179 TUF).

If the public prosecutor is informed of such offences, he or she will inform the president of CONSOB, and, likewise, if CONSOB acquires elements implying the existence of an offence, it will pass on to the public prosecutor any documents it acquires. Furthermore, CONSOB may join the prosecution as a plaintiff and apply for a sentence ordering the payment of a specific sum, established on equitable terms, indemnifying the damage caused to the integrity of the market.

§3. Administrative Liability of Companies

755. Legislative Decree No. 231 of 8 June 2001 introduced into the Italian legal system the administrative liability of legal persons, companies, and associations, for certain types of offences committed in the interest, or for the benefit, of an entity either: (i) by persons who have powers of representation or perform functions with respect to administering and running the entity or one of its autonomous organizational units; or (ii) by persons who are under the management or supervision of persons belonging to the first category. The long list of offences for which companies are thus administratively liable is gradually increasing (the list appears in Legislative Decree No. 231/2001 and has been repeatedly extended). The list already includes the corporate offences referred to in the CC and the offences of insider trading and manipulation mentioned in the TUF.

For corporate offences, the company will be held to account if the offence is committed in the interest of the company by directors, general managers, or liquidators, or by persons under their supervision, in any case in which the act would not have occurred if they had supervised in accordance with the duties inherent in their position.

In all cases in which the offences listed are committed by persons who have powers of representation or who perform functions with respect to managing and running the entity or one of its autonomous organizational units, the company will not be liable if it is proven that:

(a) the governing body adopted and effectively implemented before the act was committed models of organization and management such as to avert offences of the type that occurred;
(b) the task of supervising the functioning and observance of the models, and updating them, was entrusted to a body of the entity endowed with autonomous powers of initiative and control;
(c) the persons committed the offence by fraudulently eluding the models of organization and management;
(d) the competent body was not responsible for failing to supervise or doing so adequately.

756. Just like other entities vested with administrative liability, companies may be subject to pecuniary fines, sentences affecting their activities (prohibiting their activity; suspending or withdrawing authorizations, licences, or concessions; prohibiting dealings with the public administration; excluding or withdrawing benefits, loans, contributions, or subsidies; and prohibiting the advertising of goods or services), confiscation of assets, or publication of the sentence.

Although the liability of entities is defined as 'administrative', whether or not any such liability arises is something that has to be ascertained by the competent criminal court as far as the offences to which it refers are concerned. In this respect, the rules applied will be either the rules of the criminal procedure Code or the specific rules established in Legislative Decree No. 231/2001.

Selected Bibliography

General Introduction

A) The Italian Legal System

Bognetti, G. *La Costituzione economica italiana*. Milano: Giuffré, 1995.

Cappelletti, M., J.H.Merryman & J.M.Perrillo. *The Italian Legal System*, Stanford, California: Stanford University Press, 1967.

Cassese, S. *La nuova Costituzione economica*. Roma – Bari: Laterza, 2015.

Cicconetti, S.M. *Le fonti del diritto italiano*. Torino: Giappichelli, 2007.

Crisafulli, V. *Lezioni di diritto costituzionale*, Vol II of *L'ordinamento costituzionale italiano*. Padova: Cedam, 1993.

Della Cananea G., and G. Napolitano (eds). *Per una nuova Costituzione economica*. Bologna: Il Mulino, 1998.

Di Plinio, G. *Il common core della deregulation: dallo Stato regolatore alla Costituzione economica sopranazionale*. Milano: Giuffré, 2005.

Miranda, A. *A Short introduction to the Italian Legal System*, Vol. I of *Historical Background and Modern Legal Thought*. Giappichelli, 2014.

Paladin, L. *Le fonti del diritto italiano*. Bologna: Il Mulino, 1996.

Sorrentino, F. (a cura di) *Trattato di diritto amministrativo: Le fonti del diritto amministrativo*. Padova: Cedam, 2004.

B) The evolution and General Features of Italian Company Law

Angelici, C. *La riforma delle società di capitali: lezioni di diritto commerciali*. Padova: Cedam, 2003.

Associazione Preite G. Olivieri, Presti G. & F. Vella (a cura di)., *Il diritto delle società*. Bologna: Il Mulino, 2004.

Cera, M., P. Benazzo and S. Patriarca. *Il diritto delle società oggi. Innovazioni e persistenze*. Torino: Utet2011.

Buonocore, V. *Le società. Disposizioni generali*. Milano: Giuffré, 2008.

Campobasso, G. *Diritto commerciale*, Vol. 2 *Diritto delle società*, 8TH ED. Torino: Utet, 2011.

Campobasso, G.F. *La riforma delle società di capitali e delle cooperative*. Torino: Utet, 2004.

Cottino, G. *Diritto societario*, Padova: Cedam, 2011.

Di Sabato, F. *Diritto delle società*. Torino: Giuffrè, 2005.

Ferrara F. & F. Corsi *Gli imprenditori e le società*. Milano: Giuffrè, 2011.

Ferri, G. *Le società*, in Vassali, F. (a cura di) *Trattato di diritto civile*, Torino: Giuffrè, 1987.

Ferri, G. & M. Stella Richter Jr. *Profili attuali di diritto societario europeo*. Milano: Giuffrè, 2010.

Galgano, F. *Il nuovo diritto societario*, in GALGANO F (a cura di) *Trattato di Diritto commerciale e di diritto pubblico dell'economia*. Padova: Cedam, 2003.

Gambino, A. & D.U. Santosuosso. II Società di capitali, 4th ed. Milano: Giuffrè, 2014.

Libonati, B. *Diritto commerciale. Impresa e società*. Milano: Giuffrè, 2005.

Mucciarelli, F. *Società di capitali, trasferimento della sede sociale all'estero e arbitraggi normativi*. Milano: Giuffrè, 2010.

Ungari, P. *Profilo storico del diritto delle società anonime in Italia*. Roma: Bulzoni, 1974.

VV, A.A. *La società commerciale Europea, Atti del Convegno di Villa Pignatelli*. Napoli: Jovene, 1968.

C) The Italian International Private Law

Angelici, C. *Società costituite o operanti all'estero*, in *Enciclopedia Giuridica Treccani*. Vol. XXIX. Roma: Treccani, 1993.

Ballarino, T. *Manuale breve di diritto internazionale privato*. Padova: Cedam, 2016.

Mosconi, F. & C. Campiglio *Diritto internazionale privato e processuale*. Torino: UTET, 2015.

Picone, P. *Diritto internazionale privato e diritto comunitario*. Padova: Cedam, 2004.

Pocar, F. *Il nuovo diritto internazionale privato italiano*. Milano: Giuffrè, 2002.

Santamaria A., *La società nel Diritto Internazionale Privato*. Milano: Giuffrè, 1983.

PART I: Corporations

A) The Società per Azioni – S.p.A. ('Public Company Limited by Shares')

Abbadessa P. & G.B. Portale (eds). *Il nuovo diritto delle società*. Vol. 4. Torino: Utet, 2007.

Selected Bibliography

Angelici, C. *La riforma delle società di capitali, Lezioni di diritto commerciale.* Padova: Cedam, 2003.

Angelici, C. *La società per azioni. Principi e problemi, in Trattato di diritto civile e commerciale.* Cicu – Messineo: Giuffrè, 2012.

Associazione Preite, *Il diritto delle società.* Bologna: Il Mulino, 2012.

Bianchi, G. *Amministratori e sindaci.* Torino,: Utet, 2010.

Bianchi, L.A. & P. Marchetti. *La disciplina delle società quotate.* Vol. 3. Milano: Giuffrè, 1999.

Bonfante, G., D. Corapi, G. Marziale, R. Rordorf & V. Salafia (eds). *Codice commentato delle società.* Milano: IPSOA, 2007.

Buonocore, V. *Le società. Disposizioni generali.* Milano: Giuffrè, 2008.

Cagnasso, O. & L. Panzani. *Trattato delle nuove s.p.a.* Vol. V. Zanichelli, 2013.

Campobasso, F. *Diritto commerciale.* Vol. 2. of *Diritto delle società.* 5th ed. Torino: Utet, 2002.

Canessa, N. *Amministrazione e controllo nella società per azioni e nella società a responsabilità limitata: responsabilità e strumenti di protezioni.* Padova: Cedam, 2007.

Carriello, V. *Il sistema dualistico.* Torino: Giappichelli, 2012.

Colombo, G.E. & G.B. Portale (eds). *Trattato delle società per azioni.* Vol. 10. Torino: Utet, 2009.

Corapi, D., *Gli statuti delle società per azioni.* Milano: Giuffrè, 1971

Corsi, F. *Le nuove società di capitali.* Milano: Giuffrè, 2003.

Cottino, G., G. Bonfante, O. Cagnasso & P. Montalenti. *Il nuovo diritto societario.* Vol. 3. Bologna: Zanichelli, 2004.

Di Sabato, F. *Diritto delle società.* Torino: Giuffrè, 2005.

Ferrara, F. & F. Corsi. *Gli imprenditori e le società.* Milano: Giuffrè, 2006.

Ferri, G. *Le società*, in Vassali, F. (a cura di) *Trattato di diritto civile*, Torino: Giuffrè, 1987.

Galgano, F. *Il nuovo diritto societario*, in Galgano F (a cura di) *Trattato di Diritto commerciale e di diritto pubblico dell'economia.* Padova: Cedam, 2003.

Ianniello, B. *Amministrazione e controllo nelle s.p.a. non quotate. I modelli alternativi.* Milano: Giuffrè, 2011.

Lo Cascio, G. (ed). *La riforma del diritto societario.* Vol. 10. Milano: Giuffrè, 2003.

Marchetti, P., L.A. Bianchi, F. Ghezzi & M. Notari, *Commentario alla riforma delle società.* Vol. 9. Milano: Giuffrè, 2005.

Montalenti, P. *Società per azioni corporate governance e mercati finanziari.* Milano: Giuffrè, 2011.

Montalenti P. and S. Balzola, *La società per azioni quotata.* Bologna: Zanichelli, 2010.

Nazzicone L. and S.Providenti. *Amministrazione e controlli nella società per azioni.* Milano: Giuffrè, 2010.

Niccolini, G. & A. Stagno d'Alcontres. *Società di capitali. Commentario.* Vol. 3. Napoli: Jovene, 2004.

Platania, F. *I conferimenti nelle S.p.A.* Milano: Giuffrè, 2011.

Santosuosso, D.U. *La riforma del diritto societario, autonomia privata e norme imperative nei DD. Lgs. 17 gennaio 2003, nn. 5 e 6,* Milano: Giuffrè, 2003.

VV., A.A. Amministrazione e controllo nel diritto delle società. Liber Amicorum Antonio Piras. Torino,: Giappichelli, 2010.

Zanardo, A. *Delega di funzioni e diligenza degli amministratori nella società per azioni.* Padova: Cedam, 2010.

B) The Società a responsabilità limitata - S.r.l. ('Limited Liability Company')

Baldussi, G. *Autonomia statutaria e governance nella società a responsabilità limitata.* Torino: Giappichelli, 2013.

Belviso, U. *Scopo mutualistico e capitale variabile nelle società cooperative, Quaderni di giurisprudenza commerciale.* Milano: Giuffrè,2012.

Bione M., R. Guidotti & E. Pederzini (eds). *La nuova società a responsabilità limitata.* Padova: Cedam, 2012

Bonora, S. *La responsabilità del socio 'gestore' di società a responsabilità limitata.* Milano: Giuffrè, 2013.

Buonocore, V. '*La società a responsabilità limitata*'. In La riforma del diritto societario. Edited by A. Bassi, V. Buonocore & G. Pescatore. Torino: Giappichelli, 2003.

Caccavale, C. & F.M. Magliulo. *La riforma della società a responsabilità limitata.* Milano: IPSOA, 2007.

Cagnasso, O. *La società a responsabilità limitata.* Padova: Cedam, 2014.

Ibba, C. & G. Marasà, *Trattato delle società a responsabilità limitata.* Vol. 8. Padova: Cedam, 2009 -2014

Mazzon, R. Le società a responsabilità limitata. Orientamenti giurisprudenziali. Padova: Cedam, 2013.

Mozzarelli, M. *Responsabilità degli amministratori e tutela dei creditori nella s.r.l.* Torino: Giappichelli, 2007.

Nicodemo, M. *Società per azioni, società a responsabilità limitata.* Torino: UTET, 2006.

Petroboni, G. *Le competenze gestorie dei soci nella società a responsabilità limitata.* Padova: Cedam, 2011.

Santoro, V. (ed). *La nuova disciplina della società a responsabilità limitata.* Milano: Giuffrè, 2003.

Sarale, M. (ed). *Le nuove s.r.l.* Bologna: Zanichelli, 2007.

Selected Bibliography

Stella Richter, M. Jr. '*La società a responsabilità limitata. Disposizioni generali. Conferimenti. Quote*'. In AA.VV. *Diritto delle società di capitali, Manuale breve*. Milano: Giuffrè, 2003.

Vanessa, N. *Amministrazione e controllo nella società per azioni e nella società a responsabilità limitata: responsabilità e strumenti di protezioni*. Padova: Cedam, 2007.

C) The Societa' in Accomandita per Azioni – S. A.p. A. (Limited Partnership by shares)

Barcellona, E., R. Costi & F.G. Stevens. '*Della società in accomandita per azioni*' in GALGANO, F. (a cura di) *Commentario del Codice civile Scialoja-Branca*. Roma: Foro italiano, 2005.

Galgano, F. (diretto da) *Società in accomandita per azioni. Società a responsabilità limitata. Trasformazione e fusione delle società* in *Trattato di diritto commerciale e di diritto pubblico dell'economia*. Padova: Cedam, 1985.

Massimiliano, N. *Società in accomandita per azioni, società cooperative e consortili. Le operazioni straordinarie*. Torino: Utet, 2007.

Niccolò, A. '*La società in accomandita per azioni*' in *Diritto delle società*. Milano: Giuffrè, 2006.

Santoro, V. & M. Sandulli (a cura di) '*Società per azioni, società in accomandita per azioni*', in *La riforma delle Società*. Vol. 2. Torino: Giappichelli, 2003.

D) The Societa' Europea – S. E. ('European Company')

Arnò, G. & S. Cancarini. *La società europea: la disciplina comunitaria e il suo recepimento in Italia e nei principali Stati membri*. Milano: Egea, 2007.

Bonfante, G. *La nuova società co-operativa*. Bologna: Zanichelli, 2010.

Bordogna, L. & F. Guarriello. (a cura di), *Aver voce in capitolo. Società Europea e partecipazione dei lavoratori nell'impresa*. Roma: Edizioni Lavoro, 2003.

Capriglione, F. (a cura di) *La nuova disciplina della società europea*. Napoli: CEDAM, 2008.

Corapi, D. & F. Pernazza (eds). *La Società Europea. Fonti comunitarie e modelli nazionali*. Torino: Giappichelli, 2011.

Draetta, U.& F. Pocar. (eds). *La Società europea. Problemi di diritto societario comunitario*. Milano: Giuffrè, 2002.

Ficari, L. (ed.). *Società Europea, diritti di informazione e partecipazione dei lavoratori*. Milano: Giuffrè, 2006.

Principe, A. (ed.). *Lo statuto legale di società europea*. Napoli; ESI, 2002.

Vasquez, F. *Presente e futuro della società europea e della Società Cooperativa europea*. In *Europa e democrazia industriale* edited by G.Arrigo, G.Barbucci, W. Buschak, W.Cerfeda, F.Vasquez. Roma: Ediesse, 2004.

E) The Società Cooperativa and the Mutual Insurance Company

Bonfante, G. *Imprese cooperative*. In Commentario Scialoja-Branca, Bologna-Roma: Zanichelli, 1999.

Bonfante, G. *La riforma della cooperazione*. In *La riforma delle società. Profili della nuova disciplina*. Ambrosini, S. (a cura di)Torino: Giappicchelli, 2003.

Bonfante, G. La società cooperativa. Padova: Cedam, 2014.

Buonocore, V. *Diritto della cooperazione.* Bologna: Il Mulino, 1997.

Campobasso, G.F. *La riforma delle società di capitali e delle cooperative*.Torino: UTET, 2004.

Ceccherini, A. & S. Schiro'. '*Società cooperative e mutue assicuratrici*'. In *La riforma del diritto societario.* G.,Lo Cascio.(a cura di) Milano: Giuffré, 2003.

Cerioli, S.L., P. Costanzo & A. Sanguinetti. *La riforma delle società cooperative. Disciplina civilistica e fiscale. Adempimenti contabili.* Milano: Egea, 2006.

Vella, F. & R. Genco. *Il diritto delle società cooperative.* Bologna: Il Mulino, 2011.

PART II: Partnerships

A) The società semplice ('Non-business Association')

Campobasso, G. *Diritto Commerciale. Diritto delle società.* vol. II. Torino: Utet, 2002.

Cottino, G. *Diritto Commerciale. Le società.* vol. I. Padova: Cedam, 1999.

Ferrara, F. & F. Corsi. *Gli imprenditori e la società*, 13th ed. Milano: Giuffré, 2006.

Selected Bibliography

Ferri, G. *Manuale di diritto commerciale.* Torino: Utet, 2006.

Galgano, F. *'Le società in genere. Le società di persone'*. In *Trattato di diritto civile e commerciale,* edited originally by F. Cicu, F. Messineo & L. Mengoni and now by P. Schlesinger. 3rd ed. Milano: Giuffrè, 2007.

Galgano, F. *Società semplice*. In *Digesto discipline privatistiche. Sezione commerciale.* vol. XIV. Torino: UTET, 2003.

Ghidini, G. *Società semplice*. In *Enciclopedia giuridica Treccani*. vol. XXIX. Roma: Treccani, 1993.

B) Chapter 2. The Società in Nome Collettivo ('General Partnership')

Buonocore, V. '*La società in nome collettivo*'. In Commentario al codice civile, edited by P. Schlesinger. Milano: Giuffrè, 1995.

Bussoletti, M. & E. Fazzutti. *'Società in nome collettivo'*. In Digesto delle discipline *privatistiche* – Sezione commerciale. Vol. XIV. 4th ed. Torino: Utet, 1997.

Cottino, G. & O. Cagnasso. *Le nuove società di persone*. Bologna: Zanichelli, 2014.

Di Sabato, F. 'Società in nome collettivo'. In *Enciclopedia Treccani.* vol. XXIX. Roma, 1993.

Guerrera, F. *Società in nome collettivo.* In *Enciclopedia del Diritto,* vol. XLII. Milano: Giuffrè, 1990.

C) The Società in Accomandita semplice ('Limited Partnership')

Conforti, C. *La società in accomandita semplice*. Milano: Giuffrè, 2005.

Mazzanti, R. *La società in accomandita semplice.* Milano: SEAC, 2007.

Rivolta, G. C. M. '*In tema di società in accomandita semplice*' in *Studi in onore di Pietro Schlesinger*. Milano: Giuffrè, 2004.

PART III: Common Rules

A) Groups of companies

Angelici, C. *La riforma delle società: profili della nuova disciplina*. Torino: Cedam, 2003.

Bassi, A. *I gruppi di imprese.* In *Manuale di diritto commerciale*, edited by V. Buonocuore. Torino: Giappichelli, 2004.

Berta, G. (ed.). *I gruppi societari*, Torino: Giappichelli, 2011.

Carriello,V. *Direzione e coordinamento di società.* In *Società di Capitali*. Niccolini G., Alcontres A. S. (a cura di) Vol. 3. Napoli: Jovene, 2004.

Di Majo, A. *I gruppi di società. Responsabilità e profili concorsuali*, Milano: Giuffrè, 2012.

Galgano, F. & G. Sbisà. *Direzione e coordinamento di società. Art. 2497-2497septies*. 2nd ed. Zanichelli, 2014.

Lamandini, M. *Controllo, influenza dominante e direzione unitaria, commento sub artt. 2359 -2359bis*. In *Società di Capitali*, edited by Niccolini G., Alcontres A. S. Vol. 3. Napoli: Jovene, 2004.

Lemme, G. *Il diritto dei gruppi di società. Manuali dell'Associazione Disiano Preite*, Il Mulino, 2013.

Scognamiglio, G. *Autonomia e coordinamento nella disciplina dei gruppi di società*. Torino: Giappichelli, 1996.

Tombari, V. *Diritto dei gruppi di imprese*. Milano: Giuffrè, 2010.

Valzer, A. *Le responsabilità da direzione e coordinamento di società*. Torino: Giappichelli, *2011*.

B) Conversion, merger and division

Attanasio, A. (ed.). *Fusione e scissione di società: aspetti civilistici, tributari e contabili*. Forli: Experta, 2008.

Gonfalonieri, M. *Trasformazione, fusione, conferimento, scissione e liquidazione della società*. Milano: Il sole 24 ore, 2008.

Enna, G. *Fusione, scissione e scorporo : aspetti giuridici, rilevazioni contabili, fiscalità, profili procedurali, principi contabili nazionali e internazionali*. Napoli: Sistemi Editoriali, 2007.

La Marca, E. *La fusione e la scissione delle società*. In *Lezioni di diritto commerciale comunitario*. edited by M. Cassottana & A. Nuzzo. Torino: Giappichelli,, 2006.

C) Winding-up and liquidation

Bonfatti, S. & L. Panzani *La riforma organica delle procedure concorsuali*. Milano: IPSOA, 2008.

Caiafa,A. *La legge fallimentare riformata e corretta: dalla legge 12 maggio 2005, n. 80 al d.lgs. 12 settembre 2007, n. 169*, Padova: Cedam, 2008.

Niccolini, G. 'La disciplina dello scioglimento, della liquidazione e dell'estinzione delle società di capitali'. In *La riforma delle società. Profili della nuova disciplina*. edited by S. Ambrosini. Torino: Giappichelli, 2003.

Terranova, G. *Le procedure concorsuali : problemi d'una riforma*. Milano: Giuffrè, 2004.

Selected Bibliography

Zanichelli, V. *La nuova disciplina del fallimento e delle altre procedure concorsuali : dopo il d.lg. 12.9.2007, n. 169*, Torino: UTET giuridica, 2008.

D) Criminal Rules

Alessandri, A. (ed.). *Diritto penale dell'impresa*. Torino: Giappichelli, 2007.

Bellicosa, M. *Obblighi di fedeltà dell'amministratore di società e sanzioni penali*. Milano: Giuffrè, 2006.

Cerqua, L.D., L. Luparia & G. Canzio. *Diritto penale delle società. Profili sostanziali e processuali.* Padova: Cedam, 2014.

Crespi, A. *Studi di diritto penale societario*. Milano: Giuffrè, 2010.

Maura, A. *La responsabilità civile e penale degli amministratori e dei sindaci: nuovi problemi e questioni controverse alla luce della giurisprudenza civile e penale della riforma del diritto societario*. Matelica: Halley Editrice, 2007

Musco, E. *I nuovi reati societari.* Milano: Giuffrè, 2007.

Santoriello, C. (a cura di) *La disciplina penale dell'economia*. Torino: Giappichelli, 2008.

Zannotti, R. *Il nuovo diritto penale dell'economia : reati societari e reati in materia di mercato finanziario*. Milano: Giuffrè, 2008.

Selected Bibliography

Index

The numbers here refer to paragraph numbers

Index

Index

Made in the USA
Monee, IL
18 October 2026

66037573R10157